WARCORRESPONDENT

WARCORRESPONDENT

REPORTING UNDER FIRE SINCE 1850

JEAN HOOD

For John and Alison

To buy books in quantity for corporate use
or incentives, call **(800) 962–0973**
or e-mail **premiums@GlobePequot.com.**

Text © Jean Hood, 2011
Volume © Conway, 2011

First published in Great Britain in 2011 by Conway, an imprint of Anova Books Ltd.
Published in association with the Imperial War Museum, www.iwm.org.uk
This edition published by Lyons Press in 2012

Library of Congress Cataloging-in-Publication Data is available on file.

ISBN 978-0-7627- 7993-2

Printed by Craft Print Ltd, Singapore.

10 9 8 7 6 5 4 3 2 1

Picture IDs
Frontispiece: US photographer capturing the action on Borneo during the Second World War
Page 5: Immarsat satellite phone

Author's Note
Truth is only the second casualty of war; the first is civilization, common humanity, empathy –
call it what you will. The modern war correspondent, particularly one trying to cover a civil war,
probably sees the consequences of more cold-blooded, casual, sadistic, bestial violence than any
soldier; more perhaps, than most aid workers. It follows that a number of events chronicled in this
book are shocking to read. Imagine what they were like to witness.

contents

Monday, 21 March 2011. An RSS feed from the *New York Times* arrives in the inbox with an update on the situation in Libya. These days, most people take it for granted that such up-to-the minute news from conflicts around the world will be served up via computer, mobile phone, radio, television, airport and railway station plasma screens and all the other technological triumphs of the twenty-first century. War correspondents in flak jackets talk into their microphones in front of piles of protective sandbags or among the debris of some ruined town, and if the audience is very lucky, a shell roars harmlessly past, the TV crew hit the ground, the camera carries on filming at a crazy angle, and eventually the correspondent resumes the commentary in a breathless voice. Alternatively, an anchorman, comfortably ensconced in a

War Correspondents regard war very much as a doctor regards sickness. I don't suppose that a doctor is actually glad that people are sick, but so long as sickness exists in the world he feels that he might as well get the benefit of it. It is the same with war correspondents. They do not wish anyone to be killed on their account, but so long as men are going to be killed anyway, they want to be on hand to witness the killing and, through the newspapers, to tell the world about it.

E. Alexander Powell, US War Correspondent, *Fighting in Flanders*, 1915

Introduction

studio, talks by phone to a member of the public in some trouble-spot that is either inaccessible to journalists or where events have caught the media by surprise and left the correspondents scrambling onto the first flight heading that way.

It can be argued that 'war correspondent' is a misleading term, because all war correspondents are essentially journalists who, in the course of their career, find themselves covering a war or two – or maybe a dozen – and reporting on more peaceful places and topics in between. However, in more recent years, the large number of conflicts ongoing at any one time has allowed some journalists to specialize in conflict.

Being a war correspondent – whether a reporter or photojournalist – can be addictive; over the decades many have thrived on adrenaline, danger, the thrill of the scoop – or 'exclusive' as it now tends to be called – and the comradeship that exists not just within a team but among the press corps around them. There is a dark side to the work: being in the wrong place or upsetting the wrong people can lead to injury, death, arrest or kidnap. Living conditions can be squalid, and communications – whether a lame horse in the nineteenth century or a poor satellite link-up in the

twenty-first – are deeply frustrating. Editors are demanding; governments intensely suspicious; critics – informed or otherwise – crouch ready to accuse the correspondent of either 'betraying' the troops or spinelessly spouting the military line. And there is the horror of war that must be observed, reported – and carried away like baggage.

The story of the professional war reporter began just over a century and a half ago. During that period they have given the public some of the most memorable reports, phrases and images of war. They have shaken governments and brought down generals, and all because, as William Howard Russell put it: 'I heard so from many people, and I saw it myself'.

above: 'Travoys Arriving with the Wounded at a Dressing-Station at Smol, Macedonia, September 1916', by Sir Stanley Spencer RA. In 1918 Spencer was approached by the British War Memorials Committee to complete a commission. This work is based on his experiences with the 68th Field Ambulance.

overleaf: Journalists run to safety as an Allied plane flies overhead on a bombing sortie while they are filming the aftermath of an Iraqi hit on a US tank in Badhdad.

A correspondent's first duty, within the bounds of honour and decency, is to his newspaper.

Edgar Wallace (1875–1932) in *Edgar Wallace by Himself*, 1932

If a war correspondent can be defined as a journalist who is sent by a news-gathering organization to provide eyewitness reports from a conflict zone, Special Correspondent William Howard Russell of the *Times*, who described himself as 'the miserable parent of a luckless tribe', has a good claim to be the first. His first forays into journalism came when he was a struggling young barrister, but in 1850 he covered a battle at Idstedt, an almost forgotten engagement in the political and military quagmire known as the Schleswig-Holstein Question. Four years later, the *Times* dispatched him with the 'expedition to the East' to report for the newspaper on the Crimean War (1854–56) in which, for strategic reasons, French and British forces supported Turkey against Russia.

Although Russell travelled with the British troops and lived among them, he was not embedded, nor were his dispatches censored. Shocked by the conditions endured by the soldiers, he asked his editor, John Thadeus Delane, if he should report or ignore what he

The Trailblazers:
the rise of the war correspondent

saw, and, to his credit, Delane urged him to report the truth. The consequent exposure of the inadequate medical facilities and the administrative incompetence infuriated senior commanders in the field, and their resentment extended to denying Russell all assistance, even food rations, when his baggage was lost.

At night the watchfires of the Russians were visible on our left. Great numbers of stragglers came up during the night, most of them belonging to the 4th Division. It was a cold night, and if I could intrude the recital of the sorrows of a tentless man wandering about in the dark from regiment to regiment in hope of finding his missing baggage, I might tell a tale amusing enough to read, but the incidents in which were very distressing to the individual concerned. The night was cold and damp, the watchfires were mere flashes, which gave little heat, and barely sufficed to warm the rations; but the camp of British

soldiers is ever animated by the very soul of
hospitality; and the wanderer was lucky enough to
get a lodging on the ground beside a kindly colonel,
who was fortunate enough to have a little field tent
with him, and a bit of bread and biscuit to spare after
a march of 10 miles and a fast of 10 hours.[1]

Russell, however, was a genial man who made friends among the troops. One soldier reportedly described him as 'a vulgar low Irishman, [who] sings a good song, drinks anyone's brandy and water and smokes as many cigars as a Jolly Good Fellow. He is just the

above: Captain J.M. Knap's Independent Battery 'E' Light Artillery, a Union unit at the Battle of Antietam, 1862, during the American Civil War. Photographed by Alexander Gardner.

sort of chap to get information, particularly out of youngsters'. Officers and men warmed to him, not least for his fearless willingness to describe their suffering:

> *At the present date there are no less than 3,500 sick men in the British camp before Sebastopol, and it is not too much to say that their illness has, for the most part, been caused by hard work in bad weather, and by exposure to wet without any adequate protection. Think what a tent must be, pitched, as it were, at the bottom of a marsh, into which some 12 or 14 miserable creatures, drenched to the skin, have to creep for shelter after 12 hours of vigil in a trench like a canal, and then reflect what state these poor fellows must be in at the end of a night and day spent in such shelter, huddled together without any change of clothing, and lying packed up as close as they can stow in saturated blankets. But why are they in tents? Where are the huts which have been sent out to them? The huts are on board ships in the harbour of Balaklava, and are likely to stay there. ...[2]*

Despite government attempts to discredit them, Russell's dispatches caused an outcry that brought down the government and led to massive changes in the Crimean campaign. Florence Nightingale was sent out to reorganize medical services at Scutari and *Times'* readers donated thousands of pounds to a fund that purchased supplies to ameliorate the conditions in which the troops existed. No other individual war correspondent can claim so much influence – partly for the simple reason that, after the Crimea, governments and military chiefs generally went to great lengths to manage the reporting of conflicts.

Russell was never afraid to put himself in harm's way in order to observe the action, and at the Battle of Alma he came close to being hit by shrapnel and killed when his refuge suffered a direct hit. That determination earned him a second claim to enduring fame when his eyewitness description of the charge of the Light Brigade created the definitive image of the episode, directly inspiring the poem by Tennyson that immortalizes it.

> *At the distance of 1,200 yards the whole line of the enemy belched forth, from 30 iron mouths, a flood of smoke and flame, through which hissed the deadly balls. Their flight was marked by instant gaps in our ranks, by dead men and horses, by steeds flying wounded or riderless across the plain. The first line is*

top: Men of 8th Hussars at the cooking house, photographed by Roger Fenton, whose photographic van can be seen at the left edge of the image.

above: Photograph by Roger Fenton showing the tents in the camp at Sebastopol.

broken, it is joined by the second, they never halt or check their speed an instant; with diminished ranks, thinned by those 30 guns, which the Russians had laid with the most deadly accuracy, with a halo of flashing steel above their heads, and with a cheer which was many a noble fellow's death-cry, they flew into the smoke of the batteries, but ere they were lost from view the plain was strewed with their bodies and with the carcasses of horses.... We saw them riding through the guns, as I have said; to our delight we saw them returning, after breaking through a column of Russian infantry, and scattering them like chaff, when the flank fire of the battery on the hill swept them down, scattered and broken as they were. ... It was as much as our Heavy Cavalry Brigade could do to cover the retreat of the miserable remnants of that band of heroes as they returned to the place they had so lately quitted in all the pride of life....[3]

It took 20 days for that dispatch about the cavalry action at Balaklava to reach the newspaper-reading public. Most of Europe was linked by telegraph, and a submarine cable connected France to Britain, but the nearest telegraph to the Crimea was at Bucharest. Army dispatches travelled nearly 300 miles (500 kilometres) across the Black Sea to Varna on the coast of Bulgaria, from where a mounted messenger undertook the 60-hour journey to Bucharest. By the end of the war a temporary submarine cable across the Black Sea and the linking of Varna and Bucharest reduced transmission time to and from London to around five hours. However, the electric telegraph routes were rarely made available to Russell and the other correspondents: their dispatches went by sea via Constantinople (present-day Istanbul).

After more than a year and a half reporting for the *Times* from the Crimea, Russell handed over to William Stowe, who died of cholera a month later. Russell went on to cover the remaining conflicts of the Indian Mutiny, the American Civil War and the Franco–Prussian War. The first war correspondent to be knighted, Russell died in 1907.

The American Civil War – brothers to arms

Force yourself to the rack, tug away, bear on hard, and when you are done, do not read it over, or you will throw it into the fire.

Charles Page (1838–1873) in the *New York Herald*, 25 June 1864

The newspaper industry in the USA became thoroughly established during the second half of the nineteenth century, particularly in the towns and cities of the East Coast. While large newspapers had their own salaried correspondents for home news, in 1849 the major New York titles had pooled their resources to set up a news-gathering service that would later become the Associated Press. This innovation significantly reduced the bill for telegraphy; an average 'letter' – as American dispatches were called at that time – from Washington, DC, to New York cost in the region of $100.

The outbreak of civil war in 1861 created a surge in public demand for information. The bigger newspapers dispatched their professional reporters, known as 'specials', to accompany the armies, while small-town papers may have taken advantage of freelances and enthusiastic volunteers who were following, or serving with, a locally recruited unit. While these amateurs relied on returning soldiers and the postal service to carry their material home, the professionals could afford to take their own dispatches or use the telegraph, if they had something that was top priority.

Censorship was limited, with only telegraph messages from Washington actively vetted. War correspondents considered themselves part of their chosen side's war effort and never intentionally betrayed useful information to the enemy, though in their enthusiasm they were sometimes guilty of including sensitive data such as troop movements and levels of ammunition. According to the *Commercial*[4] in Cincinnati, one Union general believed that the government would not achieve much until it had hanged a few spies 'and at least one newspaper reporter'. Both sides tried at various times to ban correspondents.

When William Howard Russell travelled to the United States in 1861, he was a welcome visitor as far as the Union side was concerned because its supporters believed that the kind of fearless, independent reporting he had displayed in the Crimea would show their cause to advantage, particularly in Britain. However, frankness proved to be a double-edged sword. At the first major engagement of the war, the First Battle of Bull Run (known to the Confederacy as the First Battle of Manassas) in July 1861, Russell found himself caught up in the panic-stricken retreat of the Union soldiers in the rear and he made no attempt to play down the ensuing chaos:

I saw a regiment of infantry blocking up the way, with their front towards Centreville. A musket was

above: Correspondents following the Union Army at their camp in Bealeton, Virginia, photographed in 1863 by Timothy H. O'Sullivan, from Alexander Gardner's studio. The *New York Herald* van stands under the trees.

opposite: William Howard Russell, photographed by Roger Fenton.

levelled at my head as I pushed to the front: 'Stop, or I'll fire.' At the same time the officers were shouting out, 'Don't let a soul pass.' I addressed one of them and said, 'Sir! I am a British subject, I am not, I assure you, running away. I have done my best to stop this disgraceful rout (as I had) and have been telling them there are no cavalry within miles of them.' 'I can't let you pass, Sir!' I bethought me of General Scott's pass. The adjutant read it, and the word was given along the line, 'Let that man pass!'[5]

When copies of the *Times* carrying Russell's dispatch reached the North it provoked outrage in the Union camp, the White House and the newspapers, leading to Russell's being banned from the Union army – and as good as expelled from the United States the following year. But not everyone despised him. General McDowell told him: 'I must confess I am rejoiced to find you are as much abused as I have been.... Bull Run was an unfortunate affair for both of us, for had I won it you would have had to describe the pursuit of the flying enemy and then you would have been the most popular writer in America and I should have been lauded as the greatest of generals.'[6]

Lacking Russell's experience and fame, but with an instinctive feel for his task, New Hampshire-born Charles Carleton Coffin had become a journalist after a succession of different careers. Unfit to serve in the army by virtue of a limp, the 37-year-old offered to report on the war for the *Boston Journal* if it paid him for any reports that it published. Following the First Battle of Bull Run he travelled overnight to Washington, to send his copy by telegraph, and his appreciative editor quickly added him to the payroll at $25 a week. He reported the war for its duration, possibly the only correspondent to do so, and soon came to realize there was nothing romantic in his profession:

> *But let me say if they were once brought into close contact with all the dreadful realities of war, if they were obliged to stand the chances of getting their heads knocked off, or blown to atoms by an unexpected shell, or bored through with a minie ball,[7] to stand their chances of being captured by the enemy, to live on bread and water, and little of it, as all of the correspondents have been obliged to do the past week, to sleep on the ground, or on a sack of corn, or in a barn, with the wind blowing a gale, and the snow whirling in drifts, and the thermometer shrunk to zero, and then, after the battle is over and the field won, to walk among the dying and the dead, to behold all the ghastly sights of trunkless heads and headless trunks, to see the human form mutilated, disfigured, torn, and mangled by shot and shell, to step in pools of blood, to hear all around sighs, groans, imprecations, and prayers from dying men, they would be content to let others become historians of the war. But this is not all; a correspondent must keep ever in view the thousands that are looking at the journal he represents, who expect his account at the earliest possible moment. If he is behindhand, his occupation is gone. His account must be first, or among the first, or it is nothing. Day and night he must be on the alert, improving every opportunity and turning it to*

> *account. If he loses a steamboat trip, or a train of cars, or a mail, it is all up with him. He might as well put his pencil in his pocket and go home.[8]*

One who endorsed that last sentiment was Charles Page. The farmer's son from a remote part of Illinois began his career as a correspondent after graduating from Cornell College. At the time of the war he reported for the *New-York Daily Tribune* where, with one reservation, he earned the approval of his editor, Horace Greeley:

> *'We are greatly pleased with your work; you are quick and graphic, and give us the news early; but, Mr Page, you are the most expensive young man the "Tribune" has ever employed.'*

> *'Early news is expensive news, Mr Greeley; if I have the watermelons and the whiskey ready when the officers come along from the fight, I get the news without asking questions.'[9]*

With the benefit of a liberal expense account, Page thought nothing of chartering steamers and trains just for himself, or simply abandoning a horse if he needed to catch a train in a hurry.

Despite having had no sleep for 24 hours, he once produced a five-column report for his newspaper, and as fast as he wrote, the printers typeset it. While recovering from an illness he wrote light-heartedly of his status as a 'special':

Ride your ten, fifteen hours; your twenty, thirty, forty, fifty miles. Fatigue is your normal condition. Sleeplessness, ditto… 'balmy sleep' is for babies… But you are a 'special'. It is far into the night when you begin. You rode all day and a part of the night, and have only now had your ablution and your supper. You begin, – 'squat like a toad'[10] before a camp-fire; a stumpy lead-pencil, and smoke in your eyes, dingy paper, and ashes puffed in your face; no part of you that has not its own special pain and torment…Your eyes will shut, your pencil will drop from nerveless fingers, but I say unto you: Write! Do you forget you are a 'special' and must write?… Was your horse stolen last night? Are your saddle-bags and all they contain missing this morning? No matter. It is a thing of course. It is a part of the misery of correspondents.[11]

Page's energy and humour shine out in his writing. After watching some percussion shells being carefully buried, he parodied Charles Wolfe's solemn poem 'The Burial of Sir John Moore after Corunna', ending with, 'we thought as we narrowed their lowly beds, and scooped out the lowly hole, that the foe and the stranger would tread o'er their heads – and perhaps get blown sky high'.[12]

However, with that dark humour went a sober grasp of the bigger reality and an admiration for those bearing the burden of war.

Headquarters. Sixth Corps, 11 miles north of Richmond, noon, Tuesday May 31, 1864.

This is the twenty-ninth day of the campaign; every day has seen more or less marching, more or less fighting. 30,000 men have been sent back on honourable furlough, 5,000 dead have been buried in honourable though obscure graves. Sedgwick and Wadsworth and many another whose memory we cannot afford to let die have fallen. Still the army is 'fighting it out on this line'.[13]

The roads are strewn with the carcasses of 6,000 horses. Actual marching has worn out 50,000 pairs of shoes. Two thirds of the men, more than 100,000, have not changed a garment since they started – have marched, and fought, and slept thirty days and thirty nights in heat and dust and rain, and have not changed a garment. They are 'fighting it out on this line'.[14]

By April 1865 Page had abandoned journalism for a job in the Department of the Treasury, but the imminent fall of the Confederate capital, Richmond, to Union forces inspired him to return to the front to report for the *New-York Daily Tribune*. All journalists' passes had been cancelled, but Page found his old permit signed by Ulysses S. Grant and joined several other veteran reporters with the same aim. With 15 miles (24 kilometres) left to go, and no transport, Page secured them all a lift in a passing four-horse wagon belonging to an officer who was an old friend. The Confederates had gone, and even before the Union troops marched in the enterprising trio were installed in the Spotswood Hotel. The War Department telegrams sent out to stop the correspondents had failed because, in Page's opinion, his many friends among the officers turned a blind eye to his movements, much as British officers in the Falklands War later did to Max Hastings's.

Page subsequently became the US Consul to Zurich and co-founded the Anglo-Swiss Milk Company, which later merged with Nestlé. He was only 35 when he died in London in 1873.

One example of an amateur correspondent was Jacob Nathaniel Raymer, a teacher from North Carolina who enlisted as a private soldier and musician in C Company of the North Carolina 4th Infantry Regiment, part of the Confederate Army. As a musician he played in concerts, but in battle he acted as a stretcher-bearer and grave-digger, which meant that he often experienced the worst aspects of the war. From the site of the pivotal Battle of Antietam (Sharpsburg), he wrote to the *North Carolina Watchman* and the *Iredell Express*:

October 6th [1862]

The enemy have thrown in their whole force on the right flank. The men become restless and uneasy, and the light of battle is seen in every face. But here comes one of Garland's aids, galloping furiously – 'General, send us reinforcements – we are falling back, and the enemy are pressing us hard in heavy force. General Anderson, hurry your brigade to Anderson's assistance.' And we are faced to the right, and away we go up the side of the mountain double

above: Alfred R. Waud, artist of
Harper's Weekly, sketching at
Devil's Den just after the Battle
of Gettysburg. Photograph by
Timothy H. O'Sullivan.

quick. We pass lots of wounded limping down the mountain, trickling blood at every step, then again a stretcher containing more desperately wounded, and as I bend over one, I catch the pale face of the gallant Garland, who is being carried down desperately wounded in the breast. He died before he reached a surgeon. He was killed on the first charge of the enemy while gallantly rallying his men before their superior force.[15]

After the Battle of Chancellorsville in May 1863, Raymer called the work of the surgeons 'butchery' and he remembered the cavalier way that amputated limbs were flung away. By the time the armies went into their winter quarters the clothing of the men was threadbare, and while the camp was efficiently laid out with rows of cabins, there was little food. The daily ration should have included 20 ounces (0.5 kilograms) of red meat, but according to Raymer they had just enough food 'to keep us from forgetting how to use our jaws, in case we should be so fortunate as to get anything which would require their services'.[16]

Of all the dispatches written in the course of the war, one of the saddest was penned after the battle of Gettysburg by Samuel Wilkeson, the veteran correspondent of the *New York Times*. Together with his friend Whitelaw Reid (*Cincinnati Gazette*), Wilkeson had travelled from Washington, DC, and had to contend with the destruction of some of the Baltimore and Ohio Railroad. Arriving at General Meade's headquarters mid-morning on the second day of the battle, the pair were lucky not to be killed when the position came under heavy fire. That night, Wilkeson was told that his son, First Lieutenant Bayard Wilkeson, had been killed the previous day when a cannonball scythed off one of his legs. Wilkeson recovered his body, buried it and wrote his dispatch on the 4th:

Who can write the history of a battle whose eyes are immovably fastened upon a central figure of transcendingly important interest – the dead body of an oldest born, crushed by a shell in a position where a battery should never have been sent, and abandoned to death in a building where surgeons dared not to stay?[17]

top: The seamen on the Union gunboat *Hunchback* pose for a photography by Mathew Brady.

above: The Kimberley (Miners) Town Guard photographed during the 124-day siege of Kimberley, which began in October 1899.

In towns where there was a sufficiently large readership to make them commercially viable, newspapers such as the *Chicago Defender* and the *Detroit Tribune* catered for the African American community. The first black correspondent to work for a major mainstream title was Thomas Morris Chester. Born in Harrisburg in 1834 to a mother who had escaped from slavery and a father who dealt in oysters, Chester had set his sights on a legal career. When the cost of college proved prohibitive, he pursued his education in Liberia, where he also edited the *Star of Liberia*. In 1863 he returned home to enlist, leading two companies of United States Colored Troops (USCT), and in August of the following year the Philadelphia Press offered him a job as a war correspondent with the Army of the James, reporting on the activities of the black troops. His first dispatch, from the headquarters of the 2nd Brigade, 3rd Division, 18th Army was dated 14 August:

> … *my attention was attracted by a huge volume of smoke, through which like flames from the centre of a volcano, a terrible blaze suddenly ascended, intermingled with dark objects which were thrown in every conceivable direction… fragments of humanity were scattered around in the immediate vicinity of the tragedy in frightful profusion.*[18]

Chester quickly discovered a distinctive voice, and like Page he had a dry sense of humour. Under the heading 'The Grand Fireworks' he wrote of the nightly artillery bombardment from both sides:

> *The enterprising managers of the firm of Grant and Lee take pleasure in announcing to the public in and around Petersburg that they are now prepared, and will continue, until further notice, to give every evening a grand exhibition of fireworks for the benefit of their respective employers. The past experience of the firm has enabled it to acquire a success in this direction which it feels satisfied a liberal-minded public will concede. The managers will not in any case hold themselves responsible for any accident which may occur to those who may be attracted, from curiosity or otherwise, to witness their exhibition.*[19]

Although as partial as any of the correspondents, Chester reported embarrassments such as desertions from his own side, and he wryly conceded the accuracy of the enemy, adding that, 'such reflections are by no means agreeable to your reporter'. On 26 January he wrote with disarming self-reference: '... and while inditing the last sentence a rebel shell came in such close proximity as to leave the impression, until I glanced around, that some part of my quarters was carried away and the aforesaid messenger injured, for he did some ludicrous feats of ground and lofty tumbling.'[20]

Chester's report of 4 April 1865, written from inside the Confederate House of Representatives in Richmond, Virginia, after the fall of the Confederate capital, must have been deeply satisfying to its author, his fellow African Americans and white abolitionists who read it: 'Seated in the Speaker's chair, so long dedicated to treason, but in the future to be consecrated to loyalty, I hasten to give a rapid sketch of the incidents which have occurred since my last dispatch....'[21]

After the war, Chester lectured as far afield as Russia and saved sufficient money to complete his law studies in England, where he became the first black American to be called to the Bar. He died in Harrisburg in 1892.

War in South Africa – In the Firing Line

But I shall wrap these lines up in a Red Cross flag and bury them among the ruins of Mulberry Grove, that, after the excavations, the unnumbered readers of the 'Daily Mail' may in the enlightened year 2100 know what a siege and a bombardment were like.

George Warrington Steevens (1869–1900) in *From Capetown to Ladysmith: An Unfinished Record of the South African War*, 1900

In 1889 the British Army had introduced a system of registration for war correspondents, which allowed them to draw food and fodder rations, gave them tacit permission to use the military telegraph for censored dispatches and entitled them to campaign medals. In addition, an article of the 1899 Hague Convention stated that: 'Individuals who follow an army without directly belonging to it, such as newspaper correspondents and reporters, sutlers, contractors, who fall into the enemy's hands, and whom the latter think fit to detain, have a right to be treated as prisoners of war, provided they can produce a certificate from the military authorities of the army they were accompanying.'

By the end of the nineteenth century, Russell's 'miserable tribe' had gone forth and multiplied considerably as newspapers proliferated. The campaign in the Sudan was closely covered, and journalists put their lives on the line for a scoop. When the situation of the British

troops besieged in Khartoum became critical in 1884, General Gordon dispatched a Nile steamer, whose passengers included the *Times'* correspondent Frank le Poer Power, to report their plight. Unfortunately, the ship was seized by the Arabs, and Power was among those murdered. Australian journalist William J. Lambie was shot and wounded in a skirmish, while the *Times* later lost a second man, the Hon. Hubert Howard, during the Battle of Omdurman in 1898. Howard's *Times* colleague, Frank Rhodes, was wounded.

Bennet Burleigh of the *Daily Telegraph*, who witnessed Howard's death, had already achieved his scoop. He simply cabled the location and result of the battle, before it had even taken place, thus allowing the news to hit the streets while the fighting still raged. He was, as his obituary allowed, a brave man who had distinguished himself at the Battle of Abu Klea as a volunteer in the trenches and a messenger. But the Glaswegian was one of the last of his kind. He died in 1914, by which time a different kind of war reporter was required – still brave, but more thoughtful and intelligent.

As the telegraph network grew and submarine cables crossed the seas, the increasing speed of communications enabled dispatches to appear in print 48 hours after their composition. This, together with the introduction of the telephone and the beginnings of wireless telegraphy, alarmed the authorities, who felt that correspondents were becoming reckless in their pursuit of news and increasingly likely to transmit information that would assist the enemy and/or embarrass their own forces. This fear was realized just before the Second Boer War (1899–1902), when on 22 September 1899 Reuters reported the precise composition of a British garrison.

Fought in South Africa and Natal, the second war, like the first, was a dispute between the British and the Dutch Boers. From October 1899 the Boers besieged three strategic British-held towns in Natal: Mafeking, Ladysmith and Kimberley. Attempts to relieve the sieges were thwarted by Boer victories against the relief forces, perhaps most famously at Spion Kop. Not until Lord Roberts had received significant reinforcements were the British able to lift the sieges and march into the Boers' territory, taking their capital, Pretoria, in June 1900. After two years of guerrilla tactics against the British, the Boers finally surrendered in May 1902.

Some 70 war correspondents from various nations were officially accredited to the British Army at the start of the war. Apart from the young Winston Churchill, the press corps included other first-rank journalists: Bennet Burleigh (*Daily Express*); Frank Rhodes, who had recovered from his injuries at Omdurman, Henry Nevinson

(*Daily Chronicle*), Henry Hiram Steere Pearse (*Daily News*), George Warrington Steevens (*Daily Mail*) and a former army private with the nom de plume of Edgar Wallace (*Daily Mail*). Headed by Lionel James and Leopold Amery, the cohort from the *Times* sported toothbrushes in their hats to distinguish themselves from lesser mortals representing the profession. Among the foreign contingent were Richard Harding Davis from the United States, and the Australians A.G. 'Smiler' Hayes and William J. Lambie, the latter working for Melbourne's the *Age* and undeterred by his narrow escape in the Sudan.

Churchill's father had expressed no great hopes for his son, prophesying that he was likely to become a 'mere social wastrel' and live 'a shabby, unhappy and futile existence'. Winston had other ideas, and at the same time as holding an army commission, he embraced a part-time career in journalism. This dual role took him to India, the North West Frontier and, in 1898, the Sudan. His motive was twofold: to see some action and to get his name noticed, a prerequisite for a political career. In 1899 he was employed by the *Morning Post* to cover the Second Boer War and given an enviable remuneration package: copyright on his dispatches and £250 per month plus all his expenses for the four-month posting. In addition, he secured complete freedom of movement and opinion.

Two weeks after his arrival, Churchill was captured by the Boers when the armoured train on which he was travelling was attacked on 15 November near Estcourt, nearly 30 miles (50 kilometres) south of Ladysmith. The commanding officer was wounded, so Churchill exhorted the soldiers to clear the line and get the train moving for the sake of the injured, allegedly with the words: 'Keep cool, men. This will be interesting for my paper.' He was held in a Pretoria prison, from where he escaped on 12 December by scaling the wall and walking unchallenged through the town. When the 23:10 goods train from Pretoria to Delagoa Bay stopped, he climbed aboard, hid under coalsacks and jumped off at dawn. His plan was to make for Lourenço Marques in neutral Portuguese East Africa – present-day Mozambique – but he was in Boer territory and he needed help. By sheer luck he asked for it at the home of a British mine manager, who told him that every one of his neighbours would have handed him back to his captors. The man sheltered him until he could be smuggled onto a train bound for Durban. After surviving a search of the train, Churchill arrived in Durban as a hero: the correspondent had become the story. The newspaper account of his escape, published as far afield as New York and New Zealand, contains less than the truth: he was protecting those who helped him.

Churchill joined an irregular cavalry unit and saw considerable action, but that brief foray into journalism had, as he had hoped, brought him to the attention of the world.

By as early as mid-June 1900 more than 40 correspondents had been killed, wounded, captured, murdered or taken ill with typhoid during the various sieges and actions that comprised the war in South Africa. Yet the tone of the memoirs of those who wrote up their experiences suggests that danger and difficulty added at least as much spice to their profession as was to be had from journalistic rivalry.

A number of reporters found themselves besieged at Ladysmith by General Joubert's forces, and little information could get out after the telegraph wire was cut on 2 November. The garrison had its own 'internal' telegraph and telephone networks, plus 160 top-class racing pigeons; and, on sunny days, the heliograph could flash Morse Code messages, though these were sometimes intercepted by the enemy. Lionel James sent his dispatches for the *Times* in triplicate by dispatch riders, some of which did get through, though when his request for a crate of pigeons was met, it only resulted in an appreciative letter of thanks from the Boers who intercepted the consignment.

Quartered in the Royal Hotel – journalists always look for the best city accommodation possible – the frustrated correspondents, headed by George Steevens, set about publishing a light-hearted newspaper for the population, with the aim of keeping up morale. The first edition of the *Ladysmith Lyre* was published on 27 November, and its opening prospectus was uncompromising:

> *The Ladysmith Lyre is published to supply a long-felt want. What you want in a besieged town, cut off from the world, is news which you can absolutely rely on as false. The rumours that pass from tongue to tongue may, for all you know, be occasionally true. In the collection and preparation of falsehoods we shall spare no effort and no expense. It is enough for us that Ladysmith wants stories. It shall have them.*

The reality of siege life was monotony and rationing, interspersed with terror as the low-lying town was exposed to heavy gunfire, particularly from the Boer gun known as 'Long Tom', which on 3 November managed to put a shell into the Royal Hotel. As well as writing the *Lyre*, Steevens wrote a brilliant journal of the siege, which was full of wry humour, even-handed in its view of the

above: A group shot of war correspondents during the Second Boer War. The young Winston Churchill is seated second from the left, middle row.

enemy and captured the tedium of the experience:

I am sick of it. Everybody is sick of it…. Weary, stale, flat, unprofitable, the whole thing. At first, to be besieged and bombarded was a thrill; then it was a joke; now it is nothing but a weary, weary, weary bore. We do nothing but eat and drink and sleep – just exist dismally. We have forgotten when the siege began; and now we are beginning not to care when it ends. For my part, I feel it will never end. It will go on just as now, languid fighting, languid cessation, for ever and ever. We shall drop off one by one, and listlessly die of old age….

So be it. I shall not be there to see….[22]

Steevens died of typhoid – then called enteric fever – on 15 January 1900 and later received a generous tribute from Lord Kitchener: 'He did his work as correspondent so brilliantly, and he never gave the slightest trouble – I wish all correspondents were like him.'[23] Alfred Farrand (*Morning Post*) and the Earl of Alva were both killed and several reporters were taken ill, mostly with typhoid, before the siege was lifted on 1 March.

The relieving force included its own quota of reporters, who were so anxious to get the news to their editors that, having heard the siege was ended, they rode back with their dispatches without actually entering the city. For Richard Harding Davis and two colleagues, who had been chasing the relieving column, it presented a golden opportunity to be the first correspondents into Ladysmith. They justified this on the grounds that only in the town

SIR WINSTON CHURCHILL, 1874–1965

In a letter to his prospective mother-in-law in 1908, Winston Churchill wrote that he was neither rich nor powerful but that he loved her daughter, Clementine Hozier, and believed he would be able to make her happy and give her the position she merited. By this time, the ambitious 33 year old, who was convinced that he would make his mark on the world, had already served as a junior cavalry officer in India, a war correspondent in the Sudan and South Africa, and, for almost eight years, a Member of Parliament. Initially he had been a Conservative, but in 1904 he had 'crossed the floor' and joined the Liberal Party, soon gaining ministerial rank.

Despite going into politics, Churchill retained his links with the army, as an officer in a yeomanry regiment, but at the outbreak of the First World War he was First Lord of the Admiralty, responsible for the Royal Navy. His enthusiasm for the disastrous Gallipoli Campaign obliged him to resign, and he went to the Western Front early in 1916 to command the 6th Battalion, Royal Scots Fusiliers and rebuild his reputation.

His political career continued during the interwar period. He rejoined the Conservatives in 1925, but many of his decisions were poor, and he fell out of favour, making his speeches from the backbenches. His support for King Edward

VIII during the abdication crisis won him few friends, and he consistently warned of the dangers of both German rearmament and of appeasing Hitler. On the day that Germany invaded Poland, Chamberlain invited Churchill to join the War Cabinet – once again as First Lord Of the Admiralty. On Friday, 10 May 1940, a few days after the German offensive against the Netherlands began, Chamberlain resigned and Churchill became Prime Minister, presiding over a government of national unity.

At 65, age gave him gravitas, but the war was physically as well as mentally demanding. He contracted pneumonia in 1943 and during his extensive foreign travels he suffered a heart attack in Washington and fever in Moscow and Malta.

Churchill will always be popularly remembered for the way he kept Britain in the war after the defeat of France. He stiffened the national resolve with speeches to Parliament and the nation that provided the most memorable soundbites since Queen Elizabeth I's 'Armada Speech' in 1588: '… if the British Empire and its Commonwealth last for a thousand years, men will still say, "This was their finest hour".'; 'Never in the field of human conflict has so much been owed by so many to so few'. Although he did not enjoy the process, he broadcast to the nation – and despite allegations to the contrary, he did not use an actor.

The Conservatives lost the 1945 election to Labour, but Churchill returned to power in 1951, and eventually retired from politics in 1955. On his death in 1965 he was given the honour of a state funeral.

As well as a soldier, war correspondent and statesman, Churchill was a talented amateur artist and a gifted writer, who won the Nobel Prize in Literature in 1953.

opposite: Churchill makes his V.E. Day broadcast, 8 May 1945.

below: Winston Churchill, correspondent for the *Morning Post* during the Boer War, on horseback.

We were racing by this time, Lambie's big chestnut mare had gained a length on my little veldt pony, and we were not more than a hundred yards away from the Mauser rifles that had closed in on us from the kopjes. A voice called out in good English: 'Throw up your hands, you d—— fools'. But the galloping fever was on us both, and we only crouched lower on our horses' backs, and rode all the harder, for even a barn-yard fowl loves liberty.

All at once I saw my comrade throw his hands up with a spasmodic gesture. He rose in his stirrups, and fairly bounded out of his saddle, and as he spun round in the air I saw the red blood on the white face, and I knew that death had come to him sudden and sharp. Again the rifles spoke, and the lead was closer to me than ever a friend sticks in time of trouble, and I knew in my heart that the next few strides would settle things. The black pony was galloping gamely under my weight. Would he carry me safely out of that line of fire, or would he fail me?

Suddenly something touched me on the right temple; it was not like a blow; it was not a shock; for half a second I was conscious. I knew I was hit; knew that the reins had fallen from my nerveless hands, knew that I was lying down upon my horse's back, with my head hanging below his throat. Then all the world went out in one mad whirl...[26]

could they be certain of finding a censor, and 'unless he said that Ladysmith was relieved, the fact that 25,000 other soldiers said so counted for idle gossip'.[24]

The censor was at his post, and a few minutes later a signal officer on Convent Hill heliographed my cable to Bulwana, where, six hours after the Boers had abandoned it, Buller's own helios had begun to dance, and they speeded the cable on its long journey to the newspaper office on the Thames Embankment.[25]

Casualties among the correspondents mounted. The British troops in South Africa included the 1st Australian Regiment, recently formed from the companies of several colonies (now states), a detachment of which was sent to reinforce the Tasmanians at Jasfontein Farm. With the detachment rode William J. Lambie and 'Smiler' Hayes. Somehow the pair became separated from the patrol they were following and found themselves surrounded by 40 Boer troops. Ignoring the calls to surrender, they spurred away.

Hayes awoke in the solicitous care of the Boers, who had already given Lambie an honourable burial. The Boer leader was vexed to find that his victims were correspondents, telling Hayes: 'Sir, you dress exactly like two British officers; you ride out with a fighting party, you try to ride off at a gallop under the very muzzles of our rifles when we tell you to surrender. You can blame no one but yourselves for this day's work.'[27]

The war ended with the signing of the Treaty of Vereeniging on 31 May 1902. During the negotiations correspondents were barred from the area, but Edgar Wallace rose to the challenge that presented.

Fortunately for me, there was a good pal of mine in the camp, a Tommy with whom I had soldiered, and, meeting him, I arranged a code of signals. He was to

PLATE LXXIX

WAR CORRESPONDENTS AT LADYSMITH

The *Daily News* Correspondent's (Mr. H. H. S Pearse) house, after being struck for a second time by a 6-in. shell from Umbuluwane. The cottage in the background was used as a rendezvous by the London journalists.

opposite: Richard Harding Davis, the American war correspondent, wearing uniform and pith helmet.

left: A reprint by the *Daily Graphic* of the *Ladysmith Lyre*, edited by George Steevens to cheer up the people of Ladysmith during the siege.

above: The shell that hit the Royal Hotel (right) during the siege of Ladysmith also wrecked the adjoining house of correspondent H.H. Pearse.

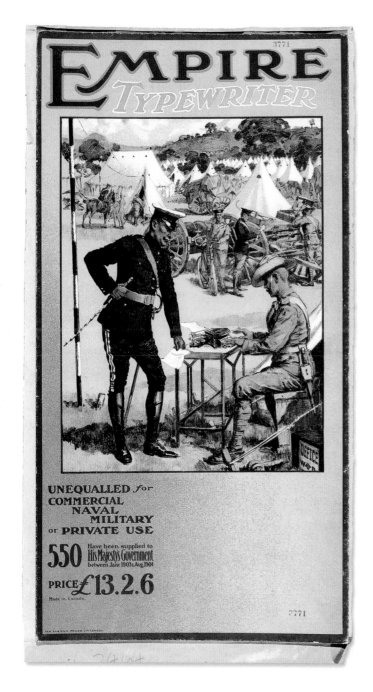

have three handkerchiefs – one red, one white, one blue. The railway ran within sight of the camp, and every morning I journeyed down to the Vaal River by train, took the next train back, keeping my eye on the camp for the signal. Red meant 'nothing doing', blue 'making progress', and the white handkerchief was to signify that the peace treaty had actually been signed. I don't know how many journeys I made on that infernal railway, but never once was the red handkerchief displayed. Then one morning, when rumour was rife that the negotiations had fallen through, I saw my friend standing on the end of the tent lines, and he was displaying a white handkerchief conspicuously. I did not wait to get back to Pretoria. Instead I sent a wire from Germiston: Contract signed....

I had been warned of the dire consequences to me should I continue sending uncensored messages; but a correspondent's first duty, within the bounds of honour and decency, is to his newspaper.[28]

The new eyewitness of war

... the camera is the eye of history.

(a comment attributed to) Mathew B. Brady (1823–1896)

Although publishing technology was insufficiently advanced to allow the publication of half-tone photographs, Roger Fenton was sent to the Crimea in 1855 to produce an official photographic record of the conflict, not for posterity but to make the war more popular at home. Photography was an expensive pursuit, but Fenton had sufficient private means to indulge in it, and he had already photographed Queen Victoria and Prince Albert. However, he was not the first photographer to record a war (images exist of the 1846–47 Mexican–American War), and the Austro-Hungarian Carol Szathmari had also taken photographs of both Russian and Ottoman Turkish troops in the Crimea in 1853, but Fenton remains the most famous, if only because so many of his images have survived.

Fenton took everything with him: bottles of chemicals, 700 glass plates, five cameras and the converted wine merchant's horse-drawn van that served as his mobile darkroom. His letters home reveal an exhausting and often frustrating five months for himself

above: The first commercially successful typewriters were developed in the 1870s. The popular Empire became available from 1892 and was marketed as suitable for use during campaigns.

opposite: Roger Fenton's assistant, Marcus Sparling, photographed by Fenton on the box of the photographic van.

and his assistant, Marcus Sparling. He fell off his horse, broke several ribs, contracted cholera and suffered from the effects of working with hazardous chemicals in the hot confines of his van during the summer.

The photographic process had to be completed within ten minutes. Nitrocellulose mixed with alcohol and ether formed the collodion base into which Fenton dissolved chloride, bromide or iodide salts. The resulting liquid was applied to one face of a glass plate, which was then light-sensitized in a bath of silver nitrate and, under red 'safe-lighting', transferred to a plate holder for insertion into the camera. The photograph had to be taken quickly, and processed immediately using benzene-1,2,3-triol, commonly known as pyrogallol. The fixing agent could be hypo (sodium thio-sulphate, formerly known as hyposulphite) or a solution of cyanide, and the resulting negative needed a gum coating for protection. The print was made at leisure by laying the negative over a sheet of albumen paper and exposing it to light.

With shutter speeds measured in seconds, rather than the hundredths of seconds essential to freeze movement, Fenton was unable to record action, and instead he photographed the camps, the desolate landscape and individuals. The primary commercial advantage of the wet collodion process was that it produced a negative from which any number of prints could be made, which was ideal for selling portraits to the sitters. He took no images of dead bodies, though he saw many, including those of friends (he mourned for the loss of several friends among the officers); he would have regarded such photographs as taboo and uncommercial. His work was exhibited and also published as engravings in books and the *Illustrated London News*.

After Fenton's departure, the fall of Sebastopol was photographed by Felice Beato and his associate James Robertson. Beato later took photographs during the Indian Mutiny and is thought to be the first photographer to include dead bodies – carefully arranged, on one occasion, to improve the composition, thus proving that even if the camera did not lie, its operators were not above tampering with the evidence. Fenton himself may have set a precedent. From the same spot he took two views of a landscape known as the Valley of the Shadow of Death, not to be confused with the valley down which the Light Brigade charged. In one image, there are cannonballs on the road as well as on the sides of the slope. On the second image, the road is clear. Serious research indicates that the photograph showing the cannonballs on the road was taken *after* that of the clear road.

Fenton abandoned photography in 1862, returned to practising law and died in obscurity seven years later.

There are parallels between Fenton's career and that of Mathew B. Brady, who created an outstanding photographic record of the American Civil War using the same process. Far less rich than Fenton, Brady worked in order to finance his photographic studies, and by the age of 22 he owned his own studio. He made his name with portraits of famous people, but passionately believed that it was his duty to his country 'to preserve the faces of its historic men and mothers'. By the time of his death he had taken photographs of 18 American presidents.

The decision to photograph the civil war was taken against the advice of his friends, and he borrowed $100,000 to set up several mobile darkrooms – again in converted vehicles – and to engage the assistants who took most of the photographs (actually credited to Brady as their employer). Operating under the same technical constraints as Fenton, the photographers could only capture still subjects, but this time there was no flinching from the cruel reality of war. In the aftermath of the Battle of Antietam (Sharpsburg) Alexander Gardner photographed dead soldiers, who were already decomposing as they lay unburied. On 20 October 1862 the *New York Times* reviewed the exhibition, 'The Dead of Antietam', of

Brady's work: 'Mr. Brady has done something to bring home to us the terrible reality and earnestness of war. If he has not brought bodies and laid them in our door-yards and along the streets, he has done something very like it.... These pictures have a terrible distinctness.'

Brady created the enduring image of the war, but, as Fenton had found, as soon as the war was over people wanted to look forwards, not back. Even the government refused to buy his pictures, and he died in poverty. 'No one,' he said, 'will ever know what I went through to secure those negatives. The world can never appreciate it. It changed the whole course of my life.'

By the time of the Second Boer War comparatively compact cameras were available, preloaded with celluloid film. The ability to take sharp images of motion action was still in the future, and there were as yet no combat photographers who went into battle with the troops in the way that Robert Capa and Larry Burrows were to do. However, camps, regiments, individuals and the after-math of battles and skirmishes were thoroughly documented by amateurs and professionals, such as the British-born, Johannes-burg-based freelance Horace W. Nicholls, who successfully sold his images to papers such as the *Graphic*.

The development of the motion picture camera allowed a great deal of footage of the Boer War to be made (although much of it was staged and shot thousands of miles away). Four genuine British film crews did dispatch cameramen to the conflict, including William Kennedy Laurie Dickson, of British Mutoscope and Biograph, who had trained in the United States under Edison. Dickson sailed to South Africa on the same voyage as Churchill, complaining bitterly in his journal about his adverse reaction to the typhoid jab. Disembarking at Durban, with the aim of reaching Ladysmith, he set off with his cart and a ton of equipment – the batteries driving the camera weighed more than 1,200 pounds (540 kilograms) alone. With such a cumbersome outfit, it was impossible for him to get close to the action, especially given the

terrain, and his telephoto lenses lacked sufficiently sharp resolution. But he filmed the progress of the army, and a minute's worth of action of the retreat from Spion Kop.

He subsequently recorded the entry into Ladysmith, but when he entered Pretoria after it had been relieved he was too late to film the ceremony. Undeterred, he resorted to staging his own flag-raising ceremony, using a larger flag than that now in Pretoria's main square, something that did not escape the notice of the audiences who saw his work in special cinemas equipped to show Biograph films. It would not be the last time a photographer found himself in trouble over a flag-raising ceremony, though Joe Rosenthal[29] did not set out to deceive at Iwo Jima in 1945. During the First World War, Geoffrey Malins would also stage scenes in his landmark film 'The Battle of the Somme' (see page 56–59).

above: Dead soldiers in front of Dunker Church, Antietam, taken during the American Civil War.

opposite: Roger Fenton's second photograph of 'The Valley of the Shadow of Death', with the cannonballs littering the ground.

As Europe slid into war in the summer of 1914 dozens of journalists hurried off to various destinations in France and Belgium, near their borders with Germany. Some had no opportunity to pack a suitcase or say goodbye to their families. The editor of the *Daily Mail* told Joseph Jeffries, 'Remember Melton Prior's words – a deceased correspondent is no use to his newspaper', before shaking his hand and adding, 'In case we don't meet again'. Many did not wait for the War Office in London to accredit them.

> Something outside myself, as it seemed, was talking now that there was no way of escape, that it was monstrous to suppose that all these bursting shells would not smash the ambulances to bits and finish the agony of the wounded, and that death is very hideous. I remember thinking also how ridiculous it is for men to kill each other like this, and to make such hells.
>
> Philip Gibbs (1877–1962) in *The Soul Of The War*, 1915

Travelling alone or in groups with colleagues and rivals, their paths frequently twining, they were an eclectic band, with various levels of reporting experience, little of which prepared them for what they would encounter. The veteran reporter of the *Times*, Harry Perry Robinson, had made his name in North America during the 1880s, reporting from the tough mining areas for American newspapers; his younger colleague, Arthur Moore had covered conflict in the

Outlaws and Captives:
the first world war

Ottoman territories and Persia. Philip Gibbs, who worked for the *Daily Chronicle*, had come to journalism via publishing, and had a best-selling novel to his name. Gibbs's slight physique and pale complexion disguised a sharp professionalism and determination; his descriptive abilities and deeply sensitive nature would translate his observations into earnest reports and searing autobiographical accounts of the war.

A journalist since leaving school, Henry Hamilton Fyfe had been an innovative editor at the *Daily Mirror* until the move to the *Daily Mail* made him 'the special correspondent with the largest newspaper public in existence to address, and a fairly free hand as to what I would write about and how'.[1] At two hours' notice, he and his wife left on the boat-train, convinced that war would be averted.

Neutral countries, particularly the USA, also sent their correspondents into the field. Frederick Palmer caught the transatlantic liner RMS *Lusitania* as soon as war was announced,

bringing with him the experience he had gained across the world. The most respected, and certainly the best paid, of the American correspondents was Richard Harding Davis, who had also covered the Second Boer War. For the duration that their country was neutral, the Americans enjoyed the freedom to report from either side.

Not all the journalists were male: Australian novelist Louise Mack had edited the *Italian Gazette* in Florence before joining the *Daily Mail*, which made her one of the first female war correspondents. The American reporter E. Alexander Powell met her early in the war, at Ghent, and described her luggage as a model of compactness: '... it consisted of a sleeping-bag, a notebook, half a dozen pencils – and a powder-puff. She explained that she brought the sleeping-bag because she understood that war correspondents always slept in the field. As most of the fields in that part of Flanders were just then under several inches of water as a result of the autumn rains, a folding canoe would have been more useful.'[2]

above: As the Germans closed in on Antwerp, troops and refugees packed onto trains to escape. This was the last train to leave the town.

Everyone travelled with expenses, generally in the form of gold sovereigns: a reliable currency in such an uncertain situation. Jeffries carried most of his in a special money belt, the remainder loose in his pockets, and he spent his first night in Brussels with the belt still round his waist and the rest of the coins in socks hidden under his pillow.

The Germans marched into Belgium on 4 August and Jeffries, who had just driven to Liège, secured his first scoop when a small cohort unsuccessfully attempted to kidnap or kill the city's commander on the night of the 5th–6th. His story written, he hurried to the telegraph office, to be told that only military traffic was permitted. In a flash of inspiration he addressed his carefully composed telegram to an official of his acquaintance at Belgium's Ministry of War, asking him to forward it to London, and he wrote in French so that it could be vetted in front of him, rather than being delayed until an English-speaking censor came on duty. It contained some factual errors, of which its author was unaware until after the war, and it was censored both in Brussels and London,

but Jeffries had the satisfaction of sending the first telegram from an Allied war correspondent at the front.

BATTLING BUREAUCRACY

On 8 August 1914 Parliament in the UK passed the Defence of the Realm Act (DORA), the wide-ranging provisions of which included severe restrictions on the publication of even the most trivial detail that, in the opinion of the censor in London, might prejudice the war effort at home or in the field.

The French, too, clamped down. Gibbs was in Paris, astonished that massive armies could be on the march while correspondents were forbidden to mention the fact. 'There was something stupefying in the veil of silence which enshrouded the operations of the legions which were being hurled against each other along the frontiers. By one swift stroke of the military censorship journalism was throttled. All its lines of communication were cut, suddenly, as when, in my office, I spoke from Paris to England, and found myself with a

opposite: A mobile army kitchen provides food to troops and correspondents on the Western Front in October 1914.

left: A party of Canadian war correspondents waiting in their official cars in the square at Hazebrouk, 28 July 1915.

overleaf: The first page of Arthur Moore's dispatch describing the retreat of the British from Mons, with the censor's changes. It was published in the *Times* on 30 August 1914.

half-finished sentence before a telephone which would no longer "march," as they say across the Channel. Pains and penalties were threatened against any newspaper which should dare to publish a word of military information beyond the official communiqués issued in order to hide the truth.'[3]

Although the British journalists had expected to gain accreditation when they reached the armies, their hopes were unexpectedly dashed by the War Office, which refused to allow any reporting from the war zone. Two highly experienced sketch-artists working for the *Illustrated London News*, Henry Charles Seppings Wright and Frederic Villiers – who had been covering wars since Afghanistan in 1879 – quickly ran up against this military hostility. France's Foreign Ministry was willing to accredit Villiers to its army, and local commanders even allowed him to sketch batteries provided he omitted specific features that might betray the location to the Germans, but the British enforced their prohibition rigorously through every possible channel. When he went to the British Embassy in Paris, the First Secretary went up to him with a letter and said: 'This is from the British

War Office; you are in touch with the correspondents here, and His Excellency would like you to tell them that they will not be allowed to go with the French armies into the field.'[4]

Heavily restricted in their movements, starved of accurate information and at risk of being shot as spies if they were captured by the advancing Germans, correspondents operated as best they could, but their reports – based on information gleaned behind their own lines – bore little relation to what was happening in the field.

Having been rebuffed in his attempt to gain accreditation to the French Army, Fyfe travelled with Arthur Moore to the British General Headquarters (GHQ) at Le Cateau, which was full of staff officers, pejoratively called 'red tabs' or 'brass hats'. Unfortunately, one of the officers had an outstanding grudge against Fyfe and he had both men arrested and paroled to appear before the Provost Marshal the following morning. For the first time they learned of the ban on correspondents and were obliged to sign an undertaking to keep out of the war zone.

Harding Davis, who was based in Brussels, remembered the confusion caused by the rumours on which they had to base their decisions. Taking cameras, telescopes and binoculars was too big a risk, because they might be mistaken for spies. Often without so much as a sandwich for lunch, 'each would depart upon his separate errand, at night returning to a perfectly served dinner and a luxurious bed. For the news-gatherers it was a game of chance. The wisest veterans would cast their nets south and see only harvesters in the fields, the amateurs would lose their way to the north and find themselves facing an army corps or running a gauntlet of shell-fire. It was like throwing a handful of coins on the table hoping that one might rest upon the winning number. Over the map of Belgium we threw ourselves. Some days we landed on the right color, on others we saw no more than we would see at state manoeuvres.'5

Not all correspondents had passports, because they were not generally required for European travel, and those who did have them found that in wartime passports did not necessarily guarantee free passage. Permits issued in one city might or might not be honoured further down the road. Improvisation was required. Fyfe and his wife drove through some thirty checkpoints on the road from Nancy to Paris flourishing a season ticket for that summer's Earls Court Exhibition in London. William Beach Thomas was temporarily imprisoned when his homemade credentials failed to convince a British officer. Jeffries had a whole sheaf of permits, which served him well, but the Rolls-Royce he hired in Paris, complete with a driver who had chauffeured the rich and famous, was sometimes his most valuable *laissez-passer*. Gibbs, who had left on the day that British reservists had been called up, favoured the document that merely authorized him to receive the daily official communiqué from the French Ministry of War.

Without official accreditation, the logistics of first obtaining and then sending home a dispatch proved a constant struggle. As Harding Davis discovered, the hardest part of being a correspondent was not avoiding bullets but trying to bribe a ride on a troop train or getting forage for a horse. Early in the war the *Daily Mail* issued an instruction by telegram to Jeffries to cover all eventualities. He was to use the telegraph until the wire went down, and the postal service while the trains were running. After that, the newspaper's official car was to shuttle between Brussels and Ostend, from where the paper's representative in Ostend would cable dispatches to London. If the submarine cable were to be cut, the representative was to send the copy by mailboat or, as a last resort, by fishing vessel.

William Beach Thomas once walked 30 miles (50 kilometres) in one day – 'on a diet of coffee and brandy and [knew] no fatigue'6 – in order to catch an afternoon train to Paris. From there he filed a dispatch to the *Daily Mail* about the Battle of the Aisne, in the belief that the engagement marked the beginning of the end of the war and not, as it proved, the moment when the troops began digging their trenches. Gibbs and his companions travelled on foot, by car, taxi, trains and dirty cattle trucks full of 'unwashed people'. Without couriers, they frequently crossed the Channel with their dispatches, stayed a few hours in Fleet Street and returned filthy, starving hungry and exhausted by lack of sleep. Others travelled around by bicycle, motorbike and horse.

One way of avoiding the cross-Channel trip was to bribe a ship's purser to take the dispatch, but before long that was made illegal – as was the next resort of the newspapers, to have their own network of couriers. The ingenious Gibbs managed to send three dispatches home through government channels by using his charm to persuade three different King's Messengers to carry a letter to the War Office along with the rest of their official correspondence. The letters were marked for the *Daily Chronicle*, care of the War Office. The ruse was then discovered.

In the procurement of transport, some were lucky. A wealthy businessman put himself and his Rolls-Royce at the service of Moore and Fyfe. Powell, the American, was chauffeured in a luxurious vehicle supplied by the Belgian government. The official car that Harding Davis and Gerald Morgan (*Daily Telegraph*) shared 'was of surpassing beauty, speed, and comfort. It was as long as a Plant freight-car and as yellow; and from it flapped in the breeze more English, Belgian, French, and Russian flags than fly from the roof of the New York Hippodrome.'7 Late for the Dover express, and wretched at the thought of losing his so-far-inseparable companions, W.M. Massey and Henry Major Tomlinson, Gibbs took his wife's suggestion and for £22 chartered a private train that whisked him in solitary state to the coast, saluted by porters at each station.

THE MONS DISPATCH

From 14 August and for much of September, the French and British clashed with German forces along the border, from the frontier with Switzerland to as far north as Mons in Belgium, in what became collectively known as the Battles of the Frontiers. The Germans pushed the French back at the battles of Lorraine, Ardennes and Charleroi, and on 23 August the British Expeditionary Force (BEF) met the Germans at Mons. Although the British held the Germans on the first day, they were obliged to retreat and

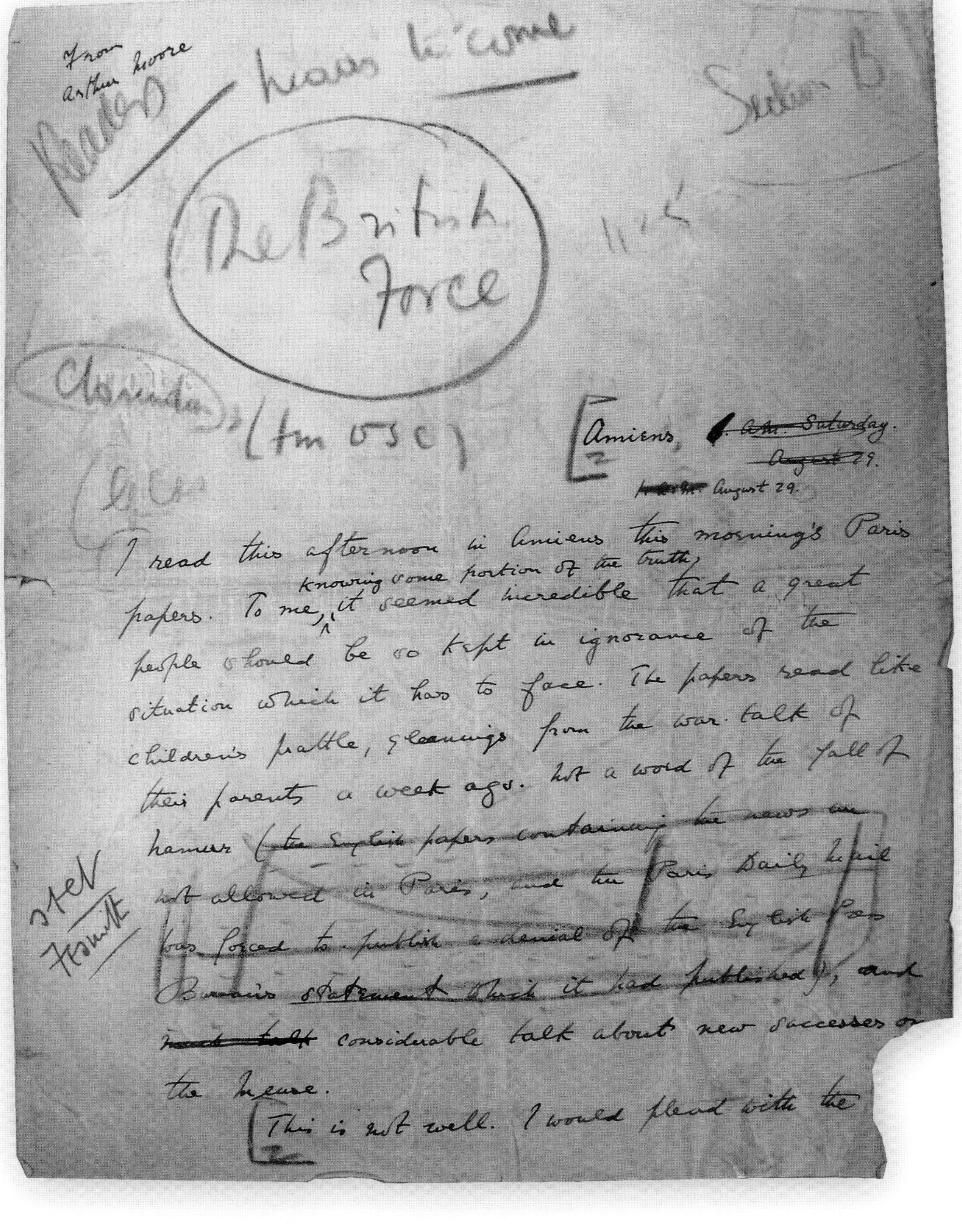
From Arthur Moore
The British Force
(fm OSC)
Amiens, ~~1 a.m. Saturday~~
~~August 29.~~
August 29.
I read this afternoon in Amiens this morning's Paris papers. To me, knowing some portion of the truth, it seemed incredible that a great people should be so kept in ignorance of the situation which it has to face. The papers read like children's prattle, gleanings from the war talk of their parents a week ago. Not a word of the fall of Namur ~~(the English papers containing the news are not allowed in Paris, and the Paris Daily Mail was forced to publish a denial of the English Press Bureau's statement which it had published)~~, and considerable talk about new successes on the Meuse.
This is not well. I would plead with the

SIR PHILIP GIBBS, 1877–1962

The fifth child of a civil servant and writer, Gibbs grew up surrounded by authors and journalists, and had his first article published in the *Daily Chronicle* when he was 17. For him, journalism was 'one of the best games in the world for any young man with quick eyes, a sense of humour, some touch of quality in his use of words, and curiosity in his soul for the truth and pageant of our human drama, provided he keeps his soul unsullied from the dirt'[41]. His pre-First World War career was varied and frenetic. He scooped the news of King Edward VII's death, gate-crashed royal events, broke into the wrong house instead of an allegedly haunted mansion, investigated anarchists, served as a literary editor and reported widely from Europe. Published in 1909, his first novel, *The Street of Adventure*, became a best seller, but profits were swallowed by a libel case brought by a former colleague who 'recognized' himself in the book.

The experience of the Western Front aged Gibbs. Official war artist William Orpen described him in 1917 as 'despondent, gloomy, nervy, realising to the full the horror of the whole business; his face drawn very fine, and intense sadness in his very kind eyes'[42].

He travelled across post-war Europe as far as Russia; in Rome he became the first journalist ever accorded a private papal interview. He had great faith in the American people and gave speaking tours in the USA. At the start of the Second World War he was an accredited war correspondent for the *Daily Sketch*, but spent most of the war with the Ministry of Information. Although he wrote numerous novels, he is best remembered for his much-quoted books about the Western Front in which he exposed the horrors once hidden by censorship.

had to fight a bitter rearguard action at Le Cateau on the 26th, during which more than 7,000 men were lost.

At Amiens, on Friday 28 August, Moore and Fyfe unexpectedly encountered some of the truth about events at Mons two days earlier when retreating troops from the 4th Division told them that a major reverse had taken place – a subject on which the newspapers were silent. Each man put pen to paper with the intention of telling the country that a greater effort was required, and Moore began with an impassioned plea to the censor to print his dispatch, assuring him that it contained nothing the Germans could not already know and that it was better for Britain to face the truth and respond to it.

A dilemma faced the pair. If they left the area at such a critical moment, they could miss an even greater scoop. But only by taking the dispatches to the mailboat in person could they ensure their safe arrival. They chose the latter course, and set off for Dieppe the following morning – only to find that the mailboat had failed to arrive. The afternoon boat sailed from Boulogne, but their car had broken down and it cost an extortionate £24 to hire another vehicle. The dispatches reached London that night and both were printed in a special Sunday edition of the *Times*.

Moore's piece had been censored overnight by the chief censor, F.E. Smith, later Lord Birkenhead, who believed it should be printed – with certain changes. However, the phrases he struck out were replaced with ellipses, and these erroneously suggested to readers that the original dispatch had contained news too dreadful to print. Smith finished the dispatch with a sentence of his own that amounted to a call for more volunteers to bolster the army.

EVADING OFFICIALDOM

Moore and Fyfe now headed for Beauvais, using a car intended for a rival correspondent, which sported a useful Belgian government permit on the windscreen. At Beauvais, a town in fear of the advancing Germans, who were by now only 4 miles (6 kilometres) away, they encountered the indignant journalist whom they had so underhandedly dispossessed – he, unable to reclaim his car, covertly scraped off the permit.

For this act they were to have cause to be grateful. On 2 September they were stopped by a German officer, but with a retreating French force nearby he could not risk a noisy exchange of fire. Having confiscated the chauffeur's gun, he graciously allowed them to proceed towards Paris on the Clermont road, knowing,

which they did not, that Clermont was in German hands. However, having been warned by locals, the pair turned round and went in search of the French Army. Had they been arrested with a Belgian pass and no official accreditation their status as civilians would have been seriously compromised.

Gibbs, too, escaped from Amiens, together with his travelling companions, Massey and Major Tomlinson, and wrote his dispatch about the Mons retreat in a troop train that was full of wounded men. The trio left Beauvais on the last train out before the town fell, and reached Paris in expectation of an imminent German occupation, from where Gibbs wrote movingly of the French capital's preparations. Instead, at the First Battle of the Marne (6–12 September) the German offensive was finally halted, and the French forces in the city were rushed to the front by every method available.

What none of the correspondents knew, nor would have been allowed to write had they known it, was that a quarter of a million French soldiers, possibly just as many Germans and more than 12,000 British soldiers were killed or wounded at the Marne. Afterwards, while walking across the battlefield with a French grave-digger, Gibbs found soggy, half-finished letters written by German soldiers to families who would never receive them, and his guide pointed out a great pyre of German bodies being cremated together, while the French and British were being laid in graves. 'Why in God's name, or the devil's,' he asked himself 'were men killing each other like this on the fields of France? ... I wondered if in that roasting mass of human flesh were any of the young men who had been kind to me in Germany ....'[8]

Most of the correspondents gradually gave up and returned home, leaving a small band of 'outlaws', as they called themselves, to play an increasingly risky game of cat and mouse with the military authorities that lasted into 1915.

When Lord Northcliffe, proprietor of the *Daily Mail*, ordered Fyfe to go to Bordeaux with the French government, the partnership with Moore was over. In Bordeaux, Fyfe joined the Red Cross as a stretcher-bearer until the authorities finally caught up with him and had him brought home. His next war posting would be to Russia. For a while Moore teamed up with Jeffries and the photographer J. Grant Marshall, but they, too, were on borrowed time. In 1915 Moore returned home, got married and was commissioned into the Rifle Brigade. He ended the war as a Royal Air Force (RAF) squadron leader. Jeffries was bitterly disappointed not to be accredited to the British Army as a correspondent in 1915, and

went to report from other fronts. Later, he calculated that he spent only 37 days in England during the war.

Ellis Ashmead-Bartlett, who later made his name reporting from the Dardanelles, was one of several correspondents to see the inside of the Cherche-Midi military prison in Paris. Others included Harding Davis and Morgan, who had been arrested by the French at Romigny. The former was in possession of a long article about the wanton destruction of Reims cathedral, while Gerald Morgan's dispatch was mainly about Gothic architecture. Each man offered to donate 5 francs to the French Red Cross for every word that their captors allowed on the wire. The officers refused, but the following morning the censor read Harding Davis's piece, authorized it for immediate transmission and complained that it should have been wired 24 hours earlier.

Despite the orders to arrest him at any port and cancel his passport if he came to England to deliver his dispatches, Gibbs always found himself welcomed at the Foreign Office by Sir William Tyrrell, Lord Grey's private secretary, who asked him about his impressions of the situation in France.

FAITHFUL TO THE TRUTH

Correspondents had been sent to find 'the facts' for populations that were eager and anxious for news, but standing in direct conflict with this pursuit of facts were the demands made by unconditional patriotism, which required the suppression of anything that would adversely affect the resolve of the public to see the war through. Gibbs's sympathy for the ordinary German soldier would not have found favour in Fleet Street, where editors wanted stories of Franco–British heroism and German atrocities to inspire the population. Fyfe wrote: 'The war atmosphere in the *Mail* office was indicated by a reproving cable Marlowe, the editor, sent me once when I had mentioned some kindly act by enemy soldiers. "Nothing wanted," he said, "about good kind Germans. There are no good Germans but dead Germans."'[9] The destruction of Louvain[10] provided a genuine example of a German atrocity, but some correspondents went further by reporting rumours as unqualified facts and creating myths that persisted long after the war.

Gibbs never stinted on his praise of the Allied troops; and, like the American reporter Stanley Washburn, he did not stoop to lurid lies of Teutonic barbarism. He found adequate ordinary horror in Belgium when he went to Funes, from where he wrote his dispatches while helping at a makeshift British hospital. Rolling up his

sleeves, he briefly became part of an ambulance unit that was attached to the Belgian cavalry to bring in the wounded from the savage fighting around Dixmude. The following short extract is from one of his dispatches:

Then Lieutenant de Broqueville spoke a word of command. 'The first ambulance must now get back.'

I was with the first ambulance, in Gleeson's[11] company. We had a full load of wounded men – and we were loitering. I put my head outside the cover and gave the word to the chauffeur. As I did so a shrapnel bullet came past my head, and, striking a piece of ironwork, flattened out and fell at my feet. I picked it up and put it in my pocket – though God alone knows why, for I was not in search of souvenirs. So we started with the first ambulance, through those frightful streets again, and out into the road to the country.

'Very hot,' said one of the men. I think it was the chauffeur. Somebody else asked if we should get through with luck.

Nobody answered the question. The wounded men with us were very quiet. I thought they were dead. There was only the incessant cannonade and the crashing of buildings. Mitrailleuses were at work now spitting out bullets. It was a worse sound than the shells. It seemed more deadly in its rattle. I stared back behind the car and saw the other ambulance in our wake. I did not see the motor-car. Along the country road the fields were still being ploughed by shell, which burst over our heads....[12]

Gibbs joined in with menial work to support the medical staff at the hospital, where 'the smell of wet and muddy clothes, coagulated blood and gangrened limbs, of iodine and chloroform, sickness and sweat of agony, made a stench which struck one's senses with a foul blow... I used to try to keep my eyes upon the ground, to avoid the sight of those smashed faces, and blinded eyes, and tattered bodies, lying each side of me in the hospital cots, or in the stretchers set upon the floor....[13]

At least as determined to see action as her male colleagues were, Louise Mack had prevailed on a reluctant Powell to drive her out to observe a minor cavalry clash at Alost (Aalst). Next moment, he

desired to go hand in hand with her in whatever happened when the Germans came marching in... Antwerp was the first and only city that I loved because she let me share her sufferings with her right through the Valley of Death, right up to the moment when she breathed her last sigh as a city, and passed into the possession of her conquerors.[15]

Having secured three passages on a boat, Fox and Jones came back for Mack but she had gone out by car, ferrying the wounded. She stayed on, disguised as a maid at her hotel, waiting on the Germans and feeling disgust at the Belgian spies now fawning over them. Only when she feared she had been betrayed did she escape from the city.

One by one the British Army picked up the remaining outlaws and expelled them, though at least two somehow evaded capture until 1916. Kitchener had ordered Gibbs's arrest; he was apprehended on the boat at Le Havre and kept for 10 days under arrest before one of the detectives guarding him sent the news back to London, where Sir William Tyrrell engineered his release and his return to England. General Bruce Williams, the commander at Le Havre, made it clear that if he were caught again he would be shot.

Those young men who had set out in a spirit of adventure went back to Fleet Street with a queer look in their eyes, unable to write the things they had seen, unable to tell them to people who had not seen and could not understand. Because there was no code of words which would convey the picture of that wild agony of peoples, that smashing of all civilized laws, to men and women who still thought of war in terms of heroic pageantry...

'Had a good time?' asked a colleague along the corridor, hardly waiting for an answer....[16]

found that they were caught in a fierce engagement – machine guns spat round them and Belgian soldiers hit the ground: '... a veteran English correspondent was giving a remarkable imitation of the bark on a tree, and my driver, my photographer and I were peering cautiously from behind the corner of a brick farmhouse. I supposed that Miss War Correspondent was there too, but when I turned to speak to her she was gone. She was standing beside the car, which we had left in the middle of the road because the bullets were flying too thickly to turn it around, dabbing at her nose with a powder-puff which she had left in the tonneau and then critically examining the effect in a pocket-mirror. "For the love of God!" said I, running out and dragging her back to shelter, "don't you know that you'll be killed if you stay out here?" "Will I?" said she, sweetly. "Well, you surely don't expect me to be killed with my nose unpowdered, do you?"'[14]

Mack later went into Antwerp at the time of the siege and waited for the inevitable, even after her male comrades at the time, Jeffries, Perry Robinson and Percival Phillips, had left. Still refusing to desert the abandoned city and determined to write something meaningful, she watched two more colleagues, Lucien Jones and Frank Fox, ride away on their bicycles, making for the Netherlands. Wondering why she had not gone with them, she walked through the city, and then:

I knew why I was there. It was because the gods had been keeping for me all these years the supreme gift of this solitary walk, when I should share her death-pangs with this city I so passionately loved.

That was the truth. I had been unable to tear myself away. If Antwerp suffered, I desired to suffer too. I

EMBEDDED JOURNALISM

Lord Kitchener finally yielded to the demands of both the public and the Americans for more information in the press, and after a short trial visit in March, five journalists were given official accreditation to go to the Western Front in June 1915: William Beach Thomas (*Daily Mail* and *Daily Mirror*), Percival Phillips (*Daily Express*), Herbert Russell (Press Association and Reuters), Harry Perry Robinson (*Times*) and, perhaps surprisingly, Philip Gibbs (*Daily Telegraph, New York Times* and others).

Gibbs's newly published book, *The Soul Of The War* (1915), ought to have enraged the War Office and destroyed any illusions the public may have been under about the war. The book gained excellent reviews and sold well, but it did not cause the anti-war sentiment that its content invited, particularly in its description of the trench warfare during the first winter of the war: 'In "Plug Street" and other lines of trenches they stood in water with walls of oozy mud about them, until their legs rotted and became black with a false frostbite, until many of them were carried away with bronchitis and pneumonia, and until all of them, however many comforters they tied about their necks, or however many body-belts they used, were shivering, sodden scarecrows, plastered with slime. They crawled with lice .... The war became a hopeless, dreary thing, without a thrill to it, except when men wading in water were smashed by shell-fire and floated about in a bloody mess which ran red through all a trench.'[17]

Now formally attached to GHQ, the war correspondents were given an honorary captain's rank and kitted out in a khaki uniform

opposite: Two of the accredited British war correspondents examine a 42-inch German 'dud' at Hoithem on 9 September 1917. Far Right is Perry Robinson with William Beach Thomas next to him.

above: Philip Gibbs (right) watching an aerial combat from a trench on 7 September 1916.

previous pages: Horse ambulances and casualties outside an advanced dressing station at Tilloy, April 1917.

above: John Warwick Brooke's photograph may have been staged, but purports to show the troops advancing down a sap during the spring battles of 1917.

opposite: Australian war correspondent C.E.W. Bean up to his knees in mud in Gird Trench, Guedencourt, on the Western Front, winter 1916–17.

similar to an officer's, with a Sam Browne belt and a plain badge on the arm, known as a green brassard, to identify them. They were billeted in a succession of relatively comfortable houses, to keep them safe but near the army, with orderlies to look after them, military cars with drivers to take them close to the front and 'conducting officers' (often soldiers considered officially too old for active service) to escort them further forward on foot. There were no more frantic drives to the coast: dispatch riders collected each day's reports and took them for transmission to their newspapers by messenger or electric telegraph. The accredited correspondents were the first 'embedded' journalists.

Significantly, the reporters were no longer paid for by their newspapers: all were now on the payroll of the War Office, with a salary that was less than Fleet Street would have paid them – the logic being that the journalists could make up the difference by writing books about their experiences, which they did.

All this cooperation came at a heavy price, and the journalists knew it. They were not there to report the truth, or at least not the whole truth; their task was to write about the 'glorious' aspects of the war: successes, heroism and resilience. GHQ would rather they had not been there, and its intense suspicion of the journalists' loyalties led to a proposal – never implemented – to screen their private letters to friends and family for anything written in invisible ink. One censor, unhappy with the role assigned to him and convinced that the public had a right to know the truth, confessed to Gibbs (who, in September 1915, had 40 pages of a report, on the disaster that was the Battle of Loos, fall victim to a blue pencil) that he was under direct orders from the chief of British Army Intelligence to waste the correspondents' time.

Frederick Palmer, who had reported the first year of the war from France, Berlin, Belgium and the Royal Navy, joined the select band attached to GHQ and was with them from early 1916 to the autumn. Unashamedly pro-Allies without hating the Germans, the American had spent time in a trench on the front line in 1914, where he recorded the daily life and the humour that those in danger employed to keep themselves sane. But by the spring of 1916, with stalemate in the trenches, that was no longer what the public wanted. Palmer saw that 'unless some new way of killing is developed, even the English public did not care to read about its own army. When my English comrades saw that a petty scandal received more space in the London papers than their accounts of a gallant air raid, they had moments of cynical depression. "But if we ever start the push they'll read every detail," said our wisest man. "It's the push that is in everybody's mind. The man in the street is tired of hearing about rehearsals. He wants the curtain to go up."'[18]

THE BLINDING FOG OF WAR

It went up at 07:30 on 1 July 1916, after a week of massive bombardment. Standing in a field of beet the correspondents could see nothing of the front line through the smoke of the final 'softening-up' shelling, but a lark was singing its heart out and a squadron of aircraft flew past. Half an hour later they could still see nothing, but they knew the advance must have taken place. Literally and metaphorically they were in the fog of war, dependent on GHQ to evaluate the events of the day and inform them.

The resulting newspaper articles gave no indication that during the battles of the Somme that summer more than a million men were killed or wounded, and on that first day the British exceeded 57,000 casualties, one-third of them fatal. The opening action was written up by all the correspondents – with varying degrees of ultimately misplaced confidence – based on the lies they had been told. 'The proportion of our losses in the

early stages of this battle due to rifle fire will be found to be very small,' wrote Perry Robinson in a dispatch for the *Times* that displayed a degree of linguistic camouflage on somebody's part, though surely anyone with a modicum of intelligence could have read something between the lines. 'The greatest factor has been machine-guns, and next to that the heavy artillery. It was the massing of artillery and the hidden machine-gun positions which prevented us from making more progress on the northern part of the front of our attack.'[19]

Gibbs realized within a couple of days that any hope of an advance had been an illusion and that the British had only a salient to show for their massive effort. While being shown the southern part of the battlefield and seeing the dead, mostly Germans but including some of the Gordons and Manchesters outside Montauban, he had received the impression that British losses were very light. The truth about the failure further north, around Gommecourt, arrived with rumour, accompanied by the wounded who had been in action there. The same realization hit Beach Thomas at the same time and left him: '... thoroughly and deeply ashamed of what I had written, for the very good reason that it was untrue. Almost all the official information was wrong. The vulgarity of enormous headlines and the enormity of one's own name did not lessen the shame.'[20]

The correspondents could not issue retractions – the censors would not have passed them. Besides, they had other concerns. None of them would have wished to facilitate a German victory, even though Gibbs cannot have been the only one to have realized long before the Somme that 'like the dead bodies of the Frenchmen and the Englishmen who lay quite close, [the German casualties] had been done to death by the villainy of statecraft and statesmen, playing one race against another as we play with pawns in a game of chess'.[21] Most journalists identified themselves with the armies in the field, in which they had friends, neighbours and relatives fighting. Gibbs had a brother serving as an artillery officer on the Western Front, and there was also a concern for the feelings of families back home – a debate that still continues. In fact, the correspondents were just one part of a huge conspiracy of silence that, for different reasons, prevailed during the war, from the High Command, which had no idea how to conduct this new type of warfare, down to the ordinary soldier, who, when home on leave or to recuperate, said nothing because nobody would be able to comprehend what was happening.

Neither could the correspondents report the news that the Germans had offered a truce for the sake of the wounded and had sent their own stretcher-bearers to help collect injured British soldiers. Also taboo was Gibbs's first-hand knowledge that on 17 July the British had shelled their own men, who had been digging on the road to Longueval, and that at the Battle of Loos in September 1915 chlorine gas was used against the Germans – or would have been had the wind not changed and blown it back at their own men.

From then until the war was over Gibbs remained – with one exception – a mute eyewitness to men suffering from shell-shock and the knowledge that more than a few would be shot as cowards. He met shell-shock cases in hospital, and described a sergeant major he met near Thiepval, who was: 'convulsed with a dreadful rigor like a man in epilepsy, and clawed at his mouth, moaning horribly, with livid terror in his eyes. He had to be strapped to a stretcher before he could be carried away. He had been a tall and splendid man, this poor, terror-stricken lunatic.'[22]

During the major and protracted campaigns being a war correspondent was not a comfortable experience. Often cold, wet, tired and in danger – although nothing like as much as the troops – they spent the day in the field, observing the distant action and talking with the men, before returning, covered in mud, to exchange notes with their colleagues about their different experiences. There were occasions when the pressure of deadlines and censorship frayed tempers, and comradeship turned sour – usually over small matters. Percival Phillips' face would turn red and white as, lips tightly compressed, pulse throbbing in his forehead, he confronted the task of completing his two columns for the *Morning Post* in just 90 minutes.

Briefings over, the correspondents scattered to their individual rooms and their typewriters began to clatter 'like a machine gun' in 'furious spasms of word-fire'. Gibbs did battle with his hated Corona, a machine he regarded as an instrument of torture for its ability to twist its ribbon into a knot. There was no time to refine the prose; as each page was written it was taken downstairs to the waiting censors by the orderly, who would return with the changes and tell them how many minutes they had left.

The correspondents became well aware that the public at home had little faith in the truthfulness of what they were writing. The troops, who had access to certain British newspapers, had even less faith, suspecting that most of what passed for eyewitness reporting was written behind the line and based on material supplied by GHQ. The War Office had its own official journalist, Lieutenant Colonel (later Major General) Ernest Swinton, who churned out propaganda under the pseudonym 'Eyewitness'. Gibbs wrote sober articles (he was accused by his editor of being too dark), but his dispatches could never convey what he witnessed and subsequently described in excoriating prose in his books.

At the other extreme, Beach Thomas incurred the hatred and contempt of the troops because of his purple, sometimes incoherent, prose; his way of putting himself centre-stage in dispatches; and the prominence given to his name, at a time when most Fleet Street journalists were bylined as 'our special correspondent'. They lampooned him and his style mercilessly in the *Wipers Times*, a trench publication that was produced by the officers and men on a discarded Belgian printing press.

On 5 July 1916 the *Daily Mail* proudly proclaimed 'Mr Beach Thomas's Finest Despatch', and its correspondent did not disappoint: '... Our attack at Gommecourt, the northern end of the frantic battle, was as heroic as anything in the war. I know the trenches there well and happen to have personal acquaintances with some of those engaged. I had played cricket with them ... I have not the hardihood to write more. Heroism could no further go ...' He was, as war artist William Orpen recognized, an unlikely war correspondent; his first love was the countryside, and when he and Robinson spent a night in the field to watch the destruction of a fortified village, his clear memory was of the quail and the larks.

FROM CIVILIZATION AT THE CHATEAU TO THE FIELDS OF ARMAGEDDON

The countryside around Amiens, and particularly the river and canal, offered an escape from the war, though not from the sound of the guns. Palmer would go to the cathedral, or try to get a table at the little Restaurant des Huîtres. There were social events at GHQ, but sometimes Palmer and Gibbs just walked the canal towpath in the evening, vowing to talk about anything but the war, yet always coming back to the subject.

There were occasional opportunities for leave. Palmer went to London just before the Somme campaign opened, and again when the action temporarily subsided – returning as a passenger in one of the aircraft being flown out to replace losses. Gibbs, too, mentions a weekend at home, but his longest period away came in the autumn of 1916 when he was sent back to England to recuperate from trench fever, caused by body lice. On 26 December, the *Chronicle's* editor gave a dinner in his honour, and at that event, which was attended by the Prime Minister David Lloyd George, Gibbs gave a speech of uncensored frankness about the war on the Western Front, and afterwards spoke directly to Lloyd George. The following day, the Prime Minister had breakfast with Charles Prestwich Scott, editor of the *Manchester Guardian*, who recorded the statesman's comments in his diary:

> *I listened last night, at a dinner given to Philip Gibbs on his return from the front, to the most impressive and moving description from him of what the war (on the Western Front) really means, that I have heard. Even an audience of hardened politicians and journalists were strongly affected. If people really knew, the war would be stopped tomorrow. But of course they don't know, and can't know. The correspondents don't write and the censorship wouldn't pass the truth. What they do send is not the war, but just a pretty picture of the war with everybody doing gallant deeds. The thing is horrible and beyond human nature to bear and I feel I can't go on with this bloody business.*[23]

top: Tank officers at Poperinghe read the latest news in the *Daily Mail*, 26 September 1916.

above: Morale-boosting poster issued by the *Daily Mirror*.

This was from a man whose War Office set the terms and conditions under which correspondents could work and whose commander-in-chief, General Sir Douglas Haig, thought that what war correspondents wanted was 'to get hold of little stories of heroism, and so forth, and write them up in a bright way to make good reading for Mary Ann in the kitchen, and the Man in the Street'.[24]

In 1917 the correspondents were based in a chateau at Rollencourt in the Pas de Calais, where they wrote up, as best they could, the huge offensives of that year, in which there was industrial-scale carnage. Fought from April to May 1917, the Battle of Arras was intended to be the assault that ended the war in 48 hours, and British gains in the first days were sufficiently marked to be reported in hyperbolic terms. By the end of the campaign, which suffered after the French were heavily defeated in the Champagne, little had been achieved and British losses (including those from Australia and Canada) exceeded 150,000, some 25,000 more than German casualties. In July, just before the Third Battle of Ypres, the Germans used mustard gas for the first time, and Gibbs had a small taste of what the troops would encounter, reporting that he 'was conscious of a burning sensation about the lips and eyelids, and for a week afterward vomited at times, and was scared by queer flutterings of the heart which at night seemed to have but a feeble beat'.[25]

During the war there had been occasional changes of personnel among the correspondents. In the spring of 1917 Beach Thomas was replaced by Fyfe for a year, who found himself rather ashamed of the luxury in which he was now quartered at Rollencourt and the facilities that were at his command when compared with the privations he had experienced in 1914. Disappointed at being so distant from the troops, Fyfe obtained permission to spend time in the trenches with a friend in the Rifle Brigade and had the chance to crawl across no man's land at night with a listening-in party.

In the autumn, the British attacked at Passchendaele as part of a campaign that Gibbs privately described as the 'Fields of Armageddon'. Perry Robinson, from well behind the action at GHQ, reported on 27 September for the *Times*, with indefensible jauntiness, that: 'It is another lovely day, and the British Army would like you at home to know that it is in the best of spirits, thank you, and enormously contented with the results of the last two days' fighting – as it has the right to be.' On 4 October he followed that with: 'At this moment it is raining hard, and one grieves for the men out there in the shell holes.... In spite of the, miserable weather, however, everywhere is the indefinable thrill which goes with victory, unmistakable, but impossible to describe.... It is good even to be wounded on such a day.'

By Christmas it was evident to everyone but the politicians that the Germans, strengthened in the west because of Russia's withdrawal from the war following the October Revolution, were planning a massive offensive in the spring of 1918. When the correspondents fell back with the army under the onslaught of Ludendorff's massed units, Gibbs packed a family into his official car and drove them out of Robeq to safety.

The declaration of war by the USA on 6 April 1917 led to the injection of tens of thousands of fresh troops. The final breaking of the German Army now seemed inevitable, and on 8 August 1918 the process began at Amiens. The Western Front correspondents went on reporting up to and beyond the Armistice, making the best of the reverses and celebrating the successes.

BEHIND THE GERMAN LINES

For Allied journalists, working behind enemy lines equated to spying, as Geoffrey Pyke quickly discovered. At the start of the conflict the Jewish law student abandoned Cambridge to report on the war for the *Daily Chronicle*. After travelling to Berlin via Denmark, on a US sailor's passport, he quickly realized that the reports of German hardships he had read back in England were mere propaganda. His foray into journalism came to an abrupt end when he was arrested after just six days spent observing troop movements and then told he would probably be shot. Held in solitary confinement, he eventually ended up at the Ruhleben internment camp, out of which he managed to tunnel. The – not entirely consistent – story of his escape, which he filed from the Netherlands, gave the *Chronicle* a scoop, and it opened up a career as a correspondent. (Instead, he pursued a different kind of inventive career, as a boffin who gave his name to Pykrete, a composite material made of ice and sawdust.)

Neutrals had the freedom to cover both sides. Arthur Ruhl, correspondent for *Collier's*, reported the early days from the Allied side, and then he crossed into Germany via the neutral Netherlands. Like Pyke, he discovered Germans to be well fed, despite a degree of rationing, and he wrote accordingly. While German journalists were rigorously excluded from the front by the German High Command, those from neutral countries such as Spain, Sweden and the USA were given week-long escorted trips, which allowed them to be: '... under fire one minute, the next shooting through some captured palace or barracks or museum of antiques. At noon the guard is turned out in your honor; at four you are watching distant shell-fire from the Belgian dunes; at eleven, crawling under a down quilt in some French hotel, where the prices of food

and wines are fixed by the local German commandant. Everything is done for you – more, of course, than one would wish – the gifted young captain-conductor speaks English one minute, French or Italian the next, gets you up in the morning, to bed at night, past countless sentries and thick-headed guards demanding an *ausweis* [pass], contrives never to cease looking as if he had stepped from a band-box, and presently pops you into your hotel in Berlin with the curious feeling of never having been away at all. It isn't, of course, an ideal way of working – not like putting on a hat and strolling out to war, as one sometimes could do in the early weeks in Belgium and France.'[26]

WAR AT A DISTANCE – THE EASTERN FRONT
Although it was far from the reach of DORA, the Eastern Front in Russia was even more shrouded in fog than the Western Front. In the opening weeks all the reporting derived from official sources,

above: British and French officers, including Perry Robinson, pay their respects at the interment of the French dramatist and war correspondent, Serge Basset, who was killed on 29 June 1917 while observing enemy positions north of Lens.

with the result that there was no mention of the disastrous Russian defeat at the Battle of Tannenberg in 1914. War correspondents had gone out to Petrograd (St Petersburg) but were kept away from the front line, where almost 80,000 Russians were killed or wounded and more than 90,000 were captured. No information was provided, and thereafter the reporters were constantly managed to an even greater degree than existed in France and Belgium, and they travelled thousands of miles in the forlorn hope of first-hand experience of the war along a front that extended down eastern Europe.

Several of those who found themselves in Petrograd in August 1914 had reported from Russia before, though few spoke the language. American correspondent Stanley Washburn found the Russian General Staff very courteous in their dealings with the press corps, even as they made the limits of press freedom crystal clear. They provided transport, facilities and organized excursions, most of which were to hospitals well behind the front – sometimes by hundreds of miles. Washburn was impressed by everything he witnessed, from the simple and virtuous lifestyles of every rank in the army to the efficiency of the medical services and the splendour of the Russian troops. It is tempting to think that he was writing with his tongue firmly in his cheek in order to fool the censors, but his dispatches were never sent to London. He brought them back in early 1915 and had them published as a book.[27]

However, he was well aware that he was being treated as a tourist during the Galicia campaign (in Austria–Hungary), commenting that the press corps did not consider a trip to a 500-year-old castle to be a substitute for visiting the Eastern Front. Neither were the effects of war as interesting as the waging of it, and he came to the wry conclusion that the round of hospital visits was intended to cure himself and his colleagues of their desire to see the front.

Rebellion was out of the question. One transgressing correspondent was abruptly returned to Petrograd in late October; two others were excluded from the next trip for unspecified misbehaviour. When the remainder pleaded eloquently for access to the front they were told that their programme was arranged – and if they did not like it, they could stay behind. Washburn and the other 'white elephants', as he called them, obediently settled down to a 30-hour train journey to Warsaw, seeing the evidence of the continuing Russian advance.

The lobby of the Bristol Hotel there became the new office of a press corps that included Granville Fortescue of the *Daily Telegraph*, Arthur Ruhl and Percival Gibbon, a colleague of Gibbs on the *Daily Chronicle*, who compared the city to Brussels on the eve of Waterloo. Rumours abounded, hard information was scarce and nobody understood the overall picture. However, there was more freedom for the correspondents, who were able to hitch a lift to the front with the Red Cross, and Washburn and Fortescue finally observed a night action in the snow.

Recalled from France, Fyfe was sent out to Petrograd late in 1914 on the strength of previous experience, but he found little to do there except learn to read Russian, until his wife, Bedelia, braved a winter journey across Scandinavia to join him. What little information Fyfe sent back to London was censored at both ends, and when in August he managed to fool the Russian censors into passing his one potential scoop – the decision by Tsar Nicholas II to appoint himself commander-in-chief of the armies as a replacement for his relative Grand Duke Nicholas – the dispatch was delayed by the British censors and in the meantime Reuters broke the news.

In Petrograd, Fyfe met novelist Arthur Ransome, who was reporting for the *Daily News*, Stanley Washburn of *The Times* and the *Chicago Tribune's* man Robert McCormick. The latter had adopted the rank of colonel, and when Washburn saw that his rank earned him a freedom of movement not accorded to other correspondents he, too, donned a uniform and styled himself 'colonel'.

The Russians began to relax their restrictions. In early 1916 Ransome and Fyfe were sent to join General Brusilov's armies, just in time to see his success in Galicia squandered when the Germans and Austrians broke through elsewhere, which obliged Brusilov to fall back with the other divisions to preserve the Russian line.

AT ALTITUDE WITH THE ALPINI

Fyfe would see a very different side of the war during a brief spell alongside Percival Phillips and the intrepid Alice Waterman, observing crack Italian troops, the Alpini, fighting the Austrians in the Dolomites. The contrast was inescapable – this war was 'fantastic, bizarre even'.

Peaks were fortified. Galleries were drilled through solid rock, with openings that gave you sight of Austrian openings in mountains opposite. From these strange gun emplacements artillerymen and machine-gunners blazed away at one another, and did little harm. Then there were trenches cut in ice, at a height where it always freezes after sunset.[28]

To reach the galleries, several thousand feet up, they travelled by *teleferica*, a rudimentary cable car for hoisting up supplies. It took Fyfe longer to get accustomed to conditions at that altitude:

above: Troops in the Carpathian forest on the Eastern Front, circa 1916.

I found the thin atmosphere trying even at midsummer. I suffered for a day or two from a form of mountain sickness. I had to wear snow-goggles to protect my eyes. My face became first scarlet and then skinless from the combined effect of sun and snow. I discovered for the first time, while I scrambled up an almost perpendicular rock face, and clung with the desperate energy of a drowning man to a rope which hung from the top – I discovered what it meant to be 47 years of age.[29]

However, there were compensations.

But to be in such sparkling, bracing air and amid such loveliness, and in the company of Alpini was

above: Italian unit climbing
a steep slope during the First
World War.

*worth more inconveniences than these. The Alpini
were Italy's finest troops. To them the defence of the
mountain frontier was given. They struck me as
being more like chamois than men. They leapt about
in places where a slip meant destruction, with not
merely a disregard of danger, but seemingly
unconscious of it. They stood on crags with eternity
around and below them just as one sees chamois
standing. They ran down slopes where their visitor
sought each separate foothold most carefully, with
an apparent longing to be dashed to pieces.*[30]

From there, it was back to the Western Front, and then to North-cliffe House in London.

BLUNDERS AND COURAGE AT GALLIPOLI

The 1915 campaign in the Dardanelles was intended to break the deadlock of trench warfare on the Western Front by establishing a second front. The plan was to capture Constantinople, force the Ottoman Turks out of the war and establish a route from the Mediterranean to the Black Sea via the Dardanelles. Russia could then receive the supplies it needed to provide more effective opposition against Germany. Ottoman territory lay on both sides of the strait, so a huge fleet was sent to force the passage by bombarding Ottoman positions. This encountered such fierce opposition in March that it was called off in favour of an amphibious landing, which would be mounted by British and French forces at Cape Helles and by the Australian and New Zealand Army Corps (ANZAC) at Gaba Tepe on the Aegean coast of the Gallipoli peninsula.

As a neutral American, Arthur Ruhl, who was writing for *Collier's* and the *New York Times*, was able to see the campaign from the Ottoman Turkish camp, where the officers were not only happy to talk freely but also to provide him with an unexpected level of comfort. The Allies provided the less welcome but entirely new experience of an air raid, courtesy of either the Royal Flying Corps (RFC) or the Royal Naval Air Service (RNAS), both of which were operating in the theatre. Hastily, Ruhl debated where he should run to in a landscape without any cover:

*It is difficult under such circumstances to sit tight,
reasoning calmly that, after all, the chances of the
bomb's not landing exactly there are a good many to
one – you demand at least the ostrich-like satisfaction
of having something overhead. So I scurried over to*

the left to get out from under what seemed his line of flight, when what should he do but begin to turn!

This was really rubbing it in a bit. To fly across as he had that morning was one thing, but to pen one up in a nice little pocket in the hills, and then on a vertical radius of three or four thousand feet, to circle round over one's head – anything yet devised by the human nightmare was crude and immature to this.[31]

The architect of the Gallipoli campaign, Winston Churchill, did not share Kitchener's mistrust of journalists and accredited several, including British correspondent Ellis Ashmead-Bartlett and the Australians Charles Bean and Keith Murdoch. As elsewhere, each was given the honorary rank of captain and the approximation of a uniform; the red-haired, blue-eyed Bean had his made by a tailor in Melbourne and he paid for it out of his clothing allowance of 15 shillings. A horse and a batman – Private Arthur Bazley, who had worked as a clerk for the *Argus* in Melbourne - were the equivalents of the orderlies and motor cars provided on the Western Front.

Oxford-educated Bean had been called to the Australian bar before he embraced journalism. By 1914 he was a high-profile figure, writing leaders for the *Sydney Morning Herald* and committed to augmenting the prestige of his young country. When the Anzac troops went ashore on 25 April, he was with them within a few hours, but the legend of the Anzacs' courage in scaling the heights and holding their positions in the face of savage fire from Ottoman Turkish positions owes far more to the vivid descriptions of his British colleague, who was full of admiration for the Australians:

Then the Australians found themselves facing an almost perpendicular cliff of loose sandstones, covered with thick shrubbery. Somewhere about half way up the enemy had a second trench, strongly held, from which poured a terrible fire on the troops below and the boats pulling back to the destroyers for a second landing party. Here was a tough proposition to tackle in the darkness, but those colonials were practical above all else and went about it in a practical way. They stopped a few minutes to pull themselves together, get rid of their packs, and charge their rifle magazines. Then this race of athletes proceeded to scale the cliff without responding to the enemy's fire. They lost some men,

but didn't worry, and in less than a quarter of an hour the Turks were out of their second position, and either bayoneted or fleeing.[32]

Ashmead-Bartlett was the superior writer. In fact, after some time the Australian newspapers decided that Bean's reports were insufficiently interesting to be worth printing. Bean himself lamented in his diary on 26 September: 'I can't write about the bayonet charges like some of the others do. Ashmead-Bartlett makes it a little difficult for one by his exaggerations, and yet he's a lover of the truth. He gives one the spirit of the thing; but if he were asked "did a shout really go up from a thousand throats that the hill was ours?" he'd have to say "no it didn't"... Well, I can't...'[33]

There was no denying Bean's commitment; when he was shot in the leg on 6 August he refused to be evacuated, and he was regularly in the trenches with his countrymen and their New Zealand allies: 'When the enemy started shelling us the guns opened heavily again, and the uproar was tremendous. You could not hear the bullets whine - it was a bit of a relief to that extent; but I was never in the midst of such an uproar... it was as if the universe was a tin lined packing case, and squads of giants with sledge hammers were banging both ends of it, and we tiny beings were somewhere inbetween.'[34]

Ashmead-Bartlett proved to be the loose cannon among the Gallipoli reporters. He had been a serving officer in the Second Boer War and had reported on the Russo–Japanese War (1904-05) before he went to the Western Front. He was unimpressed by reporting restrictions, and he had jumped at the chance to go to Gallipoli as the single representative of Fleet Street. He found things were no better, recording on 9 May: 'It is heartrending work having to write what I know to be untrue, and in the end having to confine myself to giving a descriptive account of the useless slaughter of thousands of my fellow countrymen for the benefit of the public at home, when what I wish to do is to tell the world of the blunders that are being daily committed on this blood-stained peninsula. Yet I am helpless .... Sometimes I feel it is my duty to resign and return home, but I know that if I ever did there would be little chance of the truth ever being known....'[35]

Fate almost intervened when on 26 May he found himself on HMS *Majestic* at a time of considerable concern about German submarine activity. Convinced the ship would be sunk, he and others drank the ship's store of champagne and much of the port, rather than see it lost. That night he slept on the deck with all his money

THE ART OF THE FIRST WORLD WAR

The depiction of war in art has a long history, including such well-known examples as the painted wood box from the tomb of King Tutankhamun, the Bayeux Tapestry, and Lady Elizabeth Butler's 'The Charge of the Scots Greys at Waterloo'. The vast majority of it was created well after the event, reconstructed from often heavily embellished accounts, rather than painted by eyewitnesses, and emphasizing the drama and glory of war.

During the First World War, Eric Kennington and C.R.W. Nevinson were wounded and, while recuperating, both held private exhibitions of work inspired by their service in the trenches. At the same time the head of the War Propaganda Bureau, Charles Masterman, conceived the idea of commissioning well-known artists to record the conflict from first-hand experience as observers or participants. Although the aim of the war art scheme was to emphasize Britain's liberal values through images that could be reproduced in books and exhibited at home and abroad, Masterman was not looking for the traditional narratives and grand battle canvases. Instead, the artists were given the freedom to work on their individual interpretations of the war and its effect on the whole nation. So alongside the more obvious subjects are scenes of workers in the munitions factories, casualties returning to Britain, the work of the field hospitals, and civilians in London sheltering from air raids.

The first to be sent to the front was Muirhead Bone, in August 1916, whose huge output took a serious toll on his health. Others included establishment figures such as portrait painter John Singer Sargent and the Post-Impressionist William Orpen, and more radical artists including Paul Nash, who, like Nevinson, had been on active service. All understood that they had been recruited for propaganda purposes, but if their work has one overall theme it is that of the impotence and vulnerability of life – not just human life – in the face of mechanized warfare. Nevinson's most famous work, 'Paths of Glory', was censored by the government, ostensibly because its depiction of dead British soldiers would damage morale. When it was exhibited in March 1918 he hung a diagonal banner across it proclaiming 'Censored'.

By 1918 the scheme had been absorbed into the Ministry of Information, and the Imperial War Museum, established in 1917 in London, had begun to collect records documenting the war. Housed at the Imperial War Museum, the two collections established a precedent for the ongoing artistic commemoration of wars in which British forces and civilians were and still are engaged.

opposite: 'Paths of Glory', 1917
C.R.W. Nevinson, 1889–1925
Before his appointment as an official war artist, Nevinson had been a volunteer ambulance driver on the Western Front. In this sombre, almost monochrome painting the corpses of two dead soldiers are decomposing – dust to dust – into the ground from which they are barely distinguishable. As Thomas Grey expressed it in *Elegy In A Country Churchyard*, 'The paths of glory lead but to the grave'. But these soldiers have no grave.

Nevinson's early war paintings are graphic and angular, the human beings constructed out of geometric shapes. By 1917 he had moved away from Futurism towards greater realism. His palette became more limited and his work is at the same time both softer and more starkly realistic.

below: 'The Menin Road', 1918
Paul Nash, 1889–1946
This painting is the complete antithesis of the artist's decorative pre-war images: a dystopian, geometric landscape that forces the viewer to confront the devastation wrought by war on the natural world. Pre-war leafy trees have been reduced to jagged, black stumps; concrete blocks and rusting corrugated iron in a sea of mud replace natural vegetation, a metaphor for the industrialization that has made mechanized slaughter possible. Explosions replace clouds; shafts of sunlight become gun barrels and prefigure the searchlights of the Second World War. Two figures struggle over the ground, insignificant and overwhelmed by the desolation and destruction. There is cruel irony in the title: the Menin Road is unrecognizable.

in his pyjamas. At 06:40 a torpedo was sighted and Ashmead-Bartlett was pushed into the water in the rush to escape the doomed ship. He survived and was picked up by one of *Majestic's* cutters. Subsequently, he went back to England, to replenish his lost baggage, and while there he met senior government figures, including Churchill and Asquith, as well as Kitchener, and discussed the Gallipoli campaign with them. On his return to Gallipoli he was informed that if he dared to voice criticisms again he would be sent home for good.

Ashmead-Bartlett committed his frustrations to his diary on 18 July: 'The censorship has now passed beyond all reasonable bounds. ... There are now at least four censors .... They all hold different views on what should be written, and each successive censor feels it his duty to take out something his predecessor has left in. Thus only a few dry bones are left for the wretched public. The articles and cables resemble chicken, out of which a thick nutritious broth has been extracted.'

Then he crossed the line. In September, angry at the continued mismanagement of the campaign and the refusal of the censors to allow anything critical, he wrote a private letter to the Prime Minister and gave it to Keith Murdoch, who was going on leave to England. At Marseilles, Murdoch was arrested and forced to hand over the letter. Back in Gallipoli, its author was stripped of his credentials as a correspondent by General Sir Walter Braithwaite. 'I suppose he imagined this would be a knock-out blow for me, and he seemed taken aback when I jumped up and said "May I leave at once? I have long been anxious to be relieved of my post, and have in fact applied to the N.P.A.[36] to be allowed to return." ... never have I known such an unsuitable people to whom to entrust a great campaign, the lives of their countrymen and the safety of the empire.'[37]

Who betrayed Ashmead-Bartlett and Murdoch? Bean, who described the letter as 'brilliantly written... rather overstating the case, but a great deal of it is absolutely unanswerable', was probably correct when he pointed the finger at one of the censors, whom he described in the following terms: '... the little worm of a press officer... [He] is trying to put every difficulty he can in my way... sends us orders by the private soldier from whom he gets two reports every week about our camp and who is almost certainly acting as his spy....'[38]

Murdoch, who was fully in Ashmead-Bartlett's confidence, was able to reconstruct the letter from memory and Ashmead-Bartlett secured a meeting with the Prime Minister on his return.

top: Ernest Brooks carrying his Goerz Anschütz plate camera through a trench on the Western Front, circa 1917.

above: British troops of the IX Corps landing at Sulva on the Gallipoli Peninsula before the offensive of August 1915.

As a result, the commander-in-chief, General Sir Ian Hamilton, was replaced and the troops were evacuated. Bean left only a day before the Anzacs did.

DAMNED IN ANY EVENT

All the official British war correspondents, with the exception of Ashmead-Bartlett, were offered knighthoods. Perry Robinson and Percival Phillips (an American citizen) accepted; Fyfe, who had become a committed socialist, refused; Beach Thomas and Gibbs initially agreed to decline but then accepted. Gibbs believed that his decision to accept diminished him in Fyfe's esteem, though the latter emphatically rejected the idea.

It is now fashionable to regard the official correspondents as lackeys, who happily toed the official line when they should have been telling the world about the horrors of the Western Front. It is even suggested that they really could have ended the slaughter by mobilizing public opinion against it, as Lloyd George remarked. However, that begs the question of precisely how the correspondents were supposed to publicize facts that no newspaper would

above: The 60-pounder Mark 1 Battery on a sand ridge at Cape Helles, probably in July 1915. Photographed by Lieutenant Ernest Brooks.

publish. Wireless internet, emails, Twitter, social networking sites and mobile phones that (unless jammed by government agencies) can circumvent censorship and provoke mass demonstrations, were all decades away. Correspondents in Vietnam certainly boosted anti-war sentiment, but they, of course, were not censored.

Gibbs had done his best with his book in 1915. Fleet Street's finest were among the great and the good who attended his dinner in 1917, but nobody dared to report his words, although Lord Northcliffe had published Ashmead-Bartlett's criticisms of the conduct of the Gallipoli campaign because he believed it added to his campaign of criticism against Kitchener. In fact, Gibbs, the most honest and possibly the most emotionally scarred of the correspondents, fared badly, a few of his tens of thousands of phrases, written during and after the war, seized upon as evidence against him and his colleagues.

In the early months of the war, when the presence of correspondents in France and Belgium was manifestly unwanted, there were plenty who tried hard to get to the front and obtain stories. There is no way of knowing whether, given the chance, any of them would have had the courage to go in with the first wave of an assault, or what the effect of such reporting would have been had they lived to write their accounts, but in the end they were thwarted far less by their own sense of patriotism and empathy with the troops than by a well-resourced military-political gagging machine – and, indeed, by the newspaper proprietors, who for the most part endorsed the government line enthusiastically.

War through the viewfinder

War photography either creates or attracts to itself an especial breed of men – men who are either so engrossed in their craft, or so constituted mentally and physically that the riskiness of their work has very little effect on them – and is certainly no deterrent.

Basil Clarke (1879–1947), official war correspondent

At the start of the war, press photographers and cinematographers were no more welcome than war correspondents, because published images could provide information to the enemy. However, since the Second Boer War cameras had become smaller, cheaper and were loaded with relatively robust celluloid

roll film, which made it possible for ordinary service personnel to smuggle them to the front, in defiance of the regulations.

In 1915 the War Office appointed its first official war photographer, Ernest Brooks, who had worked as a photographer for both the royal family and the *Daily Mirror*. When he joined in the Royal Navy Volunteer Reserve (RNVR) he became a logical choice to record the Gallipoli campaign.

Under instructions to photograph as much as possible, Brooks took almost 4,500 pictures and travelled thousands of miles. His images from Gallipoli include dramatic shots of naval ships, bombardments, Australians in their trenches, stretcher parties and the inglorious evacuation. From that theatre he went to photograph the Battle of the Somme, and, apart from a spell with the Grand Fleet and a foray to cover the Italian Front, he spent most of the rest of the war on the Western Front. His most memorable photographs are probably those shot in silhouette: files of men walking along the skyline, which offer a universal, almost timeless, view of men going to war. After the war he returned to his work as a royal photographer, but was suddenly dismissed and then stripped of his OBE (Order of the British Empire) in 1925 for reasons that are not yet in the public domain.

Brooks was the only stills photographer to cover the Somme, but by the end of the year others had been appointed, including (confusingly) Captain James Walker Brooke. A former photographer for the Topical Press Agency, the serious, steady Brooke had been commissioned out of the ranks and decorated for gallantry before he joined Brooks on the Western Front. In April 1917 Brooke may have taken one of the few photographs of men going into action, when he took a picture along a sap[39] as an officer of the 9th Battalion, The Cameronians led his men out (see page 42). (However, the men's equipment puts the image's authenticity in some doubt.)

Cinematographers were also employed, but it was harder for them to record men actually going into action. Although warned against faking shots, 'staging' did take place. Ivor Castle simulated images of the Canadians going into action, as did cinematographer Hilton de Witt Girdwood, whose material was censored. Oscar Bovill was dismissed for the same unprofessional behaviour.

The greatest photographic achievement of the First World War, although it ducked the issue of the obscene carnage involved, was 'The Battle of the Somme', which was shot in the summer of 1916 by Geoffrey Malins and John McDowell. Malins had been chief cameraman at the Clarendon Film Company and went to France to

report the war. After some success in covering the Belgian Army and the winter fighting in the Vosges, France, he was recruited as a War Office cinematographer. Careful study has shown that Malins staged some of the sequences in the film, and the authenticity of additional footage is suspect. Rollencourt, which was a base for photographers as well as correspondents, was also the site of a trench mortar battery school, and a former Gaumont cameraman called Bertram Brooks Carrington, who briefly served in that role in 1917, claimed to have been told by a soldier that Malins had recruited him for a sequence that was filmed at the school. In fairness to Malins, and given the limitations of his equipment and the danger in which he worked, securing quality footage at the front for a film to be shown in the cinema was probably impossible. Some dramatization was almost inevitable if a credible feature-length documentary was to emerge.

above: Frank Hurley brought exceptional creativity to his role as Australia's official photographer and produced some of the most artistic images of the war, as in this image of a line of troops on their way to the front at Passchendaele in 1917. However, his stunning pictures often owed much to technical manipulation and staging.

Malins' most difficult task was to film the springing of a mine at Beaumont Hamel at 07:20 on 1 June 1916, the opening day of the battle. Both armies regularly tunnelled under the enemy's trenches, packed a chamber with explosives and then retired to detonate the mine at a time and distance of their choosing. This charge was huge, and Malins had only one chance.

[My] hand grasped the handle of the camera. I set my teeth. My whole mind was concentrated upon my work. Another thirty seconds passed. I started turning the handle, two revolutions per second, no more, no less. I noticed how regular I was turning. (My object in exposing half a minute beforehand was to get the mine from the moment it broke ground.) I fixed my eyes on the Redoubt. Any second now. Surely it was time. It seemed to me as if I had been turning for hours. Great heavens! Surely it had not misfired. Why doesn't it go up? I looked at my exposure dial. I had used over a thousand feet. The horrible thought flashed through my mind, that my film might run out before the mine blew. Would it go up before I had time to reload? The thought brought beads of

perspiration to my forehead. The agony was awful; indescribable. My hand began to shake. Another 250 feet exposed. I had to keep on.

Then it happened.

At 7.20 a. m. this huge mine loaded with 20 tons of Aminol which took 7 months to make, was sprung under the German trenches at Beaumont Hamel. The ground where I stood gave a mighty convulsion. It rocked and swayed. I gripped hold of my tripod to steady myself. Then, for all the world like a gigantic sponge, the earth rose in the air to the height of hundreds of feet. Higher and higher it rose, and with a horrible, grinding roar the earth fell back upon itself, leaving in its place a mountain of smoke. From the moment the mine went up my feelings changed. The crisis was over, and from that second I was cold, cool, and calculating.[40]

The film, with its footage of regiments coming up to the front, dead Germans, prisoners and even a sequence in which a mortally

wounded British soldier is carried by a friend, was a sensation, with twenty million tickets sold in the first few weeks. It was screened in some 18 countries and gave many civilians their first view of war. Malins took the credit alone, and when he subsequently wrote a book about the filming he airbrushed McDowell out of the story; it is also thought that he encouraged the film's editor to discard McDowell's footage. Many who went to see 'The Battle of the Somme' at their local cinema must have been hoping to glimpse the faces of friends or family members, but the commercial success of the film also demonstrated the public's desire to engage with what they believed to be the reality of war, albeit a silent reality, through a medium that was still novel but was making rapid technological and artistic advances. Although the newsreel lagged behind newspapers because of the longer production time, it became a popular staple of the cinema – its visual images more powerful than the written word because they could be understood by the illiterate. Moving images of warfare, first seen in the Spanish–American War (1898), were now a prerequisite.

opposite: A still from Geoffrey Malin's epic 'The Battle of the Somme'. The footage is regularly used in documentaries to show men going over the top, but was almost certainly shot behind the lines.

above: This still from 'The Battle of the Somme' is believed to be genuine footage, shot on the opening day of the battle. The unidentified casualty, rescued by comrades from no man's land, died half an hour after returning to the trenches.

In August 1934 Frank Gervasi, the American-born son of Sicilian immigrants, had travelled first class from the USA to Madrid for his first posting as a foreign correspondent for the Hearst organization. On 4 October his Spanish cook informed him that a general strike had been called at midnight, the prelude to a rising against the Nationalist government. During the ruthless suppression of that ill-fated insurrection, he and his colleague lived on coffee, cigarettes and sandwiches in their office at the Palacio de Prensa, phoning dispatches to London or Paris to be forwarded to New York while sniper fire raged outside. Gervasi had an uncomfortable encounter with the authorities when he, along with Jay Allen (*Chicago Tribune*) and Rex Smith (Associated Press), was taken for interrogation. Although they were quickly freed, and their arrest blamed on an 'error', Gervasi subsequently learned that a friend and fellow journalist, Luis Sirval, had been murdered while in custody in Asturias after having exposed atrocities committed by government troops. By the time the civil war began, just over a year later, Gervasi was working in Rome.

I woke this morning to find the windows shaking from the explosion of a rebel bomb and to hear the sirens shrieking their warning of the first air raid.

Geoffrey Cox (1910–2008) in the *News Chronicle*, 10 November 1936

The Partisans:
the spanish civil war

Five months after the election to power of Spain's socialist Popular Front in February 1936, a nationwide Nationalist revolt saw success in Seville, Aragon and the Canary Islands, as well as in Spanish Morocco, which became the springboard for General Franco's invasion of the mainland with troops airlifted by Germany's Luftwaffe. Franco had the backing of both Hitler and Mussolini, ignoring international demands for all foreign powers to keep out of the war. Stalin sent in hundreds of men to provide assistance to the Spanish government. More than 60,000 volunteers, primarily French, German, Polish, Italian, American and British, flocked to join International Brigades that were set up with Soviet support.

Even more quickly on the scene were the correspondents who raced to Spain. Depending on their editors and proprietors, correspondents employed a range of terms – neutral or emotive – to distinguish the combatants. The incumbent administration became 'Reds', 'Government', 'Left', 'Loyalists', 'Socialists', 'Popular Front' or 'Republicans'; those seeking its overthrow were 'Fascists', 'Patriots', 'Rebels', 'the Right' or 'Nationalists'. Writing for the *News Chronicle*, Geoffrey Cox was happy with 'government' and 'rebels';

opposite: Positive publicity: a group of Republican militiamen near the Aragon front pose for a photograph in July 1936. The photographer, Winifred Bates, used her images to rouse support for the Republican cause in Britain.

above: General Franco addresses the crowd in the captured Catalan city of Tarragon.

Harold Cardozo had no problem with the opposing 'Reds' and 'Patriots' that was required by the *Daily Mail*; but Frances Davis had to grit her teeth when she found herself reporting for the same paper. .

Inspired by the journalism of Dorothy Thompson, Davis had made a fledgling career for herself in the USA before scraping together the fare to Europe and persuading a selection of small American papers to take articles from her on a freelance basis. Hardly had she settled in Paris than the civil war erupted in Spain and she joined the rush to Hendaye, in the French Basque Country, just over the border from the town of Irún.

At Hendaye, Davis met up with Ed Taylor of the *Chicago Tribune*, whom she had known in Paris. He introduced her to John Elliot of the *New York Herald Tribune*, Harold Cardozo of the *Daily Mail* – known as 'Major' – and Bertrand de Jouvenal, a 32-year-old French philosopher with a colourful background. Their sympathies, and those of their papers, lay mostly with the rebels, but they took Davis under their wing as they pondered how to get into Spain without the essential official passes that, perversely, could only be issued by the warring armies. Facing exactly the same problems as their predecessors back in 1914, they found similar solutions, although the consequences of getting caught were potentially far more serious.

Cardozo had a six-seater car, complete with chauffeur, and after creating some 'dazzlers' – gaudy fake passes likely to deceive unsophisticated roadside sentries – the group set off on the smugglers' trails to Pamplona with a boot that was full of typewriters. Davis showed her initiative when they were stopped in the mountains, defusing the situation by giving her cap to a small child and handing out cigarettes. In Pamplona, the four men spoke to the rebel generals, leaving her in the car with the driver. An official approached her, asked if she were a journalist and escorted her to the *comandancia*. There she was issued with her own pass and given the name of a good place to eat. Saying nothing about her pass, she directed her companions to what turned out to be a restaurant patronized by the Falange. As the meal came to an end:

top: Author George Orwell (middle, back row), with other members of the Independent Labour Party's contingent prior to leaving England, was one of the high-profile figures to join the International Brigade.

above: Jay Allen (left), who reported on the Badajoz massacre, photographed in 1941.

opposite: CBS's pioneering radio correspondent, H.V. Kaltenborn at the microphone.

… the Major in gustatory comfort eased his belt,'There! You do make yourself useful, what?' he said to me.

'She can serve in our army. She's a good soldier, isn't she?' de Jouvenal urged.

'Quite,' approved the Major, and then turning military. 'Quite. But how is she to come with us

without the proper passes? Can't have her endangering the entire manoeuvre, can we, what? Hardly can ask for a pass for a girl, to go to the front, what? Spaniards won't like it. Think we don't take their damn war seriously, what? Have to find her a ride back to France. Sorry, old girl.'

'But Major,' I tried to prevent his sweeping over me like an army tank. 'But Major, won't this do?' And I put out on the cloth, among the crumbs, the salvo conducto.

When the men's laughter subsided and the Major stopped saying 'Bloody Spaniards' it was agreed that I was officially the army's private.[1]

For Davis, the novice, it was simple to type her stories and post them to her American local newspapers. The professionals needed to dictate theirs to London or Paris from across the border in France. As a way of repaying the men for her seat in the car, Davis took their dispatches by car, bluffed her way over the frontier and used a hotel phone. Initially, the *Daily Mail* complained it was too late at night to take copy; when Davis indignantly informed them of the very real dangers she had braved, they asked her to dictate it, and then offered her a job the following day.

THE RISE OF RADIO

By 1934 around 24 million households in the USA owned a wireless set, but radio was primarily an entertainment medium and the advertisers who financed it were not interested in news. Stations such as Columbia Broadcasting System (CBS) merely fulfilled their statutory duty to provide news coverage, until the growing tensions in a Europe juddering towards war in the second half of the 1930s increased the public's appetite for information and attracted the advertising to support it.

A driving force in meeting this need was Edward R. (Ed) Murrow, CBS's London-based director of its Europe bureau, who organized live broadcasts from European cities around the time of the 1938 Munich Crisis. However, two years earlier it was another CBS legend who had achieved an impressive scoop in Spain. Famous for not reading from a script, reporter H.V. Kaltenborn had been involved with broadcasting since its beginnings in 1922. On 3 September 1936, just before he was due to return home, he became the first to speak live from a battle, when the rebels captured the strategic coastal city of Irún. The geography was such that a salient of French territory protruded into Spain, offering a superb elevated view for a broadcast. With the help of a radio technician, a telephone was found from which they could run a wire to the battlefield:

… my lines were led from a farmhouse telephone into the fighting area, where I found shelter for myself and the microphone between a haystack and a cornfield. My French technician, who was a good sport and thoroughly willing to take chances for the sake of a successful broadcast, set up his amplifier in the shelter of one of the outbuildings of the farm. Our broadcasts were booked for 4 p.m. and 11 p.m. French time. The battle began at 2 p.m, shortly after we were installed. It was at its height at 4 p.m. The broadcast did not go through because of a misunderstanding in Paris. I telephoned a succession of urgent cables: 'BATTLE CONTINUES', 'STANDING BY', 'GIVE ME LINES.' Twice between 4 and 5 o'clock the network tried to get through to me. Twice our lines were shot to pieces and had to be repaired under fire. Finally, after darkness had fallen, at 11 o'clock, when the artillery was already out of action, but with rifle and machine guns still sputtering, we got through to New York….[2]

PARTIALITY, ATROCITY AND DANGER

Davis's group came under fire from the air while driving in convoy along the Alto de Leon pass on the road towards Madrid. Cardozo ordered his driver to slam on the brakes, the car skidded sideways and everyone took shelter off the road in a field. He commented on Davis's 'exemplary coolness', though in her own account she admitted unashamedly to inward terror. But Davis was sick of the Nationalists; she wanted to do something for the Republicans.

Journalists regularly confront the question of whether they should become involved in what they are supposed to be observing. Sigrid Schultz had combined her journalism with helping Berlin's Jews escape to the USA; Philip Gibbs and Henry Hamilton Fyfe had both worked for hospitals treating the wounded. Davis returned to Paris and consulted Edgar Mowrer, a winner of the Pulitzer Prize and former president of the Foreign Press Association, who was then the bureau chief in the French capital for the *Chicago Daily News*. At his suggestion Davis travelled to Mallorca for a month. There she made notes on Italian navy operations, including troop embarkation, and opened her hotel shutters at night in defiance of a general prohibition. On the way back she was arrested and searched, but managed to conceal her notebook in a secret pocket in the lining of her coat.

Censorship rules varied. The Basques were open, trusting to fair reporting to further their cause. The Republicans in Madrid allowed the reporters free access, unescorted and in cars they provided, but censorship of all outgoing messages was strict. The censor at the tall Telefonica building on the Gran Via, the only source of lines to London and Paris, approved or modified the dispatch and then listened while the correspondent dictated it to the newspaper – change one word, and the connection would be cut. There was to be no mention of Soviet weapons or political killings. For all that, the Reuters man managed to send dispatches that included references to Republican murders of political opponents in the city.

The Nationalists were quick to impose controls on correspondents. At the head of Franco's censorship apparatus was Luis Bolin, a poacher turned gamekeeper who had been a journalist during the First World War, operating in France where he had been impressed by the British Army's control over reporting. He kept a rigid grip on who could or could not report from the Nationalist side – for example, he refused New Zealander Geoffrey Cox a permit because of the *News Chronicle's* pro-government stance. No mentions of massacres or irregular killings were permitted.

After the Nationalists captured the city of Badajoz in August 1936, the respected Jay Allen broke the story in the USA via the *Chicago Tribune*, in a piece headlined: 'Slaughter of 4,000 at Badajoz, city of horrors', which was published on 30 August:

> *They are burning bodies. Four thousand men and women have died at Badajoz since Gen. Francisco Franco's rebel Foreign Legionnaires and Moors climbed over the bodies of their own dead through its many times blood-drenched walls… After the first night the blood was supposed to be palm-deep on the far side of the lane. I don't doubt it. Eighteen hundred men – there were women, too – were mowed down there in some twelve hours. There is more blood than you would think in 1,800 bodies.*[3]

His assessment of the brutality was confirmed by the Portuguese journalist, Mario Neves, who risked going into the city just after its fall, despite being warned that the Moorish soldiers were still 'excitable'. A part of his report was published on 17 August in the *News Chronicle* in England: 'In each street there is a barricade, and each barricade is now, almost literally, a mountain of bodies. A red bloodstained wall perforated with bullets shows the grim spot where some 2000 men were executed by the insurgents.'

There was a concerted attempt in the American press to discredit Allen's story. The exposure had also rattled Franco, who realized that such orgies of bloodshed were damaging his campaign. No journalists were allowed into Toledo, but what Webb Miller, a seasoned Universal Press (UP) man, saw of the aftermath scarred him; he confided to Allen that it was enough to threaten his sanity.

Whereas during the First World War those who reported the war stood a chance of being shot or bombed, in Spain there was a real risk of being summarily executed. A telegram from UP almost cost the life of Miller in August 1936. He had been instructed to *investigate* rumours of an assassination plot, but the Nationalist censor misconstrued this as an instruction to Miller to *involve* himself in it. A month later James M. Minifie (*New York Herald Tribune*) and Denis Weaver (*News Chronicle*) were arrested as spies by African troops who had murdered their government-supplied chauffeur and guide. After being repeatedly threatened with hanging, they were taken to Franco's headquarters, forced to make false declarations of good treatment and finally expelled after a nerve-racking week.

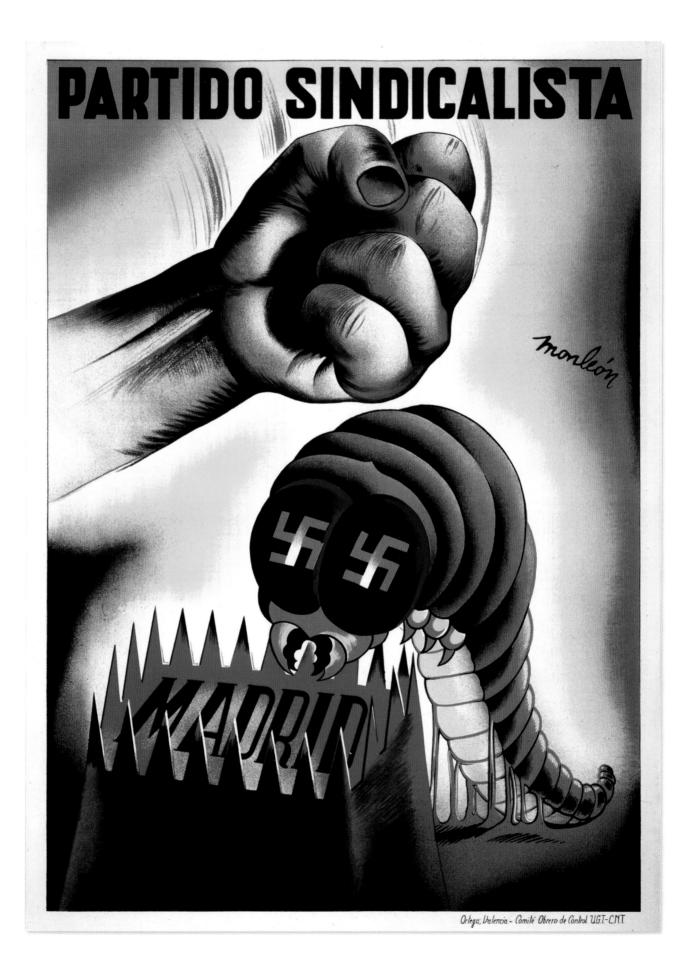

PARTIDO SINDICALISTA

monleón

MADRID

Ortega; Valencia - Comité Obrero de Control. UGT-CNT.

previous page: An allegorical Syndicalist Party poster in which the red fist of the Party is poised to smash Fascism, a swastika-eyed maggot, as it begins the assault on Madrid.

above: Vera Elkan was a pro-Republican photographer who spent two months covering the International Brigades. This picture, of an elderly woman collecting debris in an otherwise deserted street in Madrid, was taken during the winter of 1936–7.

MADRID BESIEGED

While Nationalist forces advanced on Republican-held Madrid, Geoffrey Cox arrived in Spain to replace Weaver. Oxford-educated, well travelled and inspired by the post-war writing of Philip Gibbs, the New Zealander had used every contact he had made to get a reporting job on a Fleet Street newspaper, and by sheer audacity he had secured a career with the *News Chronicle*. Spurned by the Nationalists, he grasped the chance to go to Madrid and join the other war correspondents at the (soon to be shelled) Florida Hotel on the Plaza del Callao.

The first thing Cox noticed was the camaraderie of the foreign press corps. Hardly had he arrived when a UP man took him to the censors' office to give him the opportunity to surprise London with an early dispatch, and then they went out to dine. The following day, Cox drove out towards the front with a French reporter and stood on a hill watching some bombers at work over the fields. Suddenly, government troops came running at the two men and he found himself gazing into the barrel of a rifle of a man who was kneeling on the hillside nearby:

I immediately threw up my hands into the air. A moment later I did something which nearly cost me my life. I put my hand to my pocket to pull out my handkerchief and waved it. One shot rang out. Whether it was aimed at me I shall never know, in any case it hit nobody, but immediately afterwards a man rushed forward and levelled a revolver at me. I produced my passes and my companion broke out in a torrent of explanation. But it took some minutes before all suspicion was overcome. We were then taken before the local commander and the position was explained. The soldiers, he said, had thought when we stood up that we were signalling to Fascist planes, and that when I put my hand in my pocket I was intending to draw a revolver. After the explanations were given and accepted we were treated as best friends…[4]

Cox stayed on in Madrid, even though the city was expected to fall within days. He and Henry Buckley of Reuters accepted the offer of a mattress on the floor of the British Embassy, a service for which they had to pay before leaving Spain. But Madrid held out – it was never taken – and Cox, elated at being one of just three British correspondents left in the capital, sent back a string of vivid dispatches, which described the fighting at first hand. The *News Chronicle* honoured their rookie with a coveted by-line. On 17 November he reported on the bombing of Madrid:

[which happened while] we were busy at our typewriters in the Telefonica, setting out the story of these raids, when the attack with high explosive bombs began. The building rocked like a ship struck by a heavy wave. Explosion followed explosion. Outside flares lit up the Gran Via, so that the buildings seemed to dance in a mad greenish haze. A girl, earphones still on her head, ran shrieking from the switchboard room and flung herself into the arms of her supervisor.[5]

In December Cox was recalled on leave and did not return to Spain. The experience left a lasting impression on him:

I had known in those weeks in Madrid, if not the comradeship of battle, the comradeship of shared danger. And I had tasted something more. I had sensed and felt at first hand the hopes of those millions of Spaniards who had been presented, suddenly and unexpectedly through the failure of the generals' uprising in the big cities, with a chance to take their destiny into their own hands, to build a fuller and richer life. Though the fears and strain of war obscured the future in Madrid, hope was still strong….[6]

THE BOMBING OF GUERNICA

If Jay Allen's report on the Badajoz massacre is considered to be one of the two most important dispatches sent from Spain during the civil war, the other is George Steer's[7] from Guernica. Written on 27 April 1937 and published the following day in the Times, 'The Tragedy Of Guernica' described the bombing of what, to most readers, was an obscure town in the Basque region of Spain. However, the story spawned not just decades of controversy but also one of the most famous artistic works of the twentieth century.

Steer was no stranger to controversy. His previous assignment had been to Ethiopia, from where he had revealed in 1935 that the Italians were dropping poison gas in violation of international law. The Nationalists had already expelled Steer from Spain, but it is not clear whether that was because his earlier reporting had angered Franco's Italian support or because, as his friend Peter Kemp suggested, in public and in front of his Nationalist minders, he publicly likened Spain to the toilet in his room in Toledo: 'You pull and pull, and nothing happens. You pull again, and the shit slowly rises. That's Spain for you.'

Steer went as a freelance to the besieged Basque region, installing himself in the reduced glories of the Hotel Torrontegui at Bilbao, where hot water was available only twice a week and his first meal included lentils and horsemeat. He gained the confidence of President Aguirre, who gave him carte blanche to report honestly – even a story about a massacre of prisoners that followed the bombing of Bilbao. Personal tragedy interrupted his reporting when his Anglo-Spanish wife died in London in childbirth, and when he returned to the front he had become a more reckless individual. On 25 April Steer briefed his fellow correspondents on how to deal with air attack on the road: lie still and as flat as you can. The following day, on their way to the front east of Guernica, they were surprised by a formation of Heinkels and took refuge in a fresh bomb crater while the Heinkels mounted a low-level attack on their position.

They knew there had been bombing, but only over dinner at the Torrontegui did the news come through that Guernica had been destroyed. They bolted for their cars. The city was burning. Steer took great care with his reporting, gathering eyewitness reports and teasing out the details, not rushing to submit a dispatch, nor

GUERNICA (1937),
PABLO RUIZ PICASSO 1881–1973

Spain's Republican government commissioned Picasso to create a painting for the Spanish pavilion at the 1937 Exposition Internationale des Arts et Techniques dans la Vie Moderne held in Paris, but inspiration eluded Spain's most famous living artist – until reports of the bombing of Guernica appeared in the newspapers in Paris, where Picasso was living in exile.

Monochrome like the images in the newspapers and newsreels, and even including the newsprint that stirred the artist's imagination, the huge canvas is unambiguous in its general anti-war message, and its condemnation of the Guernica bombing. The horror is clear in the form of the dismembered soldier grasping the shattered sword, his other hand displaying stigmata of the Christian martyr; the man on the far right caught between two fires, the woman on the far left holding her dead baby, and above all in the endless screaming that appears to be emitting from the human figures and the dying horse.

Interpreting the individual elements is far more difficult, and Picasso refused to unlock the symbolism. Some have seen the bull as Franco, indifferent to the suffering he has caused. The broken classical bust, a self-portrait of the artist, may stand for Spanish culture destroyed by the rebels. Others regard such interpretations as too simplistic. 'Guernica' is full of intensely Spanish iconography, of secret references, of allusions to art and religion. The flared nostrils of the horse and its upper teeth form a skull, a *memento mori*; the mother and child echo Rogier van der Weyden's 'Descent from the Cross' in the Prado Museum – of which Picasso was a director.

After the Paris exposition, 'Guernica' toured the world, first from France and then from its home at the Museum of Modern Art (MoMA) in New York: Picasso stipulated that the painting must never go to Spain until the country was a free and democratic republic. After the death of General Franco in 1975, Spain became a democratic, constitutional monarchy, and after some cavilling that this was not the republic specified by Picasso, MoMA allowed the work to go to Spain in 1981. It is now housed at the Museo Nacional Centro de Arte Reina Sofia.

above: 'Guernica', oil on canvas, 137.4in × 305.5in (349cm × 776cm), Museo Nacional Centro de Arte Reina Sofia, Madrid.

trying to suggest that he had been an eyewitness. Eschewing sensationalism he produced a lucid narrative:

... Monday was the customary market day in Guernica for the country round. At 4.30 p.m., when the market was full and peasants were still coming in, the church bell rang the alarm for approaching aeroplanes, and the population sought refuge in cellars and in the dugouts prepared following the bombing of the civilian population of Durango on March 31, which opened General Mola's offensive in the north. The people are said to have shown a good spirit. A Catholic priest took charge and perfect order was maintained.

Five minutes later a single German bomber appeared, circled over the town at a low altitude, and then dropped six heavy bombs, apparently aiming for the station. The bombs with a shower of grenades fell on a former institute and on houses and streets surrounding it. The aeroplane then went away. In another five minutes came a second bomber, which threw the same number of bombs into the middle of the town. About a quarter of an hour later three Junkers arrived to continue the work of demolition, and thenceforward the bombing grew in intensity and was continuous, ceasing only with the approach of dusk at 7.45. The whole town of 7,000 inhabitants, plus 3,000 refugees, was slowly and systematically pounded to pieces. Over a radius of five miles round a detail of the raiders' technique was to bomb separate caserios, or farmhouses. In the night these burned like little candles in the hills. All the villages around were bombed with the same intensity as the town itself, and at Mugica, a little group of houses at the head of the Guernica inlet, the population was machine-gunned for 15 minutes.[8]

The Nationalists rushed to discredit the story that the Germans had bombed Guernica – or, indeed, that anyone had – claiming that the Republicans themselves had destroyed the town, just as they had at Irún in 1936 when they could no longer defend it. Steer stuck to his story, and cited as evidence unexploded bombs marked with the name of the German factory and the date, 1936. Although the controversy persisted for decades, it is now clear that it was the Luftwaffe's Condor Legion that carried out the attack. Guernica fell shortly afterwards, and Steer stayed on for the final stand before he escaped to Paris.

LIFE GOES ON DESPITE THE WAR

Carrying a rucksack, a quantity of food, $50 in her purse, and a letter declaring she was a special correspondent for *Collier's*, a weekly magazine with some ten million readers, 28-year-old Martha Gellhorn reached Madrid in March 1937 to join Ernest Hemingway, whom she had met at Christmas in the USA. She moved into one of his rooms at the Florida Hotel and the pair began an

opposite: Devastation in Guernica, the heart of the Basque country, after the aerial bombardment which caused great loss of life. The raid was ordered to disrupt the Republican retreat to Bilbao.

above: As Nationalist forces close in on Irún, a Republican farmer continues to defend his farm. The Nationalists claimed that Republican forces had destroyed Guernica as they had Irún – to halt the Nationalist advance.

overleaf: Martha Gellhorn and Ernest Hemingway in 1937: lovers in Spain, before they married.

affair. Since it had been shelled, the hotel was no longer the comfortable billet of the previous summer, but it remained the home of the correspondents, some of whom were larger-than-life characters: the French novelist Antoine de Sainte Exupéry, the American writer John Dos Passos and the *Daily Express's* Sefton Delmer.

Unsure what to write about, Gellhorn took advice and recorded in loving detail what life was like in Madrid. Her writing had a rare quality, not so much informing the reader as quietly drawing them into the scene until they felt the death and privation endured by the ordinary people on a daily basis. *Collier's* accepted her first piece 'Only the Shells Whine', and thereafter her output grew during her periods in Madrid. Once, when she was giving a live evening broadcast to the USA from the Telefonica building, her hotel room took a direct hit from a shell.

During 1938, the world gradually lost interest in Spain, preoccupied by the conviction that a greater war was imminent. Gellhorn went to Barcelona, where she saw the hunger, the bomb craters and the injured children in the hospital, and where she went to the opera:

> *It was surprising that the singers had energy to sing, considering how little they eat. It was surprising to see such thin singers. The women were any age at all, wearing the pre-war costumes, a little mussed*

now but still brilliant and romantic. All the men were old. The young men were at the war. The opera house was full every day and everyone enjoyed the music immensely, and roared with laughter at the stale formal opera jokes, and sighed audibly at the amorous moments and shouted 'Olé!' at each curtain. We used to sit and scratch, because everyone had fleas this winter, there was no soap any more and everyone was very dirty and malodorous indeed. But we loved the music and loved not thinking about the war.[9]

By the end of the year, *Collier's* no longer wanted articles about Barcelona and Gellhorn moved on to new war zones.

THE MISERY OF THE REFUGEES

The epilogue to the Spanish tragedy was provided by another reporter at the start of a career. The BBC had lagged far behind the USA in live outside broadcasting. While CBS's H.V. Kaltenborn was speaking live to the USA from his haystack at the start of the Spanish Civil War, the BBC was reporting minor events at home using a converted laundry van as a recording vehicle. Such recordings were then taken back to the studio for vetting before transmission. But in 1939, as Franco's victorious troops pushed the shattered Republicans towards the border with France, the BBC sent its first foreign observer to the Pyrenean town of Le Perthus. That observer was Richard Dimbleby, the driving force in the BBC newsroom. On 6 April 1939 he told his audience:

> *Everyone is agitated. The headquarters of the prefect are like a beehive, day and night, and Sunday included. I've had to wait a total of nearly nine hours for two special permits. I've shown them, altogether, exactly 47 times. I've been asked if I carry arms six times, and searched for them twice. And once last night, someone mistook me for a refugee and tried to push me into a cattle truck. Perhaps that sounds vaguely amusing, but the whole refugee problem here is intensely serious and … and pathetic is the only word I can think of – unless, perhaps, tragic is better. There are thousands of them, mostly women and young children, coming over the three main entrances: Cerbère, Le Perthus and Bourg Madame. Some of them are in the last stages of exhaustion. They are hungry, starving many of them, and numb with cold. In spite of the work of relief organisations*

MARTHA GELLHORN, 1908–1998

Martha Gellhorn's career as a journalist, war corresopondent and travel writer spanned seven decades and much of the planet. Born in St Louis, Missouri, she gave up her studies in 1927 and was soon working at United Press's bureau in Paris, the perceived capital of intellectual life.

In 1937 Gellhorn teamed up with Ernest Hemingway to cover the Spanish Civil War. Her dispatches established her as one of the finest writers of her generation, and she became an inspiration to future women correspondents. She had no patience with what she described as 'all this objectivity shit', and was never afraid to be partisan, but her passion for the Spanish Republicans led her to ignore the crimes of her chosen side.

During the Second World War, Gellhorn reported from across Europe. When Hemingway took the D-Day place that should have been hers or Frank Gervasi's, she went aboard a hospital ship instead; she defied the ban on women flying on operations; she went into the liberated Dachau death camp and, using her 'cold eye and warm heart' painted a ghastly word-picture of one of the worst atrocities in human history.

Her addiction to reporting war from perspectives and in words to which ordinary people could relate took her to Vietnam, Israel for the Six-Day War, El Salvador, Nicaragua and, in 1990, Panama.

Gellhorn paid a price for her journalistic success: an unfulfilled private life further marred by numerous abortions, and regret at never finding the loving relationship of her parents. She married Hemingway in 1940, but it was a short and stormy four-year union. Her second marriage to Tom Matthews, editor-in-chief of *Time*, ended in divorce in 1963 after nine years. In failing health and almost blind she calmly committed suicide in London aged 89.

above: Martha Gellhorn, photographed in 1958.

and the scheme of evacuation which the French authorities have put into operation quite successfully, many of them have died.[10]

The experience had a profound emotional effect on Dimbleby, who had never been to a war zone before; professionally, it was a triumph for both him and the BBC. A few months later, he would be the BBC's first war correspondent, covering the action in many theatres.

Iconography of a war

Two world-renowned images of death emerged from the Spanish Civil War. One was Pablo Picasso's painting 'Guernica' (see pages 68–69), which was created for the exposition held in Paris in 1937. The other was a controversial image by a young photographer who, through the lens of his Leica, would photograph the world's conflicts, from Spain to Indo-China: Robert Capa.

The Leica revolutionized photojournalism. Still-cameras that used film rather than plates had been available early in the century, but it was the Ernst Leitz Optische Werke's invention of the 35mm camera (*Leitz camera* gave *Leica*), tested at the start of the First World War but not put into production until 1925, that gave photo-journalism a compact, robust camera capable of shutter speeds of 1/1000 second. The French magazine *Vu* sent Capa and his Leica to Spain to achieve with his images what Martha Gellhorn was doing with her words.

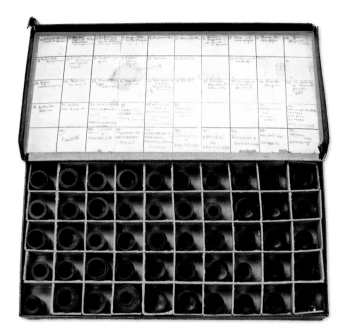

Capa's most famous photograph is 'Loyalist Militiaman at the Moment of Death, Cerro Muriano, September 5, 1936', which is better known as 'The Falling Soldier'. It is the image on which his international reputation was founded, and it shows – or at least it purports to show – a Republican soldier at the precise moment when a bullet mortally wounded him. A fine mist of doubt has always framed the image: Was it staged? Why did Capa tell conflicting stories about its genesis? Has the soldier been killed, or is he just falling over? In 2009 new research concluded that the picture was taken at Espejo, which saw no fighting. The balance of probability has shifted firmly in favour of the photograph being, in crude terms, a fake, but so strong is its resonance that it will probably continue to hold its place in the public imagination.

Capa photographed far more than combat in Spain. He had Gellhorn's empathy with civilians, the bereaved and the dispossessed. His photographs were carried as pictorial journalism spreads in magazines from *Vu* and *Life to Ce Soir* and the *Berliner Illustrirte Zeitung*. *Regards* magazine described one set of photographs, of Madrid, as 'prodigious' and pointed out to its readers that Capa had risked his life to take them. By 1938 he was being praised as the greatest war photographer in the world.

As the war in Spain came to an end, Capa stayed on in Barcelona and did not evacuate until 25 January, when, having photographed Herbert Matthews and O'Dowd Gallagher sending their final dispatches, he climbed into Matthews's car and made for Figuras, close to the border with France. Bitterly disappointed by the Nationalist victory, on the way out of Spain he photographed the weary refugees, the vanguard of those whose arrival would be broadcast by Richard Dimbleby.

TOWARDS ANOTHER WORLD WAR

The Spanish Civil War was unusual, not only because so many reporters from neutral countries took sides, but also that so many of those who supported the government did so with passionate conviction, and then felt only despair at the outcome. For this, events elsewhere in Europe were partly responsible. Italy and Germany, under Mussolini and Hitler respectively, had already become fascist states, and in 1938, with the Anschluss, Austria had followed suit. Months later, in October 1938, Czechoslovakia's Sudetenland had been ceded to Germany. For many, Spain was seen as the battleground where the advance of fascism should finally have been halted.

The rise of the totalitarian dictators, including Stalin in the Soviet Union, during the 1920s and 1930s made accurate reporting difficult – and sometimes dangerous. The foreign press corps was detested in Nazi circles, reviled by the Hitler Youth as 'horrid examples of Jewish-controlled, capitalist-inspired, communist-dominated lying venality'.[11] Quentin Reynolds risked the fury of the Nazis by reporting on the humiliating parade through Nuremburg of an Aryan girl whose crime was to wish to marry her Jewish boyfriend. Ed Mowrer was expelled for writing his book *Germany Puts The Clock Back*. George Seldes was expelled first from the Soviet Union and later from Italy. In Rome, Frank Gervasi's office was raided and one of his colleagues detained for months. Hugh Carleton Greene, the *Daily Telegraph* correspondent and future chairman of the BBC, sent back a graphic report of the infamous Kristallnacht violence that made front page news in November 1938. Ed Beattie reported on the invasion of Czechoslovakia in March the following year.

Soon the correspondents would be required to cover a world war far greater in scope than anything previously fought.

opposite: In 2007 a suitcase was found in Mexico City. It turned out to contain thousands of negatives by Robert Capa, Gerda Taro and David Seymour, almost all of them relating to the Spanish Civil War.

above: Capa's 'The Falling Soldier', 1936. The photograph became the iconic image of the Spanish Civil War and one of the most significant of the twentieth century.

What a nuisance that man Hitler makes of himself.

An anonymous lady in Liverpool speaking to Sir Philip Gibbs in 1940, from *The Pageant of the Years*, 1946

On the last day of August 1939, German tanks were massed on the Polish border ready for the following day's invasion, veiled from the eyes of curious motorists by a hessian screen next to the road to Katowice. The border was closed to all but diplomatic vehicles, and the *Daily Telegraph's* Clare Hollingworth had borrowed the British consul's car and driven into Germany to do some shopping. 'I got to the border with Germany, they were a bit surprised to see the Union Jack, but they let me in, and I went in to the nearest town. ... Fortunately for me, as I was driving along, a sudden strong gust of wind blew the screen away from its moorings and I looked into the valley and saw scores, if not hundreds, of tanks lined up ready to go into Poland.' On her return she briefed the consul, and urged him to get on to the telephone immediately to Warsaw and London. 'And I got in touch with Hugh Carlton-Greene who was my boss ... for the *Telegraph* in Warsaw.'[1]

At 08:00 on 1 September, Ed Beattie was on the phone to Amsterdam when he heard the first bombs fall on Warsaw. In a Danzig

'Warcos' Warriors:

the second world war

hotel, Associated Press's (AP) Lynn Heinzerling had: '... heard a German officer, who usually slept late, leave a call for 3:15 the next morning – Friday, Sept. 1. I realized then that it was coming. It was 4:47 a.m. by my watch when the firing started. I ran down the hotel stairs several steps at a time. The night watchman said: "*Es geht los*." (It's started.) I ran toward the Vistula River. There I saw what it was – the German warship *Schleswig-Holstein*.'[2]

On 3 September, after Germany had ignored ultimatums from both Britain and France, the Second World War began. Carleton-Green was hoisted onto the shoulders of jubilant Poles. The official at the Foreign Office to whom Beattie was talking to broke down in tears of relief when the news flash came that Poland was not alone.

The Polish campaign ended on 5 October. Sixteen days after Hitler attacked from the West, the Soviets invaded from the east. The Allied journalists had no choice other than to leave. Patrick Maitland of the *Times* and Carleton-Greene drove south in a convoy led by the *Daily Express*'s Sefton Delmer. Richard Mowrer was detained at Zaleszczyki in the Russian-occupied zone, but he escaped by swimming the Dniester River and making his way to the Romanian town of Czernowitz in just his underwear. Beattie held on until the US military attaché was told to leave, when together they found an abandoned car and headed for Romania.

The correspondents made it to Bucharest, most with no more than a rucksack and typewriter. Clare Hollingworth drove the consul general's car out of Katowice, Union Jack flying, and the consul general drove a second diplomatic car. The roads were packed with desperate Poles evacuating their cities.

Coaxed out of self-imposed retirement by Frank Gervasi, 37-year-old Robert St. John, who was supposedly too old to be a war correspondent, travelled to Budapest where he was snapped up by AP on the day that Poland was invaded.

THE 'FOURTH SERVICE'

Many of the 'warcos', as they became known, who witnessed those first weeks of the war were the less experienced ones. The veterans were fretting in London, waiting for official accreditation to the British Expeditionary Force (BEF) now established on the continent, which was accompanied by just one token journalist, Alexander Clifford.

opposite: German tanks crossing into Poland, September 1939.

above: Warco's uniform. The 'C', designating 'correspondent', embroidered on the cap can clearly be seen.

Aspiring 'warcos' trooped off to Austin Reed or Moss Brothers to be kitted out in off-the-peg uniforms complete with breeches, leather boots, peaked caps, berets and Sam Browne belts, but with leather buttons which the correspondents sometimes surreptitiously changed for brass. Later in the war, Stanley Baron of the *News Chronicle* encountered a group of American soldiers on the Siegfried Line who greeted him with: 'Jesus Christ, look what's been left over from the last war!'[3] Ed Beattie, who thought he looked like an old cavalry officer or chauffeur, remembered the 'C' embroidered in gold on the caps, and the designation 'War Correspondent', also in gold, on the shoulder tabs. This was an improvement on the 1938 design in which the cap was emblazoned with a gold 'W.C.' encircled by a chain. Black-and-white striped armbands marked 'PRESS' were issued – but not worn.

The press accredited to British forces now came under the control of the Ministry of Information's department of public relations. Correspondents again enjoyed honorary officer rank (captain, in the case of those accredited to British forces), which obliged them to salute but did not entitle them to be saluted. However, when correspondents accompanied the Dieppe Raid in 1942, they received temporary commissions and, to their consternation, were ordered to carry arms. Frank Gillard, who boarded the train in London, alighted from it in Bristol as Major Gillard complete with requisite crown on his shoulder; Quentin Reynolds became a lieutenant colonel in the US forces.

above: Alan Moorehead, photographed in 1944, wearing the war correspondent's uniform and beret.

right: Herbert David Zinman's dogtag, indicating he was part of the press corps. Zinman worked for the British government's propaganda arm, the Political Warfare Executive, and famously wrote the francophile *Instructions for British Servicemen in France 1944*.

Continuing the practice introduced in the First World War, the Ministry of Information assigned 'conducting officers' to look after small groups of 'warcos'. O'Dowd Gallagher of the *Daily Express* stigmatized those he met as caricatures of army officers, frequently if not invariably drunk. Others spoke more kindly of their chaperons: George, Marquess of Ely, made a good fourth in a rubber of bridge; the BBC's Godfrey Talbot was blessed with a captain on first-name terms with all the corps commanders, although his map-reading skills were such that in the desert Talbot was obliged to navigate; Frank Gervasi and his friends were glad to team up with Alan Moorehead and Alexander Clifford, whose conducting officer was Captain Kim Mundy, renowned for creating gourmet food in the desert out of whatever came to hand; and the marksmanship of Captain Gerry Dunn secured the liberty, and perhaps saved the lives, of four 'warcos' in France.

Censorship was tight. Everything written had to be submitted in triplicate or quadruplicate to the censors, creating delays to which official communiqués were not subject. American reporters were particularly critical of a censorship policy that seemed to be based on an assumption that the enemy was so stupid that even a simple phrase describing the River Thames as 'pointing the way to London' had to be struck out. Photographs of bomb sites had to show at least one property still standing; the Germans could be hated from Monday to Saturday, but not on Sunday; RAF losses were embargoed – an untenable policy during the Battle of Britain, of which journalists and anyone resident in the southeast of England often had a grandstand view.

The French were equally paranoid – they refused Richard Dimbleby permission to state that he was reporting from the French Army in France, despite his expostulation that everyone knew that both he and the French Army were in France. When the USA joined the war, press correspondents under its control – and not just the American ones – were allowed far more freedom to travel around (right to the front) and were extended greater trust. According to Alexander Berry Austin, the Canadians were particularly good to any correspondent accredited to them: '...They will be fully trusted, treated with complete frankness, and given every proper facility for their work. The sole restriction on their writings will be that they shall not contain information of value to the enemy.'⁴ And the devil, as always, was in the detail.

To limit the numbers on specific operations and ensure that every media organization could carry the story, correspondents were often assigned to pools, obliging them to share their information. Where competition existed, it flourished, and not always honourably. Universal News's Ronnie Noble scooped the first footage of the Free French forces at Bir Hakeim in 1942, under Luftwaffe attack, only to be informed that the news had been sent two days earlier. He subsequently learned that the footage had been faked 50 miles (80 kilometres) behind the lines.

Cable was still the prime means of communication with employers, as well as for sending dispatches, and it remained sufficiently expensive for the word-count to have to be minimized by sending messages in 'cablese'. For example, Latin suffixes, prefixes and elisions were pressed into service:

Pro— = to/for/for the attention of
—ward/—wards = up/to/in the direction of
Cum— = with
—est = most
sevening = seven p.m.
et— = and
un— = no
up— = up

This contributed to a certain type of humour among the correspondents. According to Denis Johnston, an apocryphal exchange of cables went around the press corps in the Western Desert:

Editor: why unnews
Correspondent: unnews good news
Editor: unnews unjob
Correspondent: upshove job arsewards

In the decades since the First World War, technology had developed to the extent that the BBC now had transportable disc-recording machines that could be operated from a car or a truck. A steel or sapphire cutter would transcribe the electrical impulses created by the voice into modulated grooves on 'acetates', the name given to the double-sided recording discs made out of aluminium and coated with a thin layer of nitrocellulose lacquer. The discs would then be sent to London or played back at 78rpm over a radio link to BBC receiving stations in England. In October 1939 a report on the BEF was sent back, from an undisclosed location in France, by Richard Dimbleby:

We are standing in the pouring rain at the side of a French road, a road squelching with mud.... It is a grey, cold, dismal day. A few lorries only are splashing by to and from the forward areas. And coming down the road towards us is a battalion that I know to be of a famous Irish regiment. They are marching in threes and in their full battle dress and kit they blend with the dripping green grass of the roadside and the brown of the haystacks.⁵

American war reporters were issued with wire recorders. These were forerunners of the tape recorder, which captured sound onto fine magnetic wire wound onto a spool. By 1943 the BBC had developed the Midget disc recorder, which was sufficiently portable, at 40 pounds (18 kilograms), to be carried into action. Furthermore, the correspondent could operate it without an engi-

neer. The BBC Midget looked like a portable gramophone player from the previous decade, and it demonstrated its worth from the D-Day landings until the end of the war.[6]

Although it had only one war correspondent abroad, the BBC established its first overseas office in mid-1940, in a bug-infested slum in Cairo:

[which had] a lift that remains permanently fixed between the first and second floors, so that you have to go up by the unlit staircase, falling over the sacks and bundles that have been left there temporarily by the sleepers. Then, passing a Cave of Ali Baba on the first floor, you reach a mysterious medical man's apartment on the second. The story is current that he is the City Agent for an expensive lunatic asylum,

and those seen going in and out lend colour to this theory. On the third floor comes the BBC and above this we never penetrate. All I can say is that as you sit at your desk pondering over the problems of War Reporting, American visitors look in from time to time and present you with a visiting card that reads: Mademoiselle Fifi, Hostess and Social Activities. On receipt of this card you say nothing, but silently point upwards. And the callers nod and steal away and are never seen again.[7]

CHAOS ON THE CONTINENT
Shortly after the German assault on the Netherlands began on 10 May 1940, Morley Richards of the *Daily Express* caught the last boat out of Amsterdam. Hundreds of people had packed onto the

river ferry to Ijmuiden, then into coaches that drove through the darkness without headlights; the driver of Richards' coach had shot his way out of trouble before unloading his passengers onto a cargo ship bound for Britain.

Ronnie Noble, a young cameraman, persuaded a French pilot to fly him from Paris to Arras. It was Noble's first experience of his new trade and for two weeks he filmed the retreat towards Boulogne, during which the Luftwaffe strafed and bombed roads filled with civilians. Then he discovered something about his job that was to stay with him:

> *The horror of working, of pointing a camera at people and things, completely ignoring their feelings, and my own too: recording film events I would rather not ever see. When a person is stricken to the marrow with grief I must get a 'close-up'. When my French friend lay dead it was my job to take a shot of his body being carried away, an abstract shape on a stretcher, silhouetted against the flames of burning Boulogne. Yet it must be done: my job as a news cameraman is to film the facts and report facts. The camera can lie, but in war it doesn't have to – the truth is propaganda enough.*[8]

Quentin Reynolds was informed that his application to receive accreditation from the French Army must be accompanied by six photographs and a recommendation from the American ambassador. Frustrated by French bureaucracy, Reynolds concocted a cable to 'uncle' Franklin D. Roosevelt asking him to expedite his 'nephew's' accreditation, and showed it to the head of the press section at the French Foreign Ministry, Pierre Comert, hoping to bluff him into issuing a pass on the spot. Unfortunately, Comert insisted on actually sending the telegram. It shall never be known what the US President made of the cable from a stranger claiming kinship, but the pass came through and Reynolds went to the front. There, from a forward pillbox, he observed an aerial dogfight before hitching a lift to Beauvais with the American film star Robert Montgomery, who was serving with the American Field Service (AFS). Finding Beauvais in flames, he helped Montgomery to evacuate the stretcher cases, then he left on the last hospital train bound for Paris, from where he made his way to London.

On Friday, 17 May, along the border between France and Belgium, Geoffrey Cox was outside a café with colleagues, watching the refugees leave, just as bombers came over, forcing them to run to the foot of a tower and lay there pressed to the wall:

opposite: Ed Murrow of CBS broadcasting from London under the vigilant supervision of the censor, who could cut him off at a second's notice.

above: Article on Ed Murrow, whose radio pieces 'This – is London' were popularly received in America.

overleaf: Fred Bayliss of British Paramount News (right) and his assistant setting up their tripod-mounted camera in February 1940 while attached to the British Expeditionary Force.

Above the cannonading of the guns the roar of engines came closer. Then came the roar and quake of the first bombs. The earth seemed to ripple under the shock, but these had fallen on the other side of the town. Then came a steadily growing roar, getting louder and louder as bomb after bomb crashing in a line that seemed to rumble right on top of us. One bomb fell just the other side of the tower. I waited for the next one. It seemed inevitable that it would be right on us. But with a shriek like tearing silk it plunged into the square a hundred yards ahead. A moment later another wave spread from the other side of town; nearer, nearer. It was as if great pieces of sky were hurtling down on us....[9]

Cox returned to Paris, evacuated staff from the *Daily Express* and, with other correspondents, boarded a liner that was waiting in the

Gironde to take British nationals and senior French personnel to Britain. Exchanging the pen for the sword, he was then commissioned into the New Zealand 5th Infantry Brigade.

The press corps was evacuated against its will on 24 May 1940. According to Noble, the choice was between being put under military arrest or walking aboard 'like gentlemen'.[10] His editor was furious at his return at such a momentous time, and Canadian cameraman Freddie Bayliss of Paramount almost lost his job for evacuating.

A fortnight later, troops were being taken off the beaches of Dunkirk, with no accredited press to record the event. Dimbleby had gone to Cairo in readiness for the expected escalation of the war. Charles Martin of Pathé News crossed the Channel by destroyer and boarded a paddle-steamer, but took hardly any footage, and instead assisted exhausted troops up the scram-

RICHARD DIMBLEBY, 1913–1965

The 'voice of the nation', as Richard Dimbleby became known, was born in Twickenham, the son of a local newspaper proprietor, and he joined the family business as a reporter.

In 1936 he wrote to the BBC's News Editor, effectively telling him how to restructure the entire news-gathering and broadcasting operation – and offering himself to help implement the changes. Six months later he was taken on, and enlivened his second routine assignment by using the mobile recording unit to capture interviews and background noises.

Dimbleby made the BBC's first foreign outside broadcast from Le Perthus in 1939. During the Second World War he reported from France, where fellow correspondent Sir Philip Gibbs remembered him at Arras as 'a stout young man bubbling over with good nature, and wit', who broke his four-poster bed while playing his accordion. He covered the action in the Western Desert, made recordings during RAF bombing missions, and was the first war correspondent to set foot in the Nazi concentration camp at Belsen in 1945.

For all his achievements, he was unpopular with the BBC: they could not cope with his large personality, self-confidence and ambitions for the Service. In September 1945 he was manoeuvred into resigning.

Less than a year later he was asked to present the radio panel game 'Twenty Questions', and a second light entertainment programme 'Down Your Way' gained him a regular audience of 10 million. Even more significantly, he commentated the 1946 Victory Parade in London for the reopened television service. He became established as the television reporter of first choice for such state occasions as the Coronation of Elizabeth II, and he fronted the long-running current affairs programme 'Panorama'. He was sometimes criticized for sounding too solemn and reverential when reporting live from state occasions, yet his hushed tones were the result of talking quietly but clearly without disturbing the proceedings.

News that he was suffering from cancer brought a deluge of letters and gifts, including champagne from the Queen. He died aged 52.

above: Richard Dimbleby perches informally on the side of a tank to interview Trooper J. Budgen in Libya on 12 June 1942.

ble-nets. Freelance David Divine, by his own admission, stole a Thames cruiser and was detailed to bring off Admiral Taylor. The cruiser stayed around and went pottering about looking for stragglers:

While we were doing that, a salvo of shells got one of the ships alongside the Mole. She was hit clean in the boilers and exploded in one terrific crash. There were then, I suppose, about 1,000 Frenchmen on the Mole. We had seen them crowding along its narrow crest, outlined against the flames. They had gone out under shellfire to board the boat, and now they had to go back again, still being shelled. It was quite the most tragic thing I ever have seen in my life. We could do nothing with our little dinghy....[11]

Following outraged representations to the War Office, a quartet of correspondents, including Bayliss and Noble, was allowed back to France, accompanied by their 'conducting officers', to travel north against the tide of retreating civilians. At Le Mans the four were bil-

leted in a luxurious, abandoned brothel and then they set off in two cars. Bayliss and Noble were in the first, with their officer, Captain Gerry Dunn; Ed Beattie and Alaric Jacob (Reuters) followed with Lieutenant Titley. At a bend in the walled road a cyclist suddenly leapt from his machine and opened fire.

I didn't realise he was firing until the car in front screeched to a halt, and Gerry Dunn opened up with his .38. From behind the stone wall came the crack of two more guns. For the space of thirty seconds or so, while the drivers frantically wrenched the two little cars around in the narrow road, Gerry held off the foe. There was a Lee Enfield in each car, for use of the driver, but as usual it was buried under a mass of knapsacks, gas masks and typewriters.

The front car got turned first, and ripped past us gathering speed, with Gerry leaning back out the front window pumping lead like a Chicago gangster making a getaway.[12]

RETREAT TO THE BLITZED HOME FRONT

After the fall of France, foreign journalists arrived in Britain as war correspondents and Ben Robertson of the *New York Herald Tribune* could hardly believe his reception when his plane landed at an RAF base and a young officer apologized for the fact that the 'acting customs officer' was on a practice flight. A pot of tea was served in the officers' mess, and Robertson decided the British had no concept of the danger they were in.

Having made himself comfortable in London's Waldorf Hotel, where dinner was served in the basement and guests were issued with gas masks and orders not to touch the blackout curtains, Robertson started to look round London. At St Paul's Cathedral he picked up a printed prayer against air-raids, and experienced a change of heart: 'I was supposed to be a hard-boiled, tough American news-

opposite: A German cameraman records the arrival of his country's forces at Dunkirk after the partial evacuation of the BEF and some of the French units.

above: Perched on railings high on a building in Fleet Street, two journalists acting as air-raid wardens scan the skies for approaching German aircraft during the Blitz.

above: London burns: a thousand tons of bombs were dropped on London by the Luftwaffe during a six-hour bombing raid on the night of 11 May 1941. Here, the Fire Brigade fight to control the conflagration engulfing Queen Victoria Street.

opposite: Blitz spirit. Audrey Russell, BBC Radio Newsreel Observer, talks to a woman whose home in southern England had just been destroyed by a V-bomb, September 1944.

paperman; I told myself I could not allow myself to be swept away in a day ... I must form a careful, unbiased opinion of what was going on. But just the same I knew from that time on that there was courage and bravery and determination in the British capital.'[13]

Correspondents were courted with excursions. One was to an RAF station, where, on arrival, tea was served in the mess, before a sherry reception, hosted by an air vice-marshal, at their hotel. Then it was back to the RAF station for dinner at 19:45, followed by a short tour before assembling on the flare path to watch the Wellington bombers take off. The reporters could either go back to the hotel or sleep on a camp-bed until the bombers returned around 04:30.

Robertson teamed up with Ed Beattie, the photographer Art Menken and journalists Helen Kirkpatrick and Hilde Marchant for regular trips down to Dover to watch the RAF take on the Luftwaffe. The sounds of the war were caught in recordings by BBC journalists, including Robin Duff and Charles Gardner – the latter was reprimanded after reporting a dogfight (to protect a British convoy) over the Channel because his tone was considered by some to be more suited to a sports commentary.

Those correspondents who headed to Dover for the day came back in the evening on what became known as 'the Blitz express'. 'It almost made us physically ill to see the enormity of the flames which lit the entire western sky,' Robertson wrote. Once, when they drove back after breakfast, they saw: '... the factories gutted and docks burning and bomb craters.... What really disturbed us was the East End itself.'[14]

Hilde Marchant of the *Daily Express* became famous for her morale-boosting reporting from the home front. She may have underplayed the panic that ensued on the night of 14/15 November 1940 after the Luftwaffe, in her words, 'guernicaed' Coventry, and she undoubtedly overstated the morale of those who returned from Dunkirk (all to please the censor), but she used her position to campaign vociferously for better bomb shelters for the tens of thousands of Londoners having to use the unsanitary and shockingly overcrowded buildings set aside for them.

The accommodation for correspondents was no safer, though those staying in hotels might have access to sleeping quarters set up in basements. The Grand Hotel in Dover was hit after Robertson and his colleagues had left it. In London, Ray Daniell of the *New York Times* was evacuated from his hotel because of an unexploded bomb. Eric Sevareid and Larry Lesuer of CBS were bombed out and had to stay with Ed Murrow, whose own office had taken a hit. The windows of Lansdowne House, where Quentin Reynolds was putting up, were blown out. Robertson was dining at The Dorchester with the socialite Lady Diana Cooper when German bombers came over Hyde Park, prompting the big anti-aircraft (AA) guns outside the hotel to crash out; Lady Diana 'winced'. In what could almost be a caricature of 'stiff-upper-lip Britain' the band struck up a medley of famous tunes.

There was little neutrality among the American press in London. Ed Murrow broadcast regularly to the USA, always beginning his pieces with 'This – is London', and he played a role in making American public opinion more pro-British. At a dinner held in Murrow's honour by CBS in New York in 1941, Archibald MacLeish, Librarian of Congress, told him: 'You burned the city of London in our houses and we felt the flames that burned it. You laid the dead of London at our doors, and we knew the dead were our dead....'[15]

Ernie Pyle also 'burned London' for an American audience in terms that earned him a wire from the president of Scripps Howard: 'your stuff not only greatest your career but most illuminating and appealing since outbreak battle britain ... your stuff talk of new york'.[16]

Reynolds, who had provided the voice-over to a 1940 short documentary entitled 'London Can Take It!', was asked by the BBC to broadcast a postscript to the nine o'clock news. He offered a satirical 'open letter' to Goebbels, mocking the Führer under the name of Mr Schickelgruber, and the BBC received thousands of appreciative letters, including one from Churchill. When Robert Capa – an enemy alien by virtue of his birth – arrived to photograph for *Collier's*, Reynolds took him to register with the police, where he announced in a comic German accent, 'I have brought you a German spy to register', which sent everyone into fits of laughter.

Capa ran into trouble almost immediately by photographing a B-17 Flying Fortress with its highly classified Norden bombsight. Hauled in front of a tribunal, he was saved by the intervention of one of the squadron pilots. After that inauspicious start, he went on to record his trademark, close-up images of ordinary people caught in war.

The experience of the Blitz quickly rubbed away any gloss of war. Beattie saw, 'too many women and kids pulled out of houses dead to get any exciting kick out of this. It's just horrible, not exciting....' Robertson, who was to be killed on a flight to Britain in 1942, compared reality with such exciting texts as 'The Charge of the Light Brigade', realizing that: '... the war I had come to know was short on glamour and long on tragedy ... out of these reflections came a sobering realization. I, too, had often been guilty of glorifying the war in my articles and books.'[17]

BALKAN BLITZKRIEG

Italy had invaded Greece in October 1940, but such was the resistance of the Greeks that Germany was compelled to intervene in April 1941. Clare Hollingworth was in Bucharest where the fascist Iron Guard went to arrest her in her flat. 'We still had a skeleton embassy – or consulate general, it may have been called ... I took all my clothes off except a blouse and I said "I'm naked, and you can't take a naked woman away", and while I was talking I got on the phone to Robin [Hankey, the consul] and Robin came very kindly ... and rescued me and took me to the embassy[18] where I camped until we left....'[19] Outside Belgrade, Serbs mistook Sam Brewer for a German paratrooper, identifying his typewriter as a radio transmitter and denouncing his papers as forgeries. His freedom was granted only when a Serbian editor, who held a reserve commission, vouched for him.

Among the most dramatic escapes by a group of war correspondents is that by AP's Robert St. John, the *New York Herald Tribune's* Russell J. Hill, CBS's Leigh White and Terence Atherton of the *Daily Telegraph*. Leaving Bucharest in 1941, they reached the coast of German-occupied Yugoslavia at Budva and hired a sardine boat to travel down the Adriatic to Corfu. A fifth correspondent, the *Daily Mirror's* Robert Esdaile Walker, elected to remain.

From Corfu, White and Atherton continued in the sardine boat and were picked up by a Greek minesweeper that was then bombed by the Germans. The other pair travelled by Greek sailing ship, and the quartet regrouped at Patros, where they took a train bound for Corinth. When the Luftwaffe machine-gunned the train, White was seriously injured and St. John slightly, but they secured a lift to Corinth in an RAF truck. In Corinth they found a hospital for White – just as the Luftwaffe bombed a train filled with wounded soldiers, creating such horrific carnage that they resolved not to leave White there.

In another condemned RAF truck, the four correspondents joined the British Army in its retreat. At Argos, where White was taken to

the local hospital, the Germans attacked again from the air. Concussed and his nerve broken, St. John took refuge in a shelter, only to see:

> *… a child lying beside me with only a stump of a leg. She was bleeding badly…. A man who had been hit on the head by a block of stone moaned and foamed at the mouth. Another man had had his lungs crushed, and every time he breathed it was like the noise when you drag your fingernail across a blackboard. The last thing I remember doing was trying to get to the door for air. But there was another raid going on, and someone pulled me back. Atherton told me afterwards that I raved like a madman for an hour, completely out of my head. During that hour Atherton and Hill took turns watching me while the other went out between raids and made more arrangements about White….*[20]

Leaving White, the men escaped to Myloi where they managed to get aboard the British destroyer HMS *Havock*, which took them to Crete. When Crete was evacuated, they reached Egypt where their first act was to track down a censor – who promptly excised all references to the horrors they had described. 'We must lean over backwards,' he told them 'not to make war seem horrible. Death by bullet wounds is alright. Death by cremation is not very pleasant to think about.'[21]

Shortly afterwards, St. John was perplexed to receive a congratulatory cable from AP over a 'bombing of Belgrade' dispatch, which he had never sent. It was followed by a letter, written on toilet paper by Walker from Kotor (modern-day Montenegro), which said that, as promised at Budva, he had sent dispatches to both the *Daily Mirror* and AP, and that he doubted he would leave Yugoslavia alive. Sunderland flying boats had been sent to pick them up, but the British had given up their places in favour of Yugoslav collaborators.

Walker survived and went on to play a dual role as correspondent and agent. White, too, recovered to carry on his career, and Hill continued to report from the front. St. John returned to New York where the anti-communist hysteria of the 1950s ended his career in the US. He built up another from Switzerland and died in 2003 at the age of 100. Atherton, whose reporting provided him with cover for espionage work, joined the Special Operations Executive (SOE) and returned to Yugoslavia in February 1942, only to be murdered for the gold he was carrying.

THE 'WARCOS' AFLOAT

Two of the best-known correspondents to serve at sea were John Nixon of Reuters and Larry Allen of AP. Nixon was the first to be accredited to the Royal Navy. Allen reported from the Royal Navy's Mediterranean Fleet for two torrid years from September 1940, always too close for comfort to the action. When, in January 1941, the Germans repaid HMS *Illustrious* for her air squadrons' devastating raid on the Italian fleet at Taranto the previous November, Allen and Alexander Massey Anderson, of Reuters, were the only two 'warcos' on board. Allen witnessed the first part of the attack from the bridge:

> ... where part of the time I was flat on my face, my hands folded across my head, while splinters of steel swept the carrier's decks and the 'thump, thump' of anti-aircraft guns mingled with the spine-chilling scream of the dive bombers and the crash of bursting bombs. The second time the Germans came over, a low-flying Stuka dropped a bomb which exploded near the starboard side of the ship. The blast threw a column of water over the bridge and hurled me down a hatchway to aviation intelligence quarters one deck below. A sheet of fire burned my face....[22]

The carrier was so badly damaged that she limped off to the USA for repairs, and Rear Admiral Lumley Lyster allegedly described Allen as the 'darling' of the Mediterranean Fleet for sticking to his post. Undeterred, Allen took his typewriter aboard HMS *Warspite* and watched the Battle of Cape Matapan in March.

Earlier the same month Nixon had been sent to the destroyer HMS *Eskimo* to cover the raid on the Lofoten Islands, off the coast of Norway near the Arctic Circle, and he was seasick for the only time. Long after his death it was revealed that *Eskimo's* routine interception of an armed trawler during the operation had resulted in the capture of a rotor for an Enigma coding machine. Two months later, on 24 May, 'Eye-Witness', as Nixon was known to the public, was aboard the brand new battleship HMS *Prince of Wales* – and it was from her deck that he became the only 'warco' to witness the Royal Navy's single worst disaster of the war, when the *Bismarck* exchanged fire with HMS *Hood*:

> Suddenly orange-gold flame belched from Hood's great forward guns with a deep-throated roar. Within three seconds puffs of black smoke shot out from the Bismarck – she had opened up, too. Then our own giant guns began firing, just below me, like a volcano

bursting into eruption. Dense clouds of yellow cordite smoke rose up round the bridge, and momentarily I could see nothing. But it soon cleared, and looking to my left I saw Hood, still surging forward on a course approximately parallel to ours. Fountains of water suddenly shot up in her wake. Hood sped on, leaving the subsiding water rapidly behind.

> Then Hood was hit.... What happened next is the kind of nightmare you don't want to see twice in a lifetime. There came a terrific explosion, and the whole vast ship was enveloped in a flash of flame and smoke, which rose high into the air in the shape of a giant mushroom. Sections of funnels, mast and other parts hurtled hundreds of feet into the sky, some falling on the Prince of Wales. Most landed back on the sea and quickly disappeared. One had an impression of bows tilted high in the air, and two or three minutes after Hood was hit all that remained, apart from bits of wreckage, was a flicker of smoke and flame on the water's surface.[23]

Allen's run of good fortune began to desert him at the end of 1941. Aboard HMS *Galatea* with Alexander Massey Anderson, he endured seven hours of German dive-bombing off the Libyan coast before *U557* put a torpedo into the light cruiser's hull. She capsized and went down with the loss of 470 men, including Anderson. Allen struggled in the water until a young British sailor aboard a raft saved his life: 'He passed a heavy rope under my armpits, tied it around my neck, and flung the end to the quarter-deck of the destroyer. Three others slowly pulled me out of the oily mass and flopped me aboard like a wet fish. They cut off all my clothes and carried me to the mess deck below where there were nearly 100 other survivors. I felt a sharp sting in my left arm as the ship's doctor gave me an injection, and for the next ten hours lay on a mass of greasy rags, too weak to get on my feet.'[24]

Allen and Nixon were assigned to HMS *Sikh* and HMS *Zulu* respectively, covering the disastrous commando raid on Tobruk in September 1942, when the two ships were sunk on consecutive days. Nixon, who had previously reported on the loss of *Hood* and the *Bismarck*, described *Sikh's* loss as he saw it from *Zulu*:

> Hit and disabled by shore batteries the gallant crew of the Sikh still at their guns, blazing back at the land in a suicide attempt to knock out the enemy. A great fire is raging aboard her as the shells tear into her

side at a range of only one mile, but her Captain refuses to abandon ship. Sikh is doing her best to cover our retreat....

The next hour was the most terrifying I have ever experienced. With searchlights on us (Zulu) we edged up to the stationary ship and began the operation of taking her in tow.

By now the shore batteries had the range of Sikh and scored hits with practically every shell. I was convinced my last moment had come.

A shell by a million to one chance severed the steel tow line and the operation of passing a new line had to begin. ...[25]

Allen was one of *Sikh*'s survivors, all of whom became prisoners of war (POWs) in Italy. After the armistice with Italy in 1943 the guards departed from Allen's camp, but to his dismay the senior British commander ordered the POWs to wait for the Allies. Unfortunately, the Germans arrived first and transferred them to Germany, and it was not until 1944 that he regained his freedom, as part of a prisoner exchange.

THE FAR EAST

After the attack on Pearl Harbor, on 7 December 1941, the Japanese swept across the Pacific region with little serious opposition. O'Dowd Gallagher was in Singapore at the time, when the city was bombed only moments after correspondents were alerted to the idea that something important, but unspecified, had occurred. Subsequently offered a 'trip' by the military's public relations' office, most correspondents declined, content to wait for a scoop. However, Gallagher accepted, guessing that the 'trip' involved the newly arrived HM Ships *Repulse* and *Prince of Wales*, and dragged along Cecil Brown of CBS. Two days later both men were swimming for their lives in an oil-coated sea off Malaya after Japanese air strikes had sunk both capital ships with considerable loss of life among the crews.

Gallagher got out of Singapore before the Japanese captured the British colony, and thereafter he reported during the retreat of the British and their allies through the jungle as Burma fell. Particular prominence was given to the extraordinary success of three mercenary fighter squadrons, officially called the American Volunteer Groups, but popularly known as the Flying Tigers, which were raised in 1941 to fight against the Japanese. After the War Office

rescinded Cecil Brown's accreditation because of his critical reporting, Gallagher teamed up with Leland Stowe and Darrel Berrigan, wanting the support that comradeship with fellow journalists could give. During one of Stowe's missions with the Tigers, Berrigan lied to Stowe about Gallagher's whereabouts, knowing how anxious he had become about air missions since the death of a friend (see page 112).[26]

From a correspondent's perspective, the Pacific was not the easiest theatre from which to report. The war was fought across the world's largest ocean and on scattered islands, against an enemy without respect for the Geneva Convention. Trying to make sense of things in such a vast region without recourse to official briefings was impossible.

Stanley Johnston had joined the USS *Lexington* in 1942, a few weeks before the US Navy began to turn the tide of the conflict at the Battle of the Coral Sea. The engagement was hailed as the first 'no-see-um', because neither fleet could see the other and all the action was carried out by carrier-borne naval aircraft. During those preliminary weeks Johnston became integrated into the ship's company, absorbing the heritage of the carrier's name and learning how everything operated; his book, *Queen of the Flat-Tops*, offers a fine overview of life and work on a carrier during the Second World War. During air operations he listened to the radio communications; and when the aircraft landed on after raids over Bougainville, Lae and Salamaua, he questioned the pilots. Although Johnston was a print journalist for the *Chicago Tribune*, who described himself as an inveterate note-taker, he was also equipped with recording gear and was keen to exploit it.

On 7 May *Lexington*'s squadrons flew off and, in concert with aircraft from USS *Yorktown*, sank the Japanese carrier *Shōhō*. Squadron Commander Robert E. Dixon communicated the news over the radio with the coded message, 'Scratch one flat top! Dixon to carrier. Scratch one flat top!' Johnston seized on this and popularized it in a widely copied dispatch; he also recorded interviews with all the squadron commanders involved in the attack. He intended the four 20-minute disks to become supplements to the official written records, and was so pleased with them that he decided to try a recording of the following day's expected action. First, he had to deal with the noise of the ship and the shaking caused by the firing of the AA guns.

... we taped the microphone so that by cupping my hands over it and holding it close to my lips we could exclude almost any other sound and yet get a clear

recording of the voice itself. We extended the microphone line from the Commander's cabin up to the signal bridge – my battle station – and had about 400 feet of loose line there to enable me to move freely around the bridge and see everything that might happen. One of the orderlies was shown how to operate the recording machine. We rigged an intercommunications telephone between the bridge and his cabin so that he could be given directions when to start and stop the turntable.[27]

When the Japanese planes launched a counter-offensive, Johnston got more action than he had bargained on. It began with a lucky break, when two aerial torpedoes 'porpoised' under the ship, but was followed by a bomb hitting the funnel and machine guns strafing the catwalk, with Johnston 'attempting to dictate into the mike in my left hand and with the other hand make a few scribbles in my notebook while trying to see everything that happens, when a quite illogical thought passes through my mind: "There's so damned much noise here I can't hear any single explosion – it's almost like a complete silence."'

The Japanese air attacks continued relentlessly. During the afternoon, explosions ripped through the carrier, and at 17:07 orders were given to abandon ship. Johnston had been writing furiously and he now put his notes and notebook into the breast pocket of his shirt. Although they became wet during the boat trip to the cruiser USS *Indianapolis*, his scribbles – 'hen tracks', as they were known – remained legible. His other possessions including the precious disc recordings, were lost with the *Lexington*.

On his way back to San Diego, on USS *Barnett*, Johnston shared a cabin with the executive officer of *Lexington* and saw a paper that gave the estimated Japanese order of battle at Midway, *before* the battle had been fought. He copied it and gave it to his editor at the *Chicago Tribune*, who failed to clear it with the censor and published it under a false dateline with the headline 'NAVY HAD WORD OF JAP PLAN TO STRIKE AT SEA'. The story appeared after Midway, but still imperilled future intelligence gathering by as good as announcing to the Japanese that the Americans had cracked their naval code. The government wanted to prosecute the paper, but the US Navy preferred to close down the story rather than give credence to it by reacting, and in the end there was no trial.

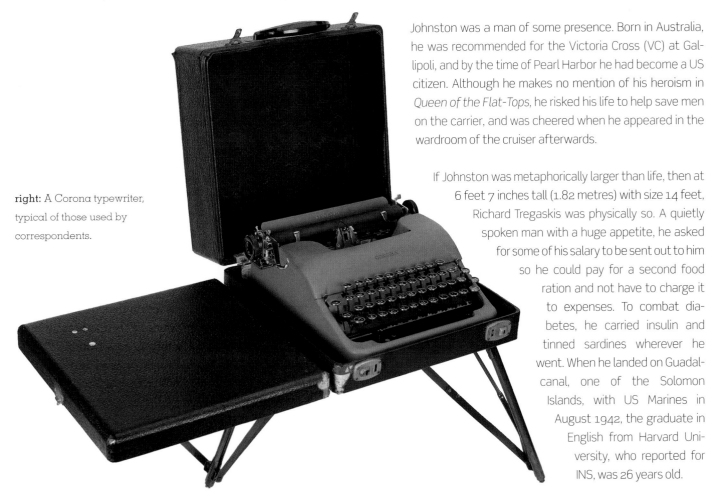

right: A Corona typewriter, typical of those used by correspondents.

Johnston was a man of some presence. Born in Australia, he was recommended for the Victoria Cross (VC) at Gallipoli, and by the time of Pearl Harbor he had become a US citizen. Although he makes no mention of his heroism in *Queen of the Flat-Tops*, he risked his life to help save men on the carrier, and was cheered when he appeared in the wardroom of the cruiser afterwards.

If Johnston was metaphorically larger than life, then at 6 feet 7 inches tall (1.82 metres) with size 14 feet, Richard Tregaskis was physically so. A quietly spoken man with a huge appetite, he asked for some of his salary to be sent out to him so he could pay for a second food ration and not have to charge it to expenses. To combat diabetes, he carried insulin and tinned sardines wherever he went. When he landed on Guadalcanal, one of the Solomon Islands, with US Marines in August 1942, the graduate in English from Harvard University, who reported for INS, was 26 years old.

The Battle of Guadalcanal stretched over six months and was vital to the defence of supply lines between the Americans and their Anzac allies. It also represented the first opportunity to defeat the Japanese on land. Tregaskis was one of two correspondents on the island and he spent seven weeks covering the initial fighting. A total absence of communication facilities prevented his filing any dispatches, and the daily pages of notes he made formed his book *Guadalcanal Diary*, which was the first the American public – and indeed the soldiers – learned about the Pacific land war, and how humour and horror were common bedfellows. On 25 August Tregaskis and Colonel Hunt ran for shelter as shells exploded close by:

> We bumped into each other at the entrance and then backed away and I said, 'You go first, Colonel.' He said politely with a slight bow, 'No, after you.' And we stood there for a few moments, arguing the matter, while the shells continued to fall. ... But the humor of that moment was soon gone. When the barrage halted, we could hear a blubbering, sobbing cry that was more animal than human. A marine came running to the dugout entrance to say that several men had been badly wounded and needed a corpsman. And the crying man kept on, his gurgling rising and falling in regular waves like the sound of some strange machine. ... His face and shoulders lay in the center of a sheet of gore. Face wounds rained blood on the ground. A deep excavation through layers of tissue had been made in one shoulder. The other shoulder, too, was ripped by shrapnel. I could see now how he made the terrible noise. He was crying, sobbing, into a pool of blood. ...[28]

Out of funds, Tregaskis radioed twice for another correspondent to relieve him, but received no acknowledgement. He eventually flew out in a B-17 Flying Fortress, enjoyed 'rest and relaxation' at Pearl Harbor, then saw his diary become a best-seller and the basis of a film that was released in late 1943. By then, Tregaskis had turned his attention to Italy.

LINES WRITTEN IN THE SAND

> the trouble about running this war is that there are too many politicians who think they are generals and too many generals who think they are politicians and too many journalists who think they are both
>
> (a notice on the door of the censors' officer in Cairo[29])

During the first few months of the war in North Africa in 1940, the Italians advanced into Egypt as far as Mersa Matruh, before the British under Field Marshal Wavell pushed them back into Libya and captured Tobruk. The latter was held even after Rommel's Afrika Korps had reclaimed most of the lost Libyan territory.

Alan Moorehead of the *Daily Express*, his close friend Alexander Clifford of the *Daily Mail*, Russell Hill, Ernie Pyle, Clare Hollingworth and, for the BBC, Richard Dimbleby and Denis Johnston, were just seven of many who served in the desert at different, sometimes overlapping, periods between 1940 and 1942. The North Africa theatre offered considerable scope to journalists. They had freedom to travel in and report from a landscape that was perceived to be exotic and exhilarating, even if much of its charm withered during the freezing nights and vicious sandstorms, or clashed with the stark reality of decomposing corpses at the roadside. As Moorehead perceptively observed, reporting from along that coastal strip of Libya was more like naval than land warfare:

> Each truck or tank was as individual as a destroyer, and each squadron of tanks or guns made great sweeps across the desert as a battle-squadron at sea will vanish over the horizon. One did not occupy the desert any more than one occupied the sea. One simply took up a position for a day or a week, and patrolled about it with Bren-gun carriers and light armoured vehicles. ... We hunted men, not land, as a warship will hunt another warship.[30]

The British headquarters was at Cairo, from where the news agencies were fed with official communiqués that could be sent rapidly by radio. It took time for those correspondents in forward positions to get their more colourful dispatches and recordings submitted to Cairo for the censor to review. For example, during Wavell's surging advance in the early weeks of 1941 Moorehead's group were constantly on the move:

> [we] typed on the backs of trucks, on beaches, in deserted houses, in gun emplacements and tents. We hoisted our typewriters on kerosene cases, on bathtubs and rolls of kit, on humps of sand and the steps of cars, or just perched them on our knees. We wrote by candlelight or lamplight, or with an electric torch shining onto the paper. And in the end we could write anywhere at any hour of the day or night – anywhere, that is, except during a bombardment, for I tried it and failed miserably.[31]

In July 1941 Wavell was replaced by Auchinleck, whose newly con-stituted Eighth Army once again pushed back the Axis forces. However, the first half of 1942 was grim for the British, with Rommel forcing them into a retreat. Gazala and Tobruk were lost, and by July Axis forces were 70 miles (110 kilometres) from the vital naval base at Alexandria. An anxious Churchill gave command of the Eighth Army to Montgomery, and in November 1942 Rommel, who was facing a war on two fronts following the Allied invasion of Morocco (Operation Torch), suffered a heavy defeat at El Alamein from which his army never recovered.

above: Alan Moorehead and Alexander Clifford photographed by Lieutenant Knight as they break camp in the vast expanse of the Western Desert in June 1942.

... driving through a thickening sandstorm, we groped about in the collection of galvanised huts for a place to sit down and write. We found the Intelligence hut at last, and a corner of the table there, and wrote. That night we slept in another iron shed, dignified with the name of Force Headquarters Mess. Other strays like ourselves had wandered in, and we bedded down around the concrete floor as soon as dinner was done. The wind ripped part of the roof off during the night, sheet by sheet, and rain splashed in. The banging of iron against iron was like an air raid, only more irritating. Bomba was a desolate place. We were glad to get back to the front.[32]

Ernie Pyle came to love the desert. In a dispatch of 8 April 1943 he wrote: 'The outstanding thing about life at the front is its magnificent simplicity. It is a life consisting only of the essentials – food, sleep, transportation, and what little warmth and safety you can manage to wangle out of it by personal ingenuity....'

THE NOMADS OF FLEET STREET

Although nominally based in Cairo, the 'warcos' were nomadic. Dimbleby tried to please the parsimonious BBC by taking a discounted room on the hot side of the city's Continental Hotel, the residence of choice for the press. However, he and his driver made sure of their comfort when they went into the desert: the BBC recording truck, nicknamed 'Belinda', was loaded with everything from fruit and beer to pressure cooker and camp-beds. In March 1941, while reporting on the final stages of the Battle of Keren in Eritrea (during which he was nearly shot on Cameron Ridge), he and his driver camped under a tree, fitting their latrine in the sand with a proper toilet seat and rigging up a canvas bath. They slept on air-beds, beneath mosquito netting, and looked up at the stars.

Moorehead and Clifford initially stayed in Cairo's fly-ridden Carlton Hotel, but when Moorehead's pregnant wife came out to join him in the autumn of 1940 the trio rented a flat on Gezira island in the Nile, the two reporters often making round trips of 1,000 miles (1,600 kilometres) to report the action. Hill recalled hours spent playing bridge with Alaric Jacob, Richard Mowrer and their 'conducting officer', the Marquess of Ely, by the light of a hurricane lamp under canvas in the press camp at Eighth Army HQ. But correspondents who were following a military campaign in the field had to make the best of things. Moorehead recalled:

REPORT RATHER THAN INTERPRET

Correspondents continued to complain about censorship for being over-zealous or for concealing unpalatable truths from the public, but the senior commanders were largely well disposed towards correspondents, seeing them as a valuable adjunct to the war effort and useful, if unwitting, pawns in their battles with the War Cabinet over the conduct of the campaign.

Once material had been censored, it was fit for use without further vetting at home. This caused serious problems for Dimbleby when his recordings, which were informed by official briefings and tended to be upbeat, proved completely at odds with the view of Churchill and the War Cabinet. 'Beg frankness stop infinite damage done minimising enemy advantages' cabled A.P. Ryan, the government's man at the BBC. A subsequent cable instructed Dimbleby to refrain from interpreting the campaign and concentrate on first-hand reporting.

Ryan's attempt to recall Dimbleby, early in 1941, was thwarted by Wavell; Auchinleck also supported the beleaguered correspondent, who could not understand why his reports, highly regarded by the commanders around him, incurred only unexplained criticism by the BBC. Nobody at Broadcasting House had ever defined his role, and the drive and determination that had allowed him to bring the front line into living rooms far from the action sometimes

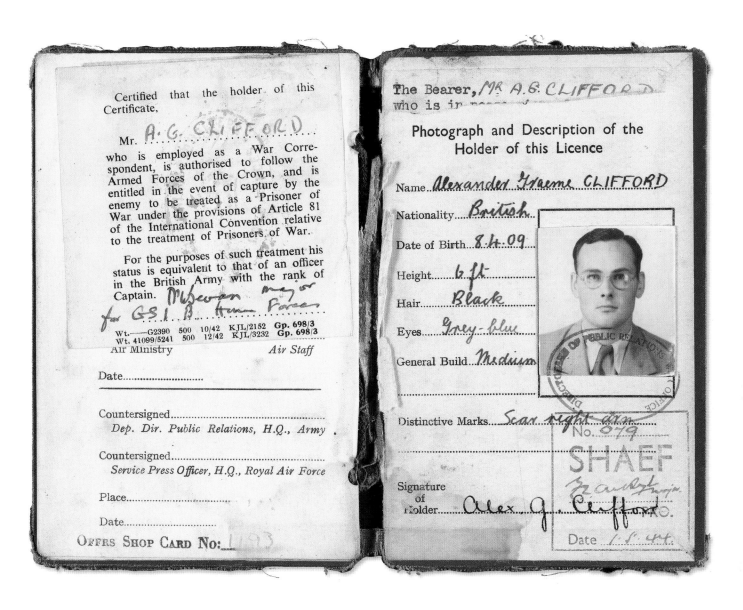

strayed into arrogance. (In 1942 Dimbleby was recalled to London, and the BBC was represented in North Africa by Irish writer Denis Johnston, Godfrey Talbot and Frank Gillard, a former teacher who had been heavily involved in schools broadcasting prior to the war.)

DANGER IN THE DESERT

Correspondents worked in a perilous environment. Loaded with plundered Italian cheese, wine, chocolate and typewriters, Moorehead, Clifford and Rex Keating – a journalist and specialist on Egypt – were returning from the battle of Beda Fomm, fought south of Benghazi in February 1941, when they came under fire from a concealed Italian battery. One vehicle was blown up and their own driver was hit in the arm. Moorehead and Clifford dragged the young man out of the car and into a ditch while Keating, under fire, ran for a first-aid dressing. The four men had to wait in the scrub

opposite: General Auchinleck welcoming the accredited warcos to GHQ on 8 July 1941 just a few days after becoming Commander-in-Chief Middle East. He told the assembled warcos he looked forward to seeing a great deal of them.

above: Alexander Clifford's press pass.

overleaf: Having dug a slit trench, a warco would eat, sleep and work in it.

until dusk when they hailed a passing Australian unit and hitched a lift to a dressing station.

In November of the same year, Russell, Mowrer, Jimmy Holburn of *Time* and a 'conducting officer' by the name of Crooke spent three days in a lumbering petrol and water tanker, vainly trying to find the forces engaged in lifting the siege of Tobruk and pausing only to sleep and to write dispatches. Returning to brigade headquarters on 22 November, they spotted some approaching cruiser tanks, which they assumed were British:

Dick Mowrer said: 'I hope they're not Germans.' I said: 'You never know. If the Germans are desperate, they might do anything.' Famous last words. Two minutes later all was confusion as shells and bullets screamed past us in every direction. Red tracer bullets literally gave colour to the scene. They would hit the ground and then shoot upwards to the sky, it may have been an illusion, but they seemed to curve as well as bounce off at angles ... within a few

seconds we found ourselves driving madly into the centre of a packed group of other trucks also driving madly.[33]

When Clare Hollingworth reached Cairo she became attached to a unit of the Long Range Desert Group (LRDG), accompanying it on expeditions to collect discarded enemy equipment. Being a woman gave her no privileges: she roughed it like the commandos and found sleeping in the sand a very comfortable experience, until the night she was woken up by the sound of German voices:

I didn't move.... We were all sleeping about thirty yards away from one another in case of bombing, and at breakfast the next morning – of bully beef and biscuits – I said to them: 'Did any of you hear German voices during the night?' and Ralph Neville, the colonel, said: 'Oh, Clare, you're making it up to make a good story when you get back...' And several of his staff said: 'No, sir, I heard German voices; in fact, I think, if you go over and look in the dune beyond this one, you'll find where they camped for a brief spell.' I said: 'Well, I sweated, and the sand was sticking to my body', and one or two of the soldiers said: 'Yes, that's how I felt, too.'[34]

Denis Johnston arrived in Egypt in June for the BBC, as the British retreated from Gazala, and as he drove in search of the forward press camp, designated by a logo resembling a 'flying arsehole', he was caught in the chaos. 'How can one describe the retreat of a modern Army? The roaring, rattling caterpillar of battered trucks and dirty men – the great transporters shouldering broken-down tanks, the RAF recovery lorries towing wrecked aircraft, the field kitchens and the ambulances, the mobile junk shops and the mass of indeterminate machinery churning the dust and spewing out petrol fumes, tangled in traffic blocks and then grinding onwards once again. The garrison of Knightsbridge[35] has assumed a mobile role.'[36]

In the Alamein box, the Marquess of Ely introduced Johnston to General Dan Pienaar, a blunt South African who was unimpressed with war correspondents in general and the BBC in particular, and who sarcastically cited a broadcast in which it had been claimed that his troops had had air cover at Gazala. Pienaar did not dispute that the sky was full of planes – 'unfortunately,' he told Johnston, 'they were not ours'. He then favoured the BBC man with his frank opinion of both the situation and Churchill's speech in Washington, DC. It was the correspondent's first interview with a commander, and he doubted he would be allowed to file a report that ran: 'Our reporter, speaking from the Alamein box, quotes General Pienaar as stating that the line cannot possibly be held and that the Prime Minister in Washington is talking balls.'[37]

Ronnie Noble filmed in North Africa, before his luck temporarily ran out at the fall of Tobruk in June 1942. Having ignored Dimbleby's advice to avoid the area, he was captured by the Italians and spent a year as a POW before the armistice with Italy allowed him to make his way back to England. He then chose to go out to film the war in the Far East. Noble's friend and rival Freddie Bayliss was killed on 8 July 1943 when the plane in which he was travelling crashed in the desert. Another to be captured was the BBC's Edward Ward; he was taken prisoner near Tobruk in November 1941 and spent the rest of the war as a POW.

IN THE FRONT LINE – DIEPPE AND TORCH

In the second half of 1942 selected correspondents were given the opportunity to participate in two amphibious landings, one of them was a disaster and the other was more successful.

The Dieppe Raid was abandoned in June after the Germans spotted the gathering fleet in the harbour, and later it was rescheduled for 19 August. 'Warcos' including Frank Gillard (BBC), Quentin Reynolds (*Collier's*) and Alexander Berry Austin (*Daily Herald*) duly presented themselves with battle dress, tin helmet, gas mask and the minimum of baggage. The object of the raid, the first amphibious landing on the European mainland, was to occupy territory, destroy defences and then withdraw after two tides. However, air cover proved to be inadequate, the fleet was discovered by a passing German convoy and resistance was heavy.

Gillard was assigned to Lord Lovat's tough No. 4 Commando, the one unit to achieve its specific objective. He was on the beach, where:

> … *the 3-inch mortar was being set up to cover our withdrawal, and to cover the slow, difficult passage of the wounded men and the stretcher-bearers down the gully and the precipitous stairs. The mortar officer, whose men were all busy hauling ammunition, grabbed me. 'Hey, would you mind?' he said, and showed me how to prepare the shells for firing. 'Why will no one bring me any smoke?' he grumbled, meaning the smoke bombs with which he could set up a smoke screen to cover us. As we*

> *worked, an enemy mortar and a machine gun began to feel for our range. Mortar shells trundled overhead, exploding among the rocks. A Spitfire flew over, and a German flak post that had been silent for some time opened fire on it. 'Can't you fix that bastard?' said the Intelligence officer to the mortar officer. We heaved the mortar round, and tried to estimate the range. As I unscrewed the tops and passed the bombs, the mortar officer popped them in, stunning my ears with such close explosions. 'I should—er—keep your head down,' he said as, in my amateur's eagerness, I dodged a little too near the mortar muzzle.*[38]

Gillard had been one of half a dozen correspondents assigned to tank landing craft, while Reynolds boarded the command ship. From the deck of HMS *Calpe*, Reynolds saw a bomb hit, just 40 feet (12 metres) away, and the concussion:

> … *threw me several feet against a steel bulkhead, and left me numb, my ears roaring. I wondered if I had been hit. Then I bit on something hard and spat out a gold filling. That seemed to be the extent of my injuries. I got to my feet with some effort, only to find that both our anti-aircraft gunners were dead…. The walking wounded were helped below to receive attention. Among them was a correspondent I knew, Wallace Reyburn of the* Montreal Standard. *He, too, had the face of a man in shock. 'I'm hit somewhere,' he mumbled as I helped him out of his bloodstained uniform. I surveyed his minor damage. 'Wally, unless you're a contortionist, you'll never be able to admire your scars,' I said, and began plucking bits of shrapnel from his buttocks. But Reyburn was not listening. 'What a story! What a story!' he suddenly burst out.*[39]

The correspondents were ordered to put a positive spin on the debacle, so Gillard reported on the air cover, only later discovering it had been a disaster.

The Dieppe Raid assisted planning for future amphibious landings, not least that which took place just a few months later, in early November: Operation Torch, the invasion of North Africa along the coast of Morocco and Tunisia. This was the first big Allied combined operation, designed to bring the Vichy French into the Allied camp, open a second front and prepare for an invasion of southern Europe.

ERNIE PYLE, 1900–1945

above: Ernie Pyle shares cigarettes with US Marines on Okinawa.

On 18 June 1945, exactly two months after Pyle's death, *The Story of G.I. Joe* received its premiere, subsequently gathering four 'Oscar' nominations. The film follows a semi-fictitious US infantry unit from Tunisia to the battle for Monte Cassino – as seen through the eyes of Ernie Pyle, played by Burgess Meredith.

Pyle was the son of a dominant mother and a weak-willed but hardworking farmer, and grew up with a streak of melancholy and a fear of proving ineffectual. Uninterested in farming and too young to serve in the First World War, he went to Indiana University where he threw himself into student journalism. An Associated Press report on the interment of a US soldier at Arlington National Cemetery gave him a vision of his ideal career, and, while working for Scripps Howard newspapers, he established himself as an authoritative aviation correspondent for the *Washington Daily News*. Six years as a roving reporter followed, and for one remarkable report he stood on a London balcony watching the bombs falling around St Paul's Cathedral.

His undisguised empathy with, and championing of, the young American GIs with whom he became embedded from 1942 won him the deep affection of both the soldiers and his audience at home. He wrote about them in an easy, conversational style as they fought their way from Tunisia to Monte Cassino and followed them after D-Day, before going to the Pacific. The throat-tightening patriotism of his reports may now seem sentimental, but he tempered it by confronting death, not in graphic terms, but through its effects on the casualty's comrades.

His long absences contributed to serious difficulties in his marriage; his wife, Jerry, had been a bright, unconventional woman when they married in 1925, but later she became increasingly unstable and died shortly after her husband.

Torch was, briefly, Walter Cronkite's baptism as a war reporter. He was on the USS *Texas* when her guns opened up on Port Loyauty, and he observed the detail of the firing, how: 'The great belch of yellow flame threatens to engulf the ship herself, and the blast of heat sears the freshman war correspondent on the bridge. The gun blows its own great smoke ring and the shell can actually be seen disappearing towards the horizon through the middle of the doughnut. Whatever has been loose on deck is sent skyward, sucked into the vacuum the explosion has left behind.'

After a brief run ashore, Cronkite returned to the ship, believing it was heading for Casablanca, but to his chagrin it headed home towards Norfolk, Virginia. Forced to make the best of a bad job, he had himself catapulted off in a small reconnaissance plane, a couple of days before the *Texas* was due to dock, thus managing to file the first uncensored story of the landings ahead of a 'warco' on USS *Massachusetts*.

Ernie Pyle followed the beaten trail to North Africa, arriving just after the main landing and staying well into 1943. A legend in the USA, the slight, gnome-faced, balding farmer's son – often referred to as a 'little guy' – always spoke for the ordinary soldier, and in a piece that echoed Page's 'fighting-it-out-on-this-line' dispatch (see page 16) he revealed his admiration of, and identification with, his subject:

The men are walking. They are fifty feet apart, for dispersal. Their walk is slow for they are dead weary, as you can tell even when looking at them from behind. Every line and sag of their bodies speaks their inhuman exhaustion. On their shoulders and backs they carry heavy steel tripods, machine-gun barrels, leaden boxes of ammunition. Their feet seem to sink into the ground from the overload they are bearing.

They don't slouch. It is the terrible deliberation of each step that spells out their appalling tiredness. Their faces are black and unshaven. They are young men, but the grime and whiskers and exhaustion make them look middle-aged. In their eyes as they pass is not hatred, not excitement, not despair, not the tonic of their victory – there is just the simple expression of being here as though they had been here doing this forever, and nothing else.[40]

Robert Capa flew to Algiers to report the war in Tunisia in the spring of 1943, and he quickly discovered an unhealthiness not

encountered in the Spanish Civil War, when within a few days he was badly bitten by bedbugs and had to be rescued from a minefield into which he had strayed to relieve himself. He joined up with Ernie Pyle, and while Pyle wrote the dispatches that created the public's warm image of the American GI, Capa photographed the dust and death – but it was nothing compared to what the two men would soon see in Italy.

ORDEAL IN ITALY

After the success of the North African campaign, the Allies turned their attention to the liberation of Europe, beginning with Italy. In July 1943 the Allies crossed the Mediterranean to take Sicily, which was to be their springboard to the mainland.

Because of his family roots in Messina, Frank Gervasi had been desperate to be among the journalists selected for the Sicily landings. Earlier in the year he had volunteered to join the new Office of Strategic Studies (OSS) as an agent but had been turned down on the grounds of his value as a war correspondent, and even when he was called up and classed as 1-A, his service was deferred for the same reason. In the event, he observed Messina – or what remained of it after 24 hours of bombing – from an altitude of several thousand feet in a B-24 Liberator on a mission to destroy the airstrip at Vibo Valentia, arriving on the island after the invasion and seeing the poverty and misery of the people.

Capa came to Sicily, after the landings and illegally. His accreditation had lapsed because *Collier's* had cabled him to return home, and to follow the army without it was a court-martial offence. Although *Life* had expressed an interest in him, no decision had been communicated to him. He learned that he had been hired only while he was photographing in the ruins of Troina.

The close relationship between the press and the military was demonstrated on the island when General George Patton assaulted a soldier in a field hospital after the man said he thought he was suffering from shell-shock. In fact, he had malaria. The 'warcos', both British and American, agreed not to file their dispatches. Demaree Bess put it succinctly: 'We're Americans first and correspondents second.' Mueller went further, asserting his intention to flatly deny the incident ever took place. By the time the story broke, three months later, Patton had made grovelling apologies, but the incident affected his career.

On 3 September, Montgomery led the Eighth Army across the Strait of Messina into the 'toe' of Italy. With him in his DUKW (the

picked off and you are the one chap who manages to escape, and you are not even a combatant. ...[41]

The Americans brought ashore a complete radio station mounted on a DUKW, which, despite drawing heavy German fire, made a run for the beach and found cover, allowing the first reports to be broadcast that same night. Frank Gillard was initially less well served by his lines of communication. As well as his typewriter he had brought with him a portable wire recorder.[42] Once recorded, the spools were sent to Malta for transmission to London – but none arrived, and his frustration was compounded when General Clark complained that the BBC was damaging morale by quoting German assertions that they were about to retake the beaches. However, when Gillard explained his problems, Clark provided him with a radio set and also authorized him to transmit 250 words a day on the general's direct line to the War Office.

The mobility of correspondents in unfamiliar, even enemy-held, territory was surprising. Having decided that the Eighth Army would not see much action in Reggio Calabria, Clifford and Moorehead set off alone in a truck, heading for Salerno in defiance of British Army orders. That they reached Salerno unhurt was probably thanks to the obliging *Carabinieri* and two British military trucks with which they joined up.

The campaign to push the Germans out of Italy was ferocious – fought along muddy valleys, on pitiless mountains and in viciously cold weather. It was costly, too, in terms of lives and injuries among correspondents and troops. British forces liberated Scafati, near Naples, on 28 September 1941, and the town appeared safe when Stewart Sale (*Reuters*), Alexander Berry Austin (*Daily Herald*), Basil Gingell (British Exchange Telegraph Agency) and William J. Munday (*News Chronicle*) entered it. They had left their jeep and were standing together on a street corner when the gun of a German half-track[43] opened fire, wounding Gingell and killing his companions outright.

amphibious truck, colloquially known as a 'duck') travelled Moorehead, Clifford and Gervasi.

A second mainland landing took place at Taranto, tucked into the inside of the 'heel' of Italy, and on 9/10 September the main invasion fleet unloaded General Mark Wayne Clark's US Fifth Army – plus British units – on the beaches of the Bay of Salerno near Naples. The armistice had come into force on 8 September, by which time the Germans, in no way fooled into pouring their troops into Reggio Calabria, were busy reinforcing the area around Salerno. Frank Gillard decided it was:

> *... the toughest assault landing of the war as far as I was concerned – more frightening in many ways than Dieppe, even. I count myself extremely lucky to be still alive because I never came closer to death than in the landing at Salerno. The actual landing itself [was] under the most intense fire on the beaches. I mean when everybody around you is*

The death of Sale provided an unexpected opening for a young Reuters correspondent from Scotland. Doon Campbell had sold himself to the agency as someone exempt from call-up, without domestic ties and willing to go anywhere, while glossing over the fact that he had been born with one forearm missing. On being told he would take Sale's place, Campbell proceeded to have all his teeth extracted in favour of dentures, used his clothing allowance to equip himself with uniform, sleeping bag and greatcoat, and flew to Foggia to join the Eighth Army via a pleasant, ration-free

Print the complete address in plain block letters in the panel below, and your return address in the space provided. Use typewriter, dark ink, or pencil. Write plainly. Very small writing is not suitable.

No. _____

To
Mrs Alex Clifford
SCAMPS HILL
LINDFIELD
Sussex
ENGLAND

From
A. G. CLIFFORD
(Sender's name)
WAR CORRESPONDENT
(Sender's address)
XXXXXXX ALLIED
PRESS
A. F. H. Q.
(Date)

(CENSOR'S STAMP)

JULY 31 1943

Dear Mama,

Heavens knows whether this sort of letter can even theoretically reach you . I dont know whether it it xxxxxxxx valid for England atall. But ever since we landed in Sicily I have been with the Americans . At first it was not technically possible to write atall and now I have only got these american lettercards . I have had no contact with the british atall.

I presume you know that I am in Sicily because I hope by now that at least some of my stories have got through and have been printed under my name with a Sicily dateline . We have had the worst communications trouble I have ever known and in my opinion the American public relations have been astonishingly inefficient about it . We used to have everything far better arranged in the western desert . I understand that all my stories about the first assault landing were lost and so it must have been days before the paper got anything from me atall. It is very disheartening because it is impossible to explain and I am sure the paper thinks I am just not trying. I have sofar heard nothing from them atall.

It has been a good and exciting campaign sofar , not very dangerous except for the landing and the first few days but touristically wonderful . Through being with the Americans I have managed to see most of the island, because they have captured the greater part of it. I know nearly every village and it is practically all the most wonderful landscape . The western end andnthe northern coast are marvellous and so are the mountains inland .

Thxx I am the only British correspondent with the Americans : I dont know what the paper thinks about it , but it was my only chance to get to Sicily right at the beginning because I had used up my turn by going to Pantelleria . I have really enjoyed it very much . I havent bothered so much about the actual fighting because I imagine people in England are less interested in the American details. But I have been able to concentrate on the background and the people and the political angle etcetera all of which interests me infinitely more .

It was rough living at first because we could only bring essentials ashore. But now we have got the hang of the country . I have been typing this by the roadside and have just exchanged my tin of luncheon rations frxx for some tomatoes onions green peppers peaches and bananas which a little boy brought along in a basket. We are living in an inland valley in a forest of oaks and cypresses which is pure theocritus xxxx . For some curious reason it hasnt been intensely hot and it would all be a wonderful summer holiday if it werent for the war .I think I am getting a little war weary . My trip home wasnt really much of a rest and I have been at it continuously ever since. It is very tiring.

Thank you very much for your airgraph and for a letter which got over here .

Love from
Dick

V···MAIL

U. S. GOVERNMENT PRINTING OFFICE : 1942 ☆ 16—28143-4

stopover in Algiers. Gervasi, meanwhile, had requested accreditation to Clark's army and was on his way to Naples.

The Allied armies pushed northwards, hampered by the rivers that flowed east-west, the bitter winter and the strong defensive lines that had been established by the Germans from the Tyrrhenian to the Adriatic. Vasto, on the Adriatic coast, had been taken in November and the press, including Johnston, Moorehead, Clifford and Campbell, were accommodated, four per room, in a building on Pinna Point that was soon christened 'Dysentery Hall'. The tea tasted of petrol, few of the windows had any glass and there were no toilets. 'In summer,' conceded Denis Johnston 'it might be quite a pleasant little resort; in winter it is open to the winds and to every blizzard that sweeps across the sea from the steppes of Central Europe. The sanitary arrangements were nonexistent and the best people generally used the deserted railway line as a lavatory. Each morning we all moved slightly farther along, until – came the time – we turned a corner, and found ourselves arriving in a station. After this, the camp authorities decided to put up a canvas contraption on a slope overlooking the rocks, from which one might observe derelict mines dashing themselves on to the beach below.'[44]

The British 'warcos' in Naples were in greater luxury at the Villa Ruffo, but the city itself, which had been entered on 1 October, was in chaos: the utilities and infrastructure had been deliberately destroyed by the retreating Germans, the harbour was full of sunken ships and homes were uninhabitable. Into the ruins came Robert Capa, who had attached himself, with *Life's* correspondent Will Lang, to the US Rangers and survived heavy shelling in the process. His indisputable courage in putting himself in harm's way and his willingness to intrude into deep grief was matched by the compassion that continued to permeate his images of death – nowhere more so than when he happened upon a queue of people outside a school and saw children's coffins with feet protruding. He was told:

These children of Naples had stolen rifles and bullets and had fought the Germans for fourteen days, while we had been pinned to the Chiunzi Pass. These children's feet were my real welcome to Europe, I who had been born there. More real by far than the welcome of the hysterically cheering crowds I had met along the road … I took off my hat and got out my camera. I pointed the lens at the faces of the prostrated women, taking little pictures of their dead babies, until finally the coffins were carried away.

Those were my truest pictures of victory, the ones I took at that simple schoolhouse funeral.[45]

On 7 October, along with Lang and fellow photographer Charles Corte of Acme News, he was close to a post office when it was ripped apart by the massive explosion of one of many German time-bombs planted in the buildings. More than 100 people died. Capa and Corte took a whole series of uncompromising photographs that were published in *Life* on 1 November, along with Lang's equally stark dispatch.

Doon Campbell had not been at Vasto for long when, on 28 December, he and his 'conducting officer' drove up the coast, across the Sangro River to Ortona, and nearly met the same fate as his predecessor, Sale. The town, which marked the eastern end of Germany's Gustav Line, had fallen that day to the Canadians after a week of some of the most savage fighting in the campaign. Leaving the jeep, they went on foot.

Suddenly an explosion nearly blew us off our feet. The few soldiers and civilians disappeared. Then four more explosions, too close for comfort.

'Better go inside,' said Ken, standing close and cool. We dived under a crumbling archway in what had once been a bank, and crouched behind a counter.

'How long does this last?'

'All depends whether it's harassing fire or a barrage,' said Ken. Then we heard a missile coming. Had this one got our name on it? The explosion threw us back.[46]

They made a run for the jeep but while driving away Campbell suffered the shock of realizing he was afraid. It took him a week to get over the fear that he would not cope in a similar future situation.

Back in late November, Richard Tregaskis had been on Mount Corno, near Venafro towards the western end of the Gustav Line and not far from Monte Cassino. A shell had exploded nearby, seriously injuring him. A field medic bandaged his head and administered morphine, but Tregaskis had to drag himself down the slope until he was recognized by an officer, and eventually he found himself in a field hospital, temporarily paralyzed on one side as a result of a brain injury. Capa had a narrow escape, also near

Venafro, when the man next to him was killed and shrapnel hit, but failed to pierce, his own uniform.

Monte Cassino itself, with its huge mountain-top abbey, was defended by some of Germany's finest troops. In the course of four months, from 17 January 1944 onwards, the Allies mounted four major assaults, and in February Martha Gellhorn joined the French forces in the area. During her wartime travels she had heard much criticism of the French, so she used one of her *Collier's* dispatches to dispel the myth that they were not good troops:

> *The French are earning their way home and they do not complain. They know exactly what they are doing and they are doing it superbly…. The mountains of Italy are horrible; to attack always against heights held by well-entrenched and well-trained enemy troops is surely the worst sort of war. Nothing can help the infantry much in the mountains: Germans dug into the stone sides of these cliffs can survive the heaviest shelling. Tanks cannot operate. So at last it is the courage and determination of a Frenchman against the courage and determination of a German. The French have been taking their objectives.*[47]

She was at Cassino on 15 February, in company with Doon Campbell who had relocated from Vasto, when the Allies called in air power to bomb the abbey in the mistaken belief that the Germans were occupying it. 'Pure theatre' Campbell called it, and when the dust obscured the action he drove to the cable head at Caserta, and rattled off 1,000 words for Reuters. As the rest of the correspondents started to arrive the radio link was lost due to a technicality, leaving Campbell's as the only dispatch to get through.

He followed it with a scoop on the contemporaneous eruption of Vesuvius, flying just 100 feet (30 metres) above the lava in a light plane put at his disposal by General Clark, and then comparing the manmade spectacle that was Cassino with the raw force of nature. The volcano won, and the piece was published under the headline 'Vesuvius More Impressive Than Battle'.

To ease the pressure on the troops at Monte Cassino, a landing was organized at Anzio. The landing was straightforward, but then the Allies became trapped on the beachhead, under a German bombardment. Pyle was one of the correspondents who went to Anzio, despite the feeling that: '… there are times when the perpetual misery and death of war, and what seems the

above: A photograph of United Press's formidable Eleanor Packard, taken in 1936 as she boarded a plane to cover the Italian invasion of Ethiopia.

previous pages left: BBC correspondent Frank Gillard using a Midget disk recorder in 1944.

previous page right: Letter sent home by Alexander Clifford describing the situation on Sicily following the Allied invasion.

above: Artillery being loaded
aboard Landing Craft Tanks
(LCTs) in preparation for D-Day.

inevitable doom of all things, has me on the ropes. I get to losing my perspective and sometimes feel it sinful if I should survive the war myself.'[48]

On 17 March a stick of 500-pound (227-kilogram) bombs landed close to the villa near Naples that was occupied by the 'warcos'. Miraculously nobody was killed or badly hurt, not even Pyle whose room was on an upper floor that took the brunt of the blast. Capa missed the event: he had received orders to proceed to Naples and London. Monte Cassino was taken on 18 May at a total cost of over 100,000 Allied casualties, representing perhaps 20 nationalities. German losses are uncertain, but above 20,000. The Allies continued on to Rome, but interest in Italy was waning. Many 'warcos' had headed for London in expectation of the Normandy landings. Moorehead and Clifford had declined the offer of a place in the Anzio landings because they were comfortable in their villa and aware that they would be recalled for the Normandy invasion whenever it happened. But everyone who remained with the Allied campaign in Italy was determined to be first into Rome.

Denis Johnston had met up with Daniel de Luce of AP, who, while not welcoming a rival journalist, was less worried about the BBC than he was by the thought of Eleanor Packard of United Press, whose whereabouts were unknown. Johnston and de Luce were eating abandoned German chocolate when: '... a very sinister thing happened. Another jeep came threading its way down the road, passed through the parked Armour, and slipped quietly off in the direction of Rome. And round the group went the fatal words, "That was Packard!"' Uninterested in press rivalry, the army units remained stationary. '...There you are! Just as Dan had feared. This was the result of standing around wasting time when we ought to have been moving on. Packard was going to take Rome single handed. And as he spoke, Dan got into his jeep and started to move off, followed by a representative of the *Stars and Stripes*.'[49]

Johnston and his sound engineer looked at one another, and for the honour of the European media they drove for Rome ahead of the army. At a papal press conference, Eleanor Packard apologized to the Pope for wearing trousers.

Also into Rome on 5 June 1944 came the second BBC man, Godfrey Talbot, who made his recording on the balcony of the Palazzo Venezia, from where Mussolini used to address the crowds. He was afterwards taken by surprise by the number of Italians who greeted him by name, having recognized his voice while listening, illegally, to BBC broadcasts throughout the war. The age of the celebrity broadcaster, begun by Richard Dimbleby and Murrow, was here to stay.

D-DAY

If the organization of the press had left much to be desired at the start of the war, by the time of the D-Day landings every effort was made to accommodate war correspondents, assigning them to army, air force and naval/merchant units. Not all were fortu-nate: Martha Gellhorn was not accredited, but she found an unofficial way to see the action; *Collier's* passed over Frank Gervasi in favour of signing Gellhorn's husband, Ernest Heming-way, in the mistaken belief his byline would improve circulation; and Walter Cronkite was supposed to be writing the lead story from the safety of London, but at the last moment he received a visit from a major in the US Army Air Force (USAAF) who went to great lengths to ensure there was nobody else in the room. Then he informed Cronkite that he had 'drawn the straw to represent

the Allied press on a very important mission. It will be dangerous. No guarantee you'll get back. But if you do, you'll have a great story. You can turn it down now, or you can come with me. And security is on – you can't tell your office.'[50]

The BBC had taken a major step forward in 1943 with the estab-lishment of its War Reporting Unit, ready for whenever the Allies returned to Europe. The corporation had covered the desert war with first just one and then two war correspondents; for D-Day the BBC intended to field more than two dozen, only two of whom were experienced. Gillard and Dimbleby had to train the new recruits – men such as Howard Marshall, who was famous as the first to provide ball-by-ball cricket commentary. After the training, it was Gillard's view that the men sent into Normandy knew far more about how to interact and operate with an army than most of the 'conducting officers'.

Secret briefings and general instructions prepared the chosen, who had no idea of dates or destinations. They could take 125 pounds (57 kilograms) of gear beyond what they could carry; they must make sure their gas masks were always accessible; the Judge Advocate General would, if required, help them make their wills; and their identification (ID) tags should include their blood group. Ernie Pyle felt his nervousness translate into physical symp-toms. A few correspondents dropped out. Capa and Hemingway partied on black-market alcohol, and Hemingway was later taken to hospital after a friend crashed while driving him home.

Doon Campbell had been recalled from Italy and informed he was being given the most important assignment that Reuters could give a correspondent: he would go with the British, but not until the bridgehead was established. There would be no 'commando stuff'. It was to be two years before he saw home again.

On 28 May correspondents received messages to report with their baggage, and Colonel Philip Astley called out the assignments. Capa would go with the 116th US Infantry to Omaha Beach; Moore-head, on an LST,[51] for Juno; Bob Reuben (Reuters), 101st American Airborne; Guy Byam and Chester Wilmot (both BBC), Leonard Mosley (Allied Newspapers) and David Woodward (*Manchester Guardian*), 6th Airborne Brigade; and Ernie Pyle had himself rede-ployed to the LST of Colonel Samuel Myers. Doon Campbell was in for a shock: 'Until this moment we had no idea who we would be with or when we would be going. He called: *Campbell, Doon – Marine Commandos, D-Day*. That's all I had. I had no training for commando work. I'd seen a film "Commando Strike At Dawn"....'[52] 'Warcos' went off to their units to be introduced and trained, which

We hit the beach; the ramps went down; the commandos, many of them with collapsible bicycles, and their faces black for camouflage, went down the ramp. I fell off the ramp, which was becoming very greasy, up to my chest in the channel, and with this pack on my back would never have made it but for a lunge forward accelerated by a push from a huge commando behind me ... I staggered up the beach, dripping wet, across a mined road into a field, the commandos racing on ahead, passing me. A lot of mortar fire, small arms fire, and I stumbled into a ditch some 200 yards from the beach.[53]

They had landed at 09:06, and Campbell was the first, the youngest and the only one-armed correspondent on a D-Day beach. Greene made it up the beach but three of Lovat's men were killed close to him. In his ditch, Campbell obeyed his instinct to unpack his typewriter and begin his first dispatch. A mortar shell hit close to the ditch, spraying the machine. Using his notebook he scribbled a report and squirmed down to the beach to give it to an officer from one of the ships to take back. It did not make it. Many reporters experienced similar problems. Having made it onto Juno Beach, another Reuters man, Charles Lynch, released a carrier pigeon carrying a message typed on lightweight paper. The bird flew straight for Berlin. Montague Taylor, also Reuters, was rather luckier with his bird: against stiff headwinds, Gustav reached Portsmouth in just over five hours with the first report: 'We are just 20 miles or so off the beaches. First assault troops landed 0750. Signal says no interference from enemy gunfire on beach.... Steaming steadily in formation. Lightnings, Typhoons, Fortresses crossing since 0545. No enemy aircraft seen.'

for Campbell meant Southampton and Lord Lovat's commandos. With him went his AP rival Roger Greene 'and he had a black patch on one eye. Right pair!'

On the evening of 5 June envelopes were opened: Operation Overlord was on, and the amphibious units boarded their various landing craft. Pyle realized he was committed: 'From a vague, anticipatory dread, the invasion now turned into a horrible reality for me.' Campbell went up on deck to sleep, debating whether or not to remove his false arm. His pack was so heavy it was hard to stand upright and he wondered what would happen if they were torpedoed. Capa went aboard the USS *Samuel Chase*, a mother ship carrying assault barges, resolved to go ashore with Company E, whom he had known in Sicily.

Dawn opened with the roar of the guns. Capa recalled a preinvasion breakfast of hot cakes, sausages and eggs that few could face. At 08:00 Campell had the first sight of France, and the captain of the landing craft went full ahead, zig-zagging until:

Among those early aircraft was B-17 Flying Fortress *Shoo Shoo Baby*, piloted by Captain R.W. Sheets and with Walter Cronkite on board. Looking down on Omaha Beach, Cronkite marvelled at the armada below him. Then the clouds closed in and it was impossible to spot the target, a bridge near Caen; the bomb bays of the squadron were open but without visibility it was forbidden to drop bombs. The aircraft returned, landing in fog with their bombs still armed – a landing Cronkite described as 'hairy'.

The reporters and photographers representing the *Times* found tremendous difficulty in getting their dispatches and reels of film back to England. The radio links were unreliable and the cross-Channel 'courier' services did not function as planned.

Campbell crawled back to his ditch. Later, he and his captain thumbed a lift and took refuge in a drainage ditch at Ouistreham, from where they could see the gliders, bombers and transport planes coming in. The following morning, sitting in a garden he wrote a memorable dispatch:

Snipers, bullets, whining shells, diving planes, and the thunder of a great naval bombardment which shoots the typewriter off my knee every few seconds, are the rather disturbing conditions under which I am writing.

I am several miles inland and a mile behind the frontline trenches. Between 9 and 10 last night the sky filled with hundreds of allied planes cheered by the men on the ground....

opposite: Reuters correspondent Doon Campbell, taken in Normandy after the D-Day landings.

above: US soldiers wading ashore from their Coast Guard landing barge under withering German fire on D-Day.

right: In December 1938 *Picture Post* hailed Capa as the greatest war photographer in the world.

opposite: One of Capa's 11 damaged, poignant images of the US assault on Omaha Beach on D-Day.

PICTURE POST

Vol. I. No. 10.   December 3, 1938

The Greatest War-Photographer in the World: Robert Capa
In the following pages you see a series of pictures of the Spanish War. Regular readers of "Picture Post" know that we do not lightly praise the work we publish. We present these pictures as simply the finest pictures of front-line action ever taken. They are the work of Robert Capa. Capa is a Hungarian by birth; but, being small and dark, he is often taken for a Spaniard. He likes working in Spain better than anywhere in the world. He is a passionate democrat, and he lives to take photographs. Over a year ago, Capa's wife, on her way back to join her husband in Paris, was killed in Spain. She was standing on the running-board of a car when it collided with a tank. Capa went to China and took pictures of the Chinese war, some of which we have already published. To-day, Capa is back in Spain, taking pictures fo. "Picture Post."

PICTURE POST   13

ROBERT CAPA, 1913–1954

Robert Capa was born Endre Friedmann in Budapest, the son of a Jewish tailor. With anti-Semitism increasing, he left for Berlin, aged 18, and worked in the Dephot agency's darkroom as well as taking his own photographs. When Berlin became an unhealthy city for a Jew he settled in Paris, where in 1934 he met another young Jewish refugee, Gerda Taro, who became his lover. He changed his name to the more Ameri-can-sounding Robert Capa, and Gerda marketed his work. His maxim was: if your photos aren't

good enough, you're not close enough.

Both left-wing sympathizers, they covered the Spanish Civil War together, primarily for pro-Republican French magazines, and Capa made his international name with *The Falling Soldier* (see page 75). In July 1937, while Capa was back in France, Gerda was killed near Brunete, outside Madrid, not by enemy fire, but in an unlucky traffic accident. After that, at the age of only 23, Capa became a more detached man, who lived life to the full but protected himself by never allowing anyone close to him.

Capa temporarily abandoned Spain during 1938 and went to China to help with the making of a documentary. It was an unhappy experience, and he returned to cover the tragic last weeks in Spain. During the Second World war he photographed the Blitz, the war in North Africa and the Italian campaign, before being selected to accompany the D-Day landings with the US 116th Infantry.

The transport ship sailed after dark on 5 June, and Capa spent the night gambling before transferring to a landing barge, his two Contax cameras wrapped in protective oilskin for the final miles to Omaha Beach. When the landing craft doors opened the men jumped out into waist-deep water under concentrated fire that killed hundreds.

Capa had just enough light to shoot on a fast shutter speed. He photographed the soldiers wading through the water and sheltering behind the heavy physical defences that the Germans had erected in the sea to hinder the expected invasion. Then, pinned down on the beach, panic set in, and he fled to the ships. On 7 June he landed

his films at Weymouth and returned to Normandy.

By the time his films reached *Life's* bureau there was less than 12 hours to process them, have them censored, and catch the US courier.

The rolls were developed and hung in the wooden drying cabinet, but in all the rush, someone closed the cabinet door, the heat built up and the delicate emulsion melted. Just 11 negatives out of 79 survived. They were less than sharp, but they showed the unvarnished truth of the first minutes of that landing. The most significant image is arguably that of the infantryman wading up to his neck, burdened by a 66-pound (30-kilogram) pack and his rifle. He has been variously identified, but is most likely Huston Riley.

Capa photographed the liberation of Paris, and in March 1945 he parachuted into Germany with the US 17th Airborne Division. Post-war he covered the USSR, the creation of Israel and finally, Vietnam where he was killed.

'C'est très joli,' said French civilians, who say of the Allied invasion: 'c'est très chic.'

It is a miracle that I am alive to write this story, that I have survived 24 hours on this bridgehead bag of wicked tricks. Bombs, shells, bullets and mines, to say nothing of booby-traps, makes each hour an age of grim experience....[54]

Capa's barge decanted its human cargo close to the Easy Red sector of Omaha Beach, and he ran off two reels while under fire before reaching the beach. Shrapnel from an exploding mortar shell cut down the men ahead of him; the next shell came closer. The hands holding his camera were shaking; his whole body started to tremble; he went into blind panic, wading through the water to an LCI (Landing Craft Infantry) that had just offloaded medical personnel. 'As I reached the deck I felt a shock, and suddenly was all covered with feathers. I thought, "What is this? Is somebody killing chickens?" Then I saw that the superstructure had been shot away and that the feathers were the stuffing from the kapok jackets of the men that had been blown up. The skipper was crying. His assistant had been blown up all over him and he was a mess.'[55]

The BBC's Robin Duff got his Midget going and recorded: 'The paratroops are landing. ... they're landing all around me as I speak.... They've come in from the sea and they're fluttering down ... and they're just about the best thing we've seen for a good many hours ... they're showering down; there's no other word for it.'[56]

The quartet who bravely went in with the Parachute Brigade, before the amphibious landing craft reached the beaches, distinguished themselves. The brigade's report 'Operations in Normandy June–September 1944' stated: 'The Brigade was lucky to have with it Guy Byam of the BBC, Leonard Mosely [sic] of Allied Newspapers who came in by parachute and Chester Wilmot of the BBC & David Woodward of the *Manchester Guardian* who travelled by glider.... All ranks on their part learned to respect the personal courage and devotion to duty of these war correspondents who shared in every way the dangers and discomforts of the soldier.'[57]

Guy Byam recorded his drop:

We're over the coast now and the run in has started – one minute, thirty seconds. Red light – green and out – get on, out, out, out fast into the cool night air, out, out, out over France – and we know that the dropping zone is obstructed. We're jumping into fields covered with poles! And I hit my parachute and lower my kitbag which is suspended on the end of a forty-foot rope from my harness. And then the ground comes up to hit me. And I find myself in the middle of a cornfield. I look around and even with a compass I can't be sure where I am – and overhead hundreds of parachutes and containers are coming down.

The whole sky is a fantastic chimera of lights and flak, and one plane gets hit and disintegrates wholesale in the sky, sprinkling a myriad of burning pieces all over the sky.[58]

Woodward was slightly injured, but not enough to prevent him writing his dispatches. Chester Wilmot landed in a field, 'with grinding brakes and creaking timbers', and bundled out of the glider with the other commandos.

The landing craft of Howard Marshall hit a mine on its way in; he had a second soaking on the way back that same day, lost his notes in the sea and recorded his impressions before he dried off. Richard Dimbleby, who had broadcast the departure of the airborne forces on the night before the landings and given a summary of the situation at noon, made a reconnaissance flight over France on the evening of 6 June.

If Campbell's breathless prose told his readers of the heavy opposition faced on the beaches, Ernie Pyle expressed the sad detail

in his quiet way. He had arrived on D-Day+1, and his dispatch, pooled like every report made in France during the landings, was the first to reach the American newspapers, describing how: 'Submerged tanks and overturned boats and burned trucks and shell-shattered jeeps and sad little personal belongings were strewn all over these bitter sands. That plus the bodies of soldiers lying in rows covered with blankets, the toes of their shoes sticking up in a line as though on drill....'[59]

Nobody bothered to object to the unaccredited Martha Gellhorn when she simply boarded a hospital ship that left for Easy Red the day after the invasion and lowered its water ambulances to recover the injured:

opposite: D-Day+4: a radio crew interviews a US soldier before he goes ashore from the landing craft.

above: Rudolph Dunbar of the Associated Negro Press interviews a group of men from a signal construction battalion in France a week after D-Day.

It will be hard to tell you of the wounded, there were so many of them. There was no time to talk; there was too much else to do. They had to be fed, as most of them had not eaten for two days; shoes and clothing had to be cut off; they wanted water; the nurses and orderlies, working like demons, had to be found and called quickly to a bunk where a man suddenly and desperately needed attention; plasma bottles must be watched; cigarettes had to be lighted and held for those who could not use their hands; it seemed to take hours to pour hot coffee, via the spout of a teapot, into a mouth that just showed through bandages.[60]

In addition to helping with the wounded on the ship, Gellhorn went out at night in one of the water ambulances, among the floating mines, to look for more wounded, while listening to the cockney chatter of the crew who manned it.

One D-Day 'warco' exchanged the keys of his clarinet for those of the typewriter. Rudolph Dunbar had been born in British Guiana in 1907 and trained at what became the prestigious Julliard School in New York. Soloist, composer and conductor, he had conducted the London Philharmonic at London's Royal Albert Hall in 1942, the first black person to do so, and he subsequently became a war correspondent for the Associated Negro Press. At D-Day he is thought to have landed with a unit of African American soldiers, on Utah or Omaha Beach; he was certainly documented in France on 13 July.

As the five Normandy fronts linked up to form the 60-mile (96-kilometre) front, the correspondents met up again. The BBC sent over a transmitter, which Frank Gillard and colleagues opportunistically housed in the turret room of the Chateau de Creully, just half a mile from where Montgomery had his HQ. Running without interruption and with a clear signal to London, the studio was open to any correspondents who wished to climb the spiral staircase, and it remained in operation until the end of the Battle of Normandy. The BBC had been slow off the mark when it came to reporting the war, but at D-day it ruled the airwaves.

HELL ON WINGS

Despite the secrecy attached to air operations, and their very high casualty rate, correspondents were allowed to cover the air war, and although the fighters were usually too small to accommodate supernumeraries, the bomber squadrons were both able and willing. The first correspondent to be killed in the Second World

War, Ralph Waldo Barnes (*New York Herald Tribune*), died on 17 November 1940 when his RAF bomber crashed into a mountain in Montenegro after losing its way in bad weather.

In September 1942 Denis Johnston became the first BBC journalist to fly on a bombing mission, when he took off from RAF Aqir, Palestine, in a B-24 Liberator piloted by Flight Lieutenant T. Pearson of 160 Squadron. He was unable to take his engineer and recording gear, so no recording was made, but he seized a second opportunity that came in January 1943, when the RAF laid on a bombing raid over the Tunisian town of Sousse especially for him. As they reached the target:

… above my head I heard a pop, and the sky was momentarily lit up.

'Christ', I said, 'if that's flak, it must have been damn near! That's the first time I've ever heard it above the noise of the engine.' Then, hastily restraining myself from further unbroadcastable comment, I signalled to Skipper to start cutting. And as we went in on our bomb run, the BBC made its first triumphant recording of a member of a bomber crew in actual flight over a target. Who it was made the remark I do not know, but clear as a bell it came over the Intercom. 'Here comes the f shit!'

Johnston's recording was never used, though it entertained the squadron when played back to them. Even if it had been fit for transmission, it would not, in fact, have been the first made by a BBC team during a raid by the RAF. Without Johnston's knowledge, Richard Dimbleby had beaten him by a few days – flying over Berlin on 6 January 1943 with 106 Squadron in a Lancaster piloted by Guy Gibson (later to earn the VC for leading 'The Dambusters' squadron on their famous operation). During the flight Dimbleby recorded the voices of the crew as well as his impressions of Berlin, and attempted to film using a cine camera. Unfortunately, a combination of cold and a malfunctioning camera spoilt that plan.

Broadcasting of the piece was delayed for two days by order of a nervous Air Ministry, but when it went out it was well received, and Bomber Command quelled all Dimbleby's apprehensions with a congratulatory telegram. More significantly, the RAF now talked only to Dimbleby within the BBC. He participated in some twenty raids, scared stiff every time – of Bomber Command's aircrew, half were killed and only 27 percent came through their service unscathed.

On 8 February 1945 Dimbleby recorded a raid on Cleves, which was to disrupt German troop and tank movements. Standing behind the Lancaster pilot, he said:

... everything that I describe to you I can see by looking behind him to port and straight ahead of us ... and now immediately in front of us there is a great white basin of light in the sky there where the target indicators have gone down below the clouds. ...We have broken cloud and can see the ground below us. And what an astounding sight it is of light immediately ahead of us as we go into Cleves. There is the town, the junction we are attacking, lit like London on its brightest day, but not lit only by the

above: Walter Cronkite with the crew of a B-26 Martin Marauder at Earls Colne on 9 February 1944 prior to accompanying them on a mission to destroy a German V1 rocket site in Freval, France.

above: Pierre Lefevre, a Free
French war correspondent
working for the BBC, broadcasts
as a Sherman Firefly tank
moves up to the battle area
during August 1944.

*light of flares. The lights of bombs that are bursting
and incendiaries that are bursting too ....* [61]

The US Eighth Air Force wanted the publicity that correspondents
could provide, and in February 1943 it trained a group of eight that
became known initially as 'The Flying Typewriters' and then as 'The
Writing 69th'. The training was thorough, and although the Geneva
Convention banned correspondents from armed combat, Walter
Cronkite enthusiastically used the spare machine gun on a B-17
Flying Fortress on 26 February 1943, during a mission targeting the
submarine base at Wilhelmshaven. His verdict was that he fired at

every German aircraft he saw but doubted he had hit any, and by the time he had finished he was surrounded by a sea of spent cartridges. Robert Post was killed, despite being seen to bail out after his B-24 Liberator was hit by heavy groundfire. He had wanted to fly in a Fortress and switched only at the last minute to give the Liberators some press recognition. Post's death ended the concept of 'The Writing 69th' as a unit, though its former members continued to fly on raids.

On the night of 2 December 1943, Ed Murrow (of 'This – is London' renown) climbed aboard Wing Commander W. 'Jock' Abercromby's Lancaster *D for Dog*, one of four war correspondents on a bombing mission to Berlin that involved 458 aircraft. He did not record the flight, as Dimbleby had done, because CBS would not allow recording devices to be used in broadcasts, and it was not until September 1944 that he ignored the prohibition. Instead, he crafted an emotive yet sober report, guaranteed to touch his American audience, which he delivered in a composed voice. That mission claimed 40 bombers and three out of five correspondents: Norman Stockton and Captain Nordhal Grieg (a Norwegian with the *Daily Mail*) were killed; Lowell Bennet of INS was shot down and spent the rest of the war as a POW, although Murrow believed at the time that he was dead.

> *I was standing just behind Jock and could see all the seams on the wings. His quiet Scots voice beat into my ears, 'Steady lads, we've been coned.' His slender body lifted half out of the seat as he jammed the control column forward and to the left. We were going down. Jock was wearing woollen gloves with the fingers cut off. I could see his fingernails turn white as he gripped the wheel. And then I was on my knees, flat on the deck, for he had whipped the Dog back into a climbing turn. The knees should have been strong enough to support me, but they weren't, and the stomach seemed in some danger of letting me down too. I picked myself up and looked out again. It seemed that one big searchlight, instead of being twenty thousand feet below, was mounted right on our wingtip.*

> *Berlin was a kind of orchestrated hell – a terrible symphony of light and flame. It isn't a pleasant kind of warfare.*[62]

The experience shook him – and it scared CBS, who forbade him to repeat the experience.

THE LIBERATION OF PARIS

In the weeks following D-Day, the Allied army fought to break out of Normandy. Doon Campbell went on with the commandos, and at the capture of Douvres boasted that he was 'writing this dispatch on German paper, using a German typewriter, and sitting in the swivel chair of the commander of the last German force to surrender within the allied bridgehead on Saturday night'.[63] But the strain was telling on him; he was ordered to rest for a week.

Capa returned to France, and with Pyle and Wertenbacker worked his way across Normandy with the US infantry, from one hedgerow to the next as the German rearguard fought hard. When they went into the newly liberated hospital at Cherbourg, which was full of American wounded, Pyle was, as always, the centre of attention, with every soldier wanting his autograph.

The desire to be in Paris for the liberation drove many correspondents onwards. On the way to the capital, Capa photographed a young, shaven-headed woman in Chartres as she carried her German lover's child along the road amid taunts of 'whore' from the crowd.

Despite the determination of the French that only their own press would have the honour of entering on the first day, Allied correspondents of many nations were there in droves, clamouring for a room at their old haunt, the Hotel Scribe, even as the Germans were still trying to leave the city. The emotion ran high that day: Alan Moorehead drove through the city, realizing that everyone in the car with him was crying, as were many of the people of Paris.

Ollie Stewart had covered the Western Desert and the Italian campaign for the *Baltimore Afro-American* and, after being held up by the last spurts of German resistance, he reached Paris for the city's liberation. With wide-eyed wonder he watched as:

> *… beautiful women dashed into the streets to kiss dusty GI lads, to throw flowers and to offer wine and fruit. I, Ollie Stewart, of sound mind and fairly sober character, do solemnly give my word that I have never been kissed so much in all my life. Almost every woman I meet on the street stops and kisses me on both cheeks. It is a beautiful custom. Rudolph Dunbar and I were walking along the street yesterday, and at least a dozen women brought their babies and children up to us to be kissed. I felt like a small-time politician running for Congress – and if I ever run for any office, I will be rather experienced*

top: Ernie Pyle and Hal Boyle (AP) on the balcony of a room at the Grand Hotel, Paris, a couple of weeks after witnessing the liberation of the French capital.

above: Brochure for the Hotel Scribe, Paris, a favourite lodging among correspondents.

in this kissing business…. We rode behind General de Gaulle up to the Arc de Triomphe as millions of people cheered, sang and applauded the Allies.[64]

As if to remind everyone that the war was not yet over the last German snipers in Paris suddenly opened up. Stewart crawled under a tank at an intersection, 'where a girl was bleeding and a baby crying as rifles, pistols and grenades took up the refrain that echoed through the city. To contrast this with the scene an hour before was almost unbelievable. We scampered out and under and later saw a crowd with a German prisoner captured on the roof. Throughout the afternoon, the hunt and fight went on,

and when this correspondent reached his hotel, he was gasping and trembling.'[65]

ALLIED SETBACKS AND CIVIL WAR IN GREECE

The Allied campaign was not all powerful. In September, Operation Market Garden, launched to cross the Rhine and capture the Ruhr, failed with very high losses at Arnhem – the 'bridge too far' immortalized in Cornelius Ryan's book and Richard Attenborough's film. Murrow, Gillard, Stanley Maxted, Wilmot, Byam and Moorehead were all there to observe that operation, transported in by the same Horsa glider, and Byam and Maxted were able to get their reports to the BBC in two days – more quickly than some of the official communiqués.

Correspondents, moreover, continued to be killed and risk their lives. Having survived two airborne operations, Guy Byam was reported missing, presumed dead, when B-17 Flying Fortress *Rose of York* was observed going down over the North Sea in February 1945 on the way back from a bombing raid.

The Russian advance had forced Germany to withdraw from Greece in the autumn of 1944, creating a power vacuum that led to civil war between the army of the Greek government, sup-

ported by Britain and the USA, and the military wing of the Greek Communist Party. During fighting in Athens the BBC was forced to relocate from its studio to a secret address, from where John Nixon broadcast under the most difficult of conditions:

This is a service message for newscasts from John Nixon. In the last two days we have kept the window of the temporary studio open while I have been speaking my dispatches so that you can hear the noises of the battle. Will you please let me know if you have had enough of this, in which case we will close the window. [sound of gunfire]

Hello BBC, this is John Nixon speaking to you from Athens. We're broadcasting the battle of Athens in a tiny bare room overlooking a large square in the heart of this suffering city. As we're British, the guerrillas regard us as enemies, so I'm not going to give the exact location or complete details. That might lead to some attempts at interference. The building is right inside the fighting area. Occasionally bullets hit the walls, both aerial masts have been hit and the aerial is down … staff sleep on the premises because it's dangerous to come and go

in the streets around. Public Relations often arrange for an armoured car to take me and our engineer, Douglas Varley, to and from this temporary studio twice a day, but armoured cars in Athens are being kept fairly busy on other work, so up to now we've taken our chance in an ordinary army staff car. In this we tear through the streets at top speed, and beside the driver sits our armed escort, a soldier with a tommy gun....We keep [the light] out in case a light should attract the attention of any neighbouring sniper. And I do my best with a torch. At this moment I am sitting on the floor so as to keep below the level of the window....[66]

It is said that Nixon once briefly paused in his broadcast because a sniper's bullet had just missed him.

THE FINAL PUSH – AND SURRENDER

Doon Campbell was with the 17th Airborne Division of the US Army when they crossed the Rhine on 24 March 1945 – sitting in a jeep secured to the floor of a glider, with a box of grenades acting as an armrest. After a three-hour tow came the release and the glider crash-landed under fire, but its occupants were unharmed and the grenades safe. It took him six hours to find the glider containing

the transmitter so he could get the story out ready for the BBC's nine o'clock news.

Richard Dimbleby saw the landings from the air and he broadcast with a measure of triumph: 'The Germans had said they were ready for airborne landings. They were not, I think, ready for anything quite as powerful and concentrated as this, the biggest airborne force ever carried in one attack. It was British and Americans flying parallel within easy sight of each other. The Halifaxes and the Stirlings towing their Horsas and Hamilcars, the Dakotas each drawing their two Waco gliders. Around us all, giving encouraging flashes in the sun, dashed the little fighters, British and American too.'[67]

The BBC 'warcos' had become arguably the most important in the field because their English language broadcasts were the only ones available to the troops in Europe.

The closeness of the BBC correspondents to Montgomery, who liked to think of them as part of his staff, led to tension between the British and the Americans when Gillard reported a press conference on 7 January 1945 at which Montgomery took credit for destroying the 'bulge' that had been created by the German offensive known as the Battle of the Bulge in the Ardennes. The Americans were understandably angry, and Gillard was attached to General Bradley's HQ in order to provide more overtly balanced coverage. To his relief, he was, with one exception, made welcome.

Bradley was particularly helpful to Gillard, taking him to the liberation of a forced labour camp near Regensberg, and then to Torgau, a small town on the Elbe River where Russian and American forces met on 25 April. There were three American correspondents with Gillard, but the only transmitter at Bradley's HQ was the BBC's and Gillard felt that it was his right to have the first use of it. In the end, they were told to toss up for the opportunity to be the one to broadcast the news live to the world. Gillard won and at 18:00 sharp: '... the announcer in London, who was Freddie Grisewood, said, "Here is the news, and right at the outset we are going over to Frank Gillard in Germany". We'd agreed that he would take five seconds to say that... (because there was no two-way communication, of course, and I couldn't hear him). Five seconds passed; I said, "East and West have met", and those were the words that went around the world.'[68]

LIBERATING THE CAMPS

The Allied advance brought about the liberation of the POW camps. During March 1945, POWs at Oflag 12 in Bavaria, among

them Edward Ward, had heard the rumours that US forces were closing in. By that time, the prisoners' captivity had become nominal, and when shells started to fall, POWs and guards alike went down to the air-raid shelters. Then the American tanks loomed out of a wood and the former prisoners were driven out of Germany. Ward described himself as feeling rather like Rip Van Winkle.

As well as freeing the POWs, Allied forces liberated the labour and death camps. For those correspondents who had accompanied the troops, this was by far their most searing experience of the war. Gellhorn went to Dachau and Ed Murrow to Buchenwald. Afterwards he described aspects of the camp to the Americans at home: '... I was told that this building once stabled eighty horses. There were twelve hundred men in it, five to a bunk. The stink was beyond all description ... in another part they showed me the children, hundreds of them. Some were only six. One rolled up his sleeve, showed me his number. D6030 it was. ... I have reported what I saw and heard, but only part of it. For most of it I have no

previous page: A British paratrooper firing from a ruined house at Oosterbeek on 23 September 1944. The photograph was taken by Sergeant D.M. Smith from the Army Film and Photographic Division who accompanied the troops dropped at Arnhem and Oosterbeek.

above: A relaxed General Montgomery talking to reporters.

opposite: Alan Wood of the *Daily Express* types a dispatch on his Remington while sitting in a ditch near Arnhem during Operation Market Garden in September 1944.

above: A correspondent makes
a recording at Belsen against
a background of bodies in a
trench.

opposite: British newspapers
celebrate the final great
offensive after crossing the
Rhine.

words.... If I've offended you by this rather mild account of Buchenwald, I'm not in the least sorry.'[69]

With no suspicion of the particular horrors that awaited them, Richard Dimbleby accompanied a platoon of soldiers and a doctor who were going to take the surrender of Belsen, and the recording he sent back to London was so graphic that the BBC hesitated to use it without independent corroboration. Dimbleby threatened to abandon broadcasting if it were not broadcast at once, and it went out. Few, if any, broadcasts have caused such shock and outrage.

> ... Inside the huts it was even worse. I have seen
> many terrible sights in the last five years, but
> nothing, nothing approaching the dreadful interior
> of this hut at Belsen. The dead and dying lay close

together. I picked my way over corpse after corpse in the gloom, until I heard one voice that rose above the undulating moaning. I found a girl – she was a living skeleton – impossible to gauge her age, for she had practically no hair left on her head and her face was only a yellow parchment sheet with two holes in it for eyes.[70]

Elsewhere, the war continued, but the Battle for Berlin was coming to its end. Rudolph Dunbar found some of Hitler's personal notepaper when he visited the Reich Chancellery and he wrote a note to his editor on it. In September, wearing his war correspondent's uniform, he became the first black person to conduct the Berlin Philharmonic, receiving a warm ovation from the mostly German audience at the orchestra's Berlin home.

WAR STILL RAGES IN THE FAR EAST

In the Far East, the Americans and their allies were taking the Japanese-held islands now that the enemy's sea and air power had been destroyed – and with them their supply lines. The Japanese were reduced to defending their home islands, including Iwo Jima, possession of which would allow the US to launch air strikes against the Japanese mainland. The outnumbered Japanese forces were firmly ensconced in Mount Suribachi, in a honeycomb of tunnels and caves, and the American victory came at the cost of almost 7,000 American dead, most of them US Marines.

On 23 February, four days after the landing, AP's photographer Joe Rosenthal took some photographs of US Marines celebrating the capture of the mountain by raising the US flag on its summit. He had heard about this act and taken his Speed Graphic camera up the mountain, in company with a couple of other photographers.

They got there too late – and, in any case, US Marine commanders had decided to replace the flag with something larger. Rosenthal, by his own account, tried to find the original group of US Marines but they had dispersed. He was left with the second group, and as the flag was planted, he took his shot. He followed it up with another of all the US Marines posing beneath the new flag.

Rosenthal was told his Iwo Jima photograph had been splashed over the front pages of various newspapers. When asked if it had been staged, and assuming that the questioner referred to the group picture, he agreed that it had. In fact, it was the flag-raising image that had become famous around the world, winning him a Pulitzer Prize for a 'frozen flash of history'. As with Capa's enigmatic 'The Falling Soldier', the image became the story, but in this case it also brought medals and fame to the US Marines in the picture, although not to those who had first raised a flag. Rosen-

thal spent half a century wearily fighting accusations of fakery. Posthumously, his reputation was officially vindicated by the award, in 2006, of the Department of the Navy's Distinguished Service Award.

When Ernie Pyle decided to report the war in the Far East he was assigned, at his request, to a light fleet carrier rather than a big ship. The USS *Cabot* was part of Admiral Marc Mitscher's Task Force 58, and her past performance encouraged Pyle to expect a dramatic cruise with every opportunity to see close-up action. In fact, the experience proved comparatively routine, and it was not the first-hand account of the attack on Tokyo that his employer wanted. Equally galling was the naval censorship that prohibited the identification of men, other than very senior officers, which made it hard for Pyle to write the kind of dispatches for which his public, and especially the enlisted men, loved him.

What he did write was disappointing; to them, he seemed to have sold out to the naval hierarchy that gave him a place in the ward-room as an honorary officer, and failed to see the real hardships of the Pacific. Despite a feeling that this would be the campaign when his luck ran out, Pyle opted to take part in the Okinawa landings with the US Marines. On 18 April 1945 he was shot through the forehead by a Japanese sniper after lifting his head while sheltering in a ditch. His death, coming just after that of Franklin D. Roosevelt, was mourned by Americans to almost the same degree as the president's.

TENACIOUS DICKEY CHAPELLE

Into the Pacific theatre came Dickey Chapelle, youngest 'warco' to be accredited to the US Navy. Her first brief experience as a war correspondent, in 1942, had been an embarrassing failure, but in 1945, still only 25, she requested accreditation to the Pacific to report for *Life Story* magazine. She had no concept of war, and the US Navy rigorously excluded women reporters from the front unless US Navy nurses were already established.

Although she wept at Honolulu when news of the heavy casualties at Iwo Jima came though, Chapelle remained resolved to report from the front. At Guam, Admiral Miller refused her permission to go forward, citing the usual argument that the front was no place for a woman. She told him that the only other people for whom it was no place was men, and that if men were being killed a woman needed to be there because only a woman would be able to tell the story to the women back home. He remained politely immovable, and she went on the hospital ship USS *Samaritan* with the nurses, her task being to photograph the wounded and document the use of blood.

The plans she had made had not worked out. Her husband was still back in the USA and she missed him, the strain exacerbated by her awareness of his infidelities. Paralyzed with shock when a Japanese Zeke bomber almost hit the *Samaritan*, she failed to capture either the attack or the shooting down of the aircraft.

Her response was to pull herself together. At night she hung helmet and life jacket in easy reach. She checked her camera, reloaded it and cushioned it between pillows to protect it in the event of the ship being hit. With practice, she learned to find the camera's controls in the dark. And she resolved never to let her emotions get in the way of her work.

Chapelle took photographs at which male 'warcos' balked. She used the F-word for the first time in her life, to make a badly

opposite: Joe Rosenthal, AP war photographer, stands with prints of his famous Iwo Jima image.

above: On his way to Okinawa in March 1945, Ernie Pyle chats to US Marines below decks.

overleaf: Just a few weeks after the atomic bomb destroyed the city, an Allied war correspondent stares at the ruins of Hiroshima.

wounded young US Marine smile, because she believed that if he smiled he would live. At the field hospital in Iwo, one casualty insisted on giving her the knife he would no longer be needing, showing her how to wear it and telling her he now felt better about her because she was armed. Her love affair with the US Marines had begun. When she heard them complaining that civilian 'warcos' were a waste of time, she delivered a tirade on the subject – and from then on she had become, as one US Marine called her, 'our girl'.

A chance to get to the front came accidentally when two officers, unaware that she had no right to be forward, took her to Mount Suribachi. She stood up on a ridge to set up her shots and came back complaining about the insects flying past her. Aghast, the officers told her they were *bullets*: she had made herself a target on the skyline.

At Okinawa she went forward to photograph the wounded, but by now the US Navy was determined to make an example of her for defying regulations. Relieved of her accreditation, she was sent home, only to learn that *Life Story* found her raw images, in the editor's words, too 'dirty'. *Cosmopolitan* bought some and the Red Cross used one to recruit blood donors. But her career was just beginning.

PEACE AT LAST IN THE PACIFIC

As the war in Europe wound down, cameraman Ronnie Noble went East, and in Calcutta he asked to accompany an RAF bomber squadron in order to film a raid. The Wing Commander took him to meet the squadron, whose greeting was less than enthusiastic:

'What is it, sir?' asked the squadron leader.

'It's a War Correspondent!' he replied. At this they guffawed and crowded round to look at me.

'Tell us about the War, old boy! Do tell us about the war!'

'Hold on, fellows – he's a cameraman!' said the CO.

'Well, why didn't you say so. We thought he was a lying journalist.'[71]

With such faith in the probity of cameramen, or at least their apparatus, the unidentified squadron accepted Noble and his heavy equipment. While he confronted his fears as the B-24 Liberator

neared Rangoon, the RAF crew decided that his courage lay not in flying on a raid but in having filmed one from the ground. The Rangoon footage was sent to London from where Noble received a cable praising his results and technique, but informing him that his work would not be used because events in Europe – the surrender of Germany – were more important.

Meanwhile, Mountbatten organized an invasion fleet at Rangoon to retake Singapore and cut off the Japanese. 'Warcos' could accompany any one of three landings, so Noble and Noel Monks opted for Singapore and boarded their invasion ship where, during a game of cards, they heard the awful news that Japan had surrendered and they were not on the spot. But the invasion drill was such that nobody had been allowed to leave the ship since the previous day. They begged and pleaded their case, but the captain was inexorable.

Noble went on to record the liberation of POWs being held in the infamous Changi Prison. He was one of the correspondents whose careers blossomed in the brave new post-war media world when television resumed its arrested development and brought the newsreel out of the cinema and into the living room.

However, possibly the biggest scoop of the Second World War was obtained by the relatively unknown Wilfred Burchett, who was to become one of the twentieth century's most controversial journalists. Burchett had grown up in Australia during the Great Depression and tramped his country doing whatever work he could find, before travelling to London and landing a job with a company that helped German Jews settle in Britain. He married one of the clients and, on the strength of some freelance articles, as well as some – unpublished – letters to newspapers denouncing the pogroms, was taken on by the *Daily Express*.

On 6 August 1945 the USA dropped the first atomic bomb, destroying the city of Hiroshima; three days later, Nagasaki was also bombed, and Japan surrendered. While hundreds of correspondents covered the signing of the surrender, Burchett caught a train to Hiroshima, in defiance of an American ban on travel to the area and despite the prevailing belief that the railway had been bombed to pieces. After 22 hours of travel, watched throughout with hostile suspicion by Japanese officers, who had returned from the war zones, and enquiring the name of each station at which the train stopped, Burchett arrived at Hiroshima in the early hours of 3 September. He filed a dispatch by Morse Code and it appeared in print three days later on 5 September. The *Daily Express* could have treated the piece as an exclusive; instead, they made it freely available, and its impact was vast:

... Those who escaped begin to die, victims of THE ATOMIC PLAGUE ...

In Hiroshima, thirty days after the first atomic bomb destroyed the city and shook the world, people are still dying, mysteriously and horribly – people who were uninjured by the cataclysm – from something I can only describe as atomic plague.

Hiroshima does not look like a bombed city. It looks as if a monster steamroller had passed over it and squashed it out of existence. I write these facts as dispassionately as I can in the hope that they will act as a warning to the world. In this first testing ground of the atomic bomb I have seen the most terrible and frightening devastation in four years of war. It makes

a blitzed Pacific island seem like an Eden. The damage is much greater than photographs can show.

In these hospitals I found people who, when the bomb fell, suffered absolutely no injuries, but are now dying from the uncanny after effects. Their hair fell out. Bluish spots appeared on their bodies. And the bleeding began, from the ears, nose and mouth....[72]

Burchett made himself unpopular with the US military authorities, which went to great but fruitless lengths to deny that 'Atomic Plague' (now called radiation sickness) existed. He never again reported from among the ranks of Western journalists and always based himself with those who were in some way opposing Western interests.

Well over 250 correspondents came to report on the Korean War (1950–1953), not all of them from the Second World War cohort. Dimbleby was at home presenting outside broadcasts for the BBC; Gellhorn chose not to cover Korea; Campbell was in Reuters' Paris bureau; Moorehead had become an author; and Murrow made just two brief visits. For others, fresh from different post-war conflicts, the lure of the front was irresistible, even if the reality was bitter to endure in the ferocious cold of the Korean winter. 'I had once seen a correspondent in the Tokyo Press Club', René Cutforth wrote, 'dressed up in his padded and bulging parka, sitting crying on the sofa surrounded by his friends, because his paper had ordered him back to Korea.... I thought of the black night, the freezing wind, the ruin, the desolation, the pervading fear and pain of that terrible land across the sea to the west. I put off my departure one day and was about to postpone it again when I realised abruptly that if I went on in that way I should never go back to Korea.'[1]

A war correspondent can never admit that he's afraid. If he does, that's the end of him in the eyes of the soldiers.

Ronnie Noble (1916–2001) in *Shoot First*, 1955

The Great Game:
korea, vietnam and the falklands

Most journalists covered the Korean War from the side of the United Nations' (UN) armies. However, there were several Westerners accredited to the Chinese People's Volunteer Army (CPVA), and reporting from that perspective from 1951 onwards. Since his famous Hiroshima dispatch, Wilfred Burchett had written approvingly of the post-war Stalinist show trials in eastern Europe and had lectured in his native Australia on the freedoms enjoyed by those countries that were now under Soviet control. At a time of deep neurosis in the USA over the perceived march of communism, and fear of a Soviet Union that now had the atomic bomb, Burchett had become a very controversial character. Also reporting on 'the other side' was Alan Winnington of the *Daily Worker*.

On the face of it, the Korean War seemed a far more simple conflict than it proved to be after the United Nations had authorized a huge multinational force, under US military command, to help the South Koreans evict Russian-backed, communist North Korean aggressors. Given the experience of working with the press corps that had

been built up during the Second World War, the theatre should have been a rewarding one for war correspondents, particularly after General MacArthur explicitly stated that he had no desire to impose wartime censorship. The press was asked to be responsible in its reporting and not to divulge military information of interest to the enemy: troop movements, fortifications, and so on.

The early weeks of the war were a disaster for the South Korean forces and for the first US troops who arrived to support them. By the end of June 1950 they had been driven out of Seoul and were still being pushed back, with the dismayed correspondents following along. Among them was Philip Deane (full name Philippe Deane Gigantès), with wartime service behind him. At the age of 18, he had fled his native Greece, entered the Royal Naval College at Dartmouth and served in the Royal Navy until 1945. Shortly after-

above: This image of US soldiers sharing a light for their cigarettes against the burning ruins of Seoul in September 1950 helped AP's Max Desfor win a 1951 Pulitzer Prize.

wards he became correspondent in Greece for the *Observer*, and in 1950 he asked to cover Korea.

Arriving in July at Daejon, Deane stepped out of his aircraft into the middle of the chaos, hitching a ride in a US Army ambulance that was taking critically wounded GIs into the town, which was full of refugees and excrement. Five thousand UN troops faced a North Korean army that was overwhelmingly superior – in both numbers and Russian hardware. Attaching himself to various infantry companies, Deane went with them into action, much to the concern of the *Observer* whose requests that he take care went unheeded. Instead, he cabled a 6,000-word dispatch that cost the newspaper £400.

Alarmed by his rashness, the paper ordered him back to base – but it was too late. Pinned down with badly wounded GIs in a farmhouse, Deane was shot as he tried to get the soldiers out in his jeep and was then taken prisoner, being beaten, kicked and yelled at:

> *… but we could not understand. When that was over we were marched to a command post on the top of a leafy hill. There were other prisoners there – six of them. Two were severely wounded. At dusk we were ordered to stand up. The two who were badly wounded were finished off, this time with a pistol. Their executioner did not aim well. It took too many bullets to kill those two G.I.s. In single file, almost naked, our hands tied behind, we set off along goat paths, bare feet over loose stones….*[2]

After a five-day march he arrived at Suwon for a round of interrogation, before being driven to Seoul and asked to broadcast a condemnation of the USA, which he refused to do. It was only on 4 August that his claim to be a correspondent was accepted, thanks to Alan Winnington who visited him before contacting his newspaper, which in turn informed the *Observer*.

Deane was taken north, via Pyongyang, with a group of prisoners that comprised British and French diplomats, soldiers, a priest, several missionaries and nuns. Any who dropped out with sickness and exhaustion were summarily executed. An American lieutenant was shot in Deane's presence for letting five men collapse. For those who survived the worst months, conditions during the second and third year of captivity varied dramatically, and in April 1953 Deane was transferred, in style, to Moscow by the Russians. In the dining car of the train, he and other survivors encountered unexpected hostility from diners and staff because they were not eating the 420-roubles' worth of food which had been decreed for

their recuperation from captivity. They explained that they did not have very much money on them, whereupon the cashier set his jaw and declared, 'I will see that you fulfil your plan'. Turning to his staff, he ordered: 'Serve.'

> *As we ploughed through course after course, as we drank bottle after bottle of champagne, the glares on the faces of our fellow-diners disappeared, to be replaced by encouraging smiles. Like spectators at a rugger match, they egged us on, sending an occasional gift bottle to show their appreciation of our efforts. With perspiration pouring from our foreheads we persevered, feeling that Anglo–Soviet relations were at stake.*[3]

Not all were as fortunate as Deane and able to survive the war. Around the time of his arrest, when correspondents – mostly non-American – were taking advantage of the lack of censorship to criticize the campaign and expose the precarious situation of UN forces, Ian Morrison wrote:

> *A serious situation has developed at Pohang on the east coast…. This Pohang affair, even if the situation is restored once again, shows up the whole weakness of the allied position in Korea. Intelligence must have been gravely at fault to permit such a situation to develop…. The Naktong River line, which is being held only with difficulty, guards the western flank of the allied bridgehead in Korea. Across the north there is no such natural barrier, only 50 miles of mountain ridges. Again one is obliged to wonder exactly how large a bridge-head the allies can expect to hold with the forces at their disposal.*[4]

The piece was published in the *Times* on 12 August 1950 – the day on which Morrison, along with Christopher Buckley (*Daily Telegraph*), was killed when their jeep hit a landmine, giving them the distinction of being the first 2 of 11 correspondents to die. Deane heard the news on a broken radio, which he covertly repaired in the building where he was being held at the time.

Ian Morrison had been an experienced correspondent, who had reported from the Far East for the *Times* since Pearl Harbor. He had come through the hardships of the jungle, suffering diseases as serious as amoebic dysentery, and recovering from spinal injuries sustained in one of two plane crashes in which he had been involved. After the war he had continued to cover the region, before

he requested a transfer to Europe for the sake of his family. He had withdrawn that request only when hostilities commenced in Korea.

General MacArthur's stated hope of open reporting withered in the face of press criticism, and he tried unsuccessfully to withdraw the accreditation of some 17 correspondents who had disparaged his campaign, as well as ordering a progressive tightening of the rules. No adverse comment on UN strategy was allowed; words such as 'retreat' became taboo. In the end, the correspondents gave up and demanded censorship. There was no point in risking their lives at the front only for their copy to vanish into the ether or to arrive in Tokyo three weeks late, often with the most significant paragraphs deleted.

MOVING THE NEWS

Getting material out of Korea was often difficult, particularly during the 'fluid' stages of the war. When Seoul was recaptured in September 1950, Reginald Thompson (*Daily Telegraph*) and Lionel Crane (*Daily Express*) hitched a lift north to Kimpo and found a

above: The static 'Peace Train' that provided accommodation for UN war correspondents during the Panmumjeom Peace Talks (top) and correspondents at work inside the train in 1951.

above: R&R in Tokyo in late 1950 and a chance for Marguerite Higgins to dress for dinner and write up a dispatch.

opposite: General Douglas MacArthur meets his match in Marguerite Higgins.

transport aircraft that was about to fly to the air base at Ashiya, Japan. They typed their dispatches during the flight, then phoned them through to Tokyo. The BBC team of Cyril Page, with his 35mm spring-wound silent cine camera, and René Cutforth knew that it would always take a week or so for their material to reach the public. Sent to Tokyo first for processing and censoring, it was then flown to London where the commentary, any effects and soundtrack had to be added.

For much of the war, the press headquarters was at Daejon, where facilities were inadequate, particularly for transmission. Lawton Glassop of the *Sydney Morning Herald* spent three weeks travelling from Daejon to the front and back, only to discover that the authorities had reneged on their promises to send his material to Tokyo by teleprinter. Another Australian reporter, Harry Gordon, regularly shuttled to and from Ashiya. Marguerite Higgins typed her copy and then slept on a table in the pressroom, and she was not the only one to fall asleep over a typewriter, oblivious to the clattering of dozens of other machines. Real sleep was a luxury because the single telephone link to Tokyo was only available to correspondents from midnight to 04:00; later, access ended at 02:00.

MacArthur had incurred further resentment by taking personal care of the chiefs of the four main news agencies, offering them facilities unavailable to the rest. Other organizations with a sizeable presence were able to spare one person to take their material back, but those who worked alone had to waste time leaving the war zone or make common cause with friendly competitors.

Gone were the Second World War days of laid-on transport. Reginald Thompson had to hitch-hike around the area, but he found a useful friend in the shape of a US infantry captain. Yet when it came to covering the entry of MacArthur into Seoul after Inchon, a glut of jeeps suddenly materialized.

THE INDEFATIGABLE HIGGINS

Despite their distinguished record, female correspondents were banned. The reasons amounted to a combination of gender stereotype, lack of 'facilities' (ladies' toilets) and the fear of press flak should any of them be killed or taken prisoner. The military had not bargained for the arrival of Franco-Irish-American 'warco' Marguerite Higgins, who in 1945 had demanded – in German – and helped to receive the surrender of the Dachau concentration camp ahead of the US Army's arrival. Beyond her blonde hair and captivating blue eyes, Higgins, based at the Tokyo bureau of the *New York Herald Tribune*, was a steely professional – a feminist who saw herself as a newsman and whose combat journalism was largely devoid of Gellhorn's lingering details, humanity and feminine perspective. Charming and seemingly detached, her sole aim was to be a great correspondent, not just a great female correspondent. That ruthless drive locked her into intense competition, as her fellow *Tribune* colleague, Homer Bigart, another veteran of the Second World War, found out in Korea. So bitter was their feud that they hardly ever spoke to one another. Bigart lamented: 'She was a real trial to me. When I came out I thought I was the premier war correspondent and I thought that she, being the Tokyo correspondent, ought to be back in Tokyo. But she didn't see things that way. She was a very brave person, foolishly brave. As a result, I felt as though I had to go out and get shot at occasionally myself. So I resented that.'[5]

Lieutenant General Walker ordered her to leave Korea because 'this is just not the type of war where women ought to be running around the front lines'. She took her case to General MacArthur, who reiterated the toilet argument and added another: swearing. He then relented, overruled his subordinate and cabled the *Tribune*: 'ban on women correspondents in korea has been lifted. marguerite higgins is held in highest professional esteem by everyone.'[6]

That courage was soon shown. She reported from the 27th US Infantry Regiment as its encampment came under fire – and, although feeling no fear, she realized that not only could she not escape, but that she was merely surprised that she was going to die. This feeling of calm enabled her to offer a relaxed answer to Colonel Michaelis, when asked how she was. After the incident was over, Michaelis wrote an encomium to her heroic conduct in helping the medics attend to the wounded, regardless of her own safety, and expressed the Regimental Combat Team's (RCT) gratitude to her for saving many seriously wounded casualties.

The disaster of the early weeks was salvaged in September by a major amphibious landing at Inchon, behind North Korean lines. Thompson arrived in Korea that day by flying boat, remarking on the stream of foul language gushing from the lips of young American cameraman Charlie Jones. The aircraft landed on the water off Inchon, and Jones learned that his twin brother and partner, Gene, had been seriously wounded by shrapnel while going in with the first wave.

Higgins had been refused permission to go on an assault ship by virtue of her gender, and told she could watch from a hospital ship, but by a stroke of luck the permit given to her by a harassed captain authorized her to board any US Navy ship. At the end of the first day, she filed one of her crisp dispatches:

…We struck the sea wall hard at a place where it had crumbled into a canyon. The bullets were whining persistently, spattering the water around us. We clambered over the high steel sides of the boat, dropping into the water and, taking shelter beside the boat as long as we could, snaked on our stomachs up into a rock-strewn dip in the sea wall.

In the sky there was good news. A bright, white star shell from the high ground to our left and an amber cluster told us that the first wave had taken their initial objective, Observatory Hill. But whatever the luck of the first four waves, we were relentlessly pinned down by rifle and automatic-weapon fire coming down on us from another rise on the right.

There were some thirty Marines and two correspondents crouched in the gouged-out sea wall….[7]

After the landings the correspondents returned to the command ship, USS *McKinley*, where Higgins' appearance was greeted with anger, until she pulled out her pass. But thereafter she was banned from the ship and relied on Keyes Beech, her most sympathetic colleague and the one who drove their shared jeep, to file her copy from the ship. Higgins slept on the dockside or with the forces, as dirty as any of them in her filthy baggy kit. By and large

prose; and the photographers, who hurled themselves around in bursts of flash bulbs 'even demanding the repetition of acts of violence if discontented in any way with their first "shot"'.[8] Like Deane, Thompson had served in the Second World War, in British Army Intelligence, but he had been released to cover D-Day as a civilian correspondent for the *Sunday Times*.

One notable departure from past practice was the routine arming of many of the front-line correspondents, which contravened the Geneva Convention. Some simply carried a gun for self-defence; others chafed to go on the offensive and spoke enthusiastically of 'getting a gook' – 'gook' being the derogatory American term for Koreans in general, but in this context it was a reference to the North Koreans.

This blurring of the lines between correspondent and combatant, and between observation and intervention, occurred elsewhere in Korea, as it has throughout the history of war reporting. Sometimes it must have required fine judgement, but there was no doubt in the mind of René Cutforth, or of the BBC cameraman Cyril Page, and Alan Dower of Melbourne's *Age*, both of whom were in Seoul shortly after Cutforth's arrival in December 1950, by which time the capital had been back in UN hands for almost three months. Cutforth had been sent as a foreign correspondent by a BBC that was unimpressed with his performance behind the desk as a sub-editor, but prior to that he had been a teacher, traveller, soldier and POW. Dower, a no-nonsense Australian, had served as a commando officer in Timor and knew how to use the gun he carried.

Cutforth and Page had been told by two different British units that they had witnessed, and in one case prevented, South Korean policemen cold-bloodedly executing men and women – and, as Brigadier Tom Brodie, commanding the 29th Independent Infantry Brigade, put it: 'I am not going to have people executed on my doorstep.'

After being shown grim evidence, the two Britons were discussing the story with Dower when they were suddenly aware of a long procession of terrified men and women being herded towards a prison by shouting policemen. All were tied with electrical flex, just like the execution victims seen earlier. Some of the women were carrying babies. Followed by his friends, Dower set off behind them and reached the prison, where:

> *... a policeman on the other side of the gate began to yap at us in a hectoring voice, and Alan suddenly*

the other – male – correspondents did not want her there. She was tough and they were threatened by her invasion of their territory. They retaliated by spreading the lie that she had achieved her professional success by sleeping with commanders as senior as General MacArthur, but she had the last laugh in 1951 when she became the first female war correspondent to win a Pulitzer Prize (for International Reporting). Perhaps fittingly it was awarded jointly to Higgins and five others, among them her rivals Bigart and Beech – a recognition of how each, in different ways, had pushed the other two.

DISILLUSION, DESPAIR AND STALEMATE

According to the *Daily Telegraph*'s Reginald Thompson, the correspondents fell into three groups: the serious commentators; the semi-literates, who looked for stunt angles but were good at getting copy back for the rewriters to turn into accomplished

opposite: A war correspondent steps from an aircraft to make a training jump on 18 September 1951.

above: Processing film in a makeshift field photo laboratory during the Korean War.

overleaf: A US F-80 Shotking Star makes a low-level napalm attack at Suan, southeast of Pyongyang.

began to shout at him. He was a very formidable figure, Alan, and he carried an obvious four-five pistol, and now he had lost his temper and was using the kind of voice which apparently meant 'Orders' to the policeman. After a minute or two the policeman unlocked the gate and in we went. A long column of prisoners was marching diagonally across the courtyard inside. At a sharp yelp from the warder they halted and knelt in the snow. What was so dreadful about them, I saw all at once, was that they looked like a company of clowns. They were bone thin, their hair stuck out gollywog fashion, their faces were green – the colour of billiard chalk – and their noses were red with cold. I've never seen human beings look more desperately ill. When we went to enter the main prison block the policeman stood in front of us yelping and shouting and holding out his rifle. Alan pushed him aside without ceremony.[9]

After words with the prison commander, Dower's verdict was succinct: 'This, my God, is a bloody fine set-up to waste good Australian lives over. I'm going to raise hell.' Having threatened to shoot the prison commander if any executions took place, he took the matter up with the UN, and that, combined with stories in the press, protests by British officers and questions in Parliament, stopped the blatant mass executions, although political killing continued more circumspectly.

However, nothing could change the view of the majority of correspondents that the corrupt South Korean government was not worth the lives spent defending it. The British and their Dominion partners had considerable compassion for the Korean civilians, but it was not shared by all the Americans.

After the successful counter-offensive that began with Inchon, and led to the retaking of Seoul, the UN forces pushed the North Koreans back over the 38th parallel. Before finding a vehicle for themselves, Reginald Thompson, the BBC's Alan Whicker and the *News Chronicle*'s Steve Barber hitched north with an ill-disciplined rookie US unit, whose behaviour angered them and whose potential to stand and fight against determined opposition they seriously questioned. As the troops entered a village:

Carelessly the G.I.s smashed the windows, while Alan and I yelled to them to stop. Meanwhile Steve had caught a G.I. in the act of taking a wrist-watch from a young Korean, and his indignation and contempt burst from him in a scathing torrent which held the G.I. spellbound, watch in hand, as though he had been stung.

'Don't you see that a watch is almost priceless to him!' roared Steve. 'It's nothing to you. Good God, man, you've got watches and cameras, everything. Besides, can't you see, man, he's a friend! A friend!' And Steve held the boy's arm where an arm band proclaimed him an admitted ally, properly police-checked. The young Korean stood, grave-faced, and accepted the watch from the shame-faced G.I. with a courteous inclination of his head and a mumbled word.[10]

Ahead of the Americans, the British had taken Sariwon, and soon the weather became as obdurate as the terrain. The correspondents and their ailing jeep carried on. Transport had to be hauled through fast-flowing water and tempers in the convoy frayed:

At some stage of the first twenty-four hours Steve abandoned us and our slow chugging jeep. It was a miracle that we kept going; that we crossed any of these crossings, and Steve hadn't the temperament for it. We were soon without the reserve gears of which Alan had boasted so proudly, and glad enough to keep moving at any speed at all in the second gear of our four-wheel-drive…. But Alan and I had become attached to his vehicle. It had served us well, it seemed for a lifetime, and in a way it might be said to have saved our lives by not packing up in the heart of the flames or the desolate hills….

Once with the courage of despair, on our way back from somewhere, we contrived to have ourselves hitched behind a general, and we shall not soon forget his face as he looked back to see what kind of appendage he had in tow, consigning us with a terrible oath to hell and the ditch. But friendship bloomed again when we met on the road a few hours later, and he waved gaily.[11]

Pyongyang fell to MacArthur's UN forces. At this point the Chinese committed significant land forces, and in November 1950 the UN was once again in headlong retreat out of North Korea and, in January, out of Seoul.

above: Five photographers returning from the failed Kaesong peace talks in July 1951: (left to right) Ronnie Noble (BBC TV), Joe Scheerschel (*Life*), James Pringle (AP), James Healey (Acme News Pictures), Gene Zenier (Warner-Pathé Newsreels).

opposite: Wilfred Burchett photographed in Korea.

Cutforth and other correspondents were in the capital as the South Koreans destroyed it ahead of the advancing Chinese, then herded their own refugees back to the city over the frozen ice of the Han River, before sabotaging the pontoon bridge and shelling the ice to stop the refugees crossing and clogging up the roads. Page and Cutforth drove out, the latter giving way to 'a half-weeping hatred of the whole Korean set-up'; they offered a lift to two small children. In Suwon, they saw a teenage boy holding onto two girls, pushing them out in front of the passing trucks then pulling them back just in time. From the front passenger seat, Page smacked him hard across the ear as the jeep passed by. The BBC audience were to see the blowing up of the pontoon bridge over the Han River in Seoul, but Page's footage of the refugees was cut. The report by Eric Downton in the *Daily Telegraph* likewise contained no reference to civilians.

The BBC also refused to air a story by Cutforth about the civilian casualties of American napalm bomb attacks. He had been with the 29th Independent Infantry Brigade when a message reached him, requesting that he go to the field hospital. A doctor met him and without preamble said:

'Look, we must have some publicity about this. Perhaps the Press can make these people wake up to a sense of their responsibilities. Look at this, I want to show you this,' shouted the doctor as we came into a clear space in front of the hospital tent.

In front of us a curious figure was standing, a little crouched, legs straggled, arms held out from his sides. He had no eyes, and his whole body, nearly all of which was visible through tatters of burnt rags, was covered with a hard black crust speckled with yellow pus. A Korean woman by his side began to speak, and the interpreter said, 'He has to stand, sir, cannot sit or lie.'

He had to stand because he was no longer covered with a skin, but with a crust like crackling which broke easily.

'That's napalm,' said the doctor....'[12]

Although television would not show the graphic horrors, the use of napalm was reported in the less squeamish print media, and like other reporters in earlier wars, Cutforth recorded his experiences in a book, which appeared in 1952 while the war was ongoing.

One place where correspondents could meet and discuss the war was the Press Club in Tokyo, to which they gravitated while on leave or on business in the capital. Cutforth found that very few shared the view of himself and *Le Monde's* Robert Guillain, that the real story of the Korean War was the suffering of the local people. Many editors had instructed their reporters to play down the humanitarian disaster.

A CONFLICT WITH CONSCIENCES

A bite from a family's supposedly tame squirrel sent Ronnie Noble to Korea in the spring of 1951. After the 1939–45 war, he had continued his cut-throat profession as a cameraman for Universal Newsreel until 1950 when, recognizing the potential of television, he jumped ship to work for the BBC, which had resumed its embryonic television service. Noble very quickly became bored with filming for children's programmes, and the squirrel incident was the final straw: he applied for the Korean front.

Noble drove into Seoul, wondering if it was possible to capture the silence and loneliness of the deserted city: 'Could people sitting in the comfort of their English homes feel any of this when they saw it on their twelve-inch screens? Never had silence and stillness affected me so.'[13] He was another who shared the compassion for the Korean civilians caught up in the war.

While trying in vain to reach the location of a heroic stand by the British 29th Independent Infantry Brigade against overwhelmingly superior Chinese forces at Imjin River, Noble filmed in a village from which all but one farmer and his family were fleeing, just as the British guns opened up 100 yards (90 metres) from the village:

I saw his eyes through the viewfinder, and felt sick at the stomach. Although he was outwardly calm, his eyes showed the panic of his soul. They flitted from side to side, moving so fast that sometimes one lagged behind and suddenly he was cross-eyed. Saliva dripped down his thin, straggly beard. As he ran to a hut one shoe fell off. He kicked off the other, and ran barefoot to his wife, who sat beside the hut. Rapidly he piled a few of their belongings on her back; she stood as quiet as a pack-mule while the load grew and grew. As a last thought, he tucked a live chicken into a blanket, and the wife set off on the trek back. He went inside the hut, and I heard moans coming from the dark interior. Then he backed out, dragging the grandmother by her armpits. Her legs were useless, and dragged limply, leaving two deep furrows in the square patch of dry dust which was their home. By a superhuman effort he hoisted her on his back and staggered past the camera on his way to Seoul. We loaded the jeep with a dozen fleeing Koreans.[14]

Later, with a combination of professionalism and emotion, Noble filmed the Royal Ulster Rifles in the immediate aftermath of their withdrawal. Half-asleep with fatigue, dirty and unshaven, some of them swore at him and told him to take the camera away. Their exhausted acting commanding officer asked him to return the next day, but Noble ('though I hated myself for insisting') persuaded him to grant permission, because he wanted the world to see them as they were, not fresh and kitted out in clean uniforms.

He filmed dirty, starving orphans and young girls offering sex to GIs. He also filmed inside the UN orphanages, and as a result of his and others' newsreel footage, television audiences in Britain and the USA sent money to charities set up to provide care for Korean orphans. 'I felt able in some way to help in this catastrophic conflict....'

Photographers and cameramen with consciences still agonized over what should and should not be filmed. Alan Lambert photographed a young mother, her unhurt baby crying in her arms, who was lying dead in the street after she was caught in crossfire in front of him. American twins Gene and Charlie Jones filmed the same scene at close range with their newsreel cameras, exclusively concerned with the technical aspects of their trade. Two more, unnamed, correspondents came on the scene and were outraged by the filming, threatening to smash the camera. '"But," said Lambert, "the Jones boys believed that they were there to show the people back home the true face of war."'[15] Gene Herrick put down his camera when US aircraft accidentally dropped napalm and conventional bombs on British forces at the Nakton River in September 1950, but this was more to do with his instinct to help the wounded.

Wilfred Burchett arrived in July 1951, with Chinese accreditation, to report on the first peace talks. He was a source of interest to the correspondents in the UN camp, all anxious for something concrete to write about, because he had first-hand knowledge of the UN POWs in North Korean camps – and information about the enemy. The truth about Burchett's veracity is hard to establish. He visited POWs, he showed his UN-accredited brethren photographs that indicated the POWs were treated infinitely better than those in South Korea, and he said he was not involved in brainwashing them, as his detractors alleged. On the other hand, Burchett's claims that, while the UN correspondents were cynically fed on a diet of lies, he was totally independent must be treated with caution. By his own account, he enjoyed the full confidence of his military and political command, and he wrote that he was: '... treated on the same basis as a local writer, although you need not spread this news outside our own circle. In other words I am relieved of financial cares and given facilities to see what I want to see, travel where I want to travel, interview who I want to interview.... I would do anything at all for this people and their government because they represent the fullest flowering of all the finest instincts in humanity.'[16]

The talks and the conflict dragged on until July 1953 when the pre-war status quo was re-established, and as the public lost interest so did the news media. The front-line journalists were not sorry to leave an inhospitable terrain and climate in which the conscientious had become frustrated, shocked and disenchanted, and the remainder had uncritically chewed the 'dope' – press releases and briefings – handed out by the military. Reginald Thompson spoke for many when he wrote:

I have become acquainted with death in many previously unimaginable forms. I remember so well arms, legs, heads, busts, buttocks, hands, in macabre confusion in the death pits. I remember men roasting alive, or starved to grotesque caricatures, disintegrating in obscene heaps. But all these memories have become mere child's play. Soon the civilians may disappear without trace as progress marches on.

There is no more war. It is old-fashioned. It began to go out with our fathers and grandfathers. The glamour is false. The illusion is gone. The writing is on the wall in letters of blood and bits, and this is the latest message from Korea.[17]

Despite the presence of cameramen and photographers, Korea had still been a war primarily for the print journalists, although out of Ed Murrow's Christmas trips had come influential documentaries that brought the war into many American homes. In Britain in 1950 only 343,882 combined television and radio licences had been issued, compared with nearly 12 million radio licences. The coronation of Queen Elizabeth II in 1953 gave a major boost to television in Britain, and a decade after Korea 10.5 million homes had a combined licence. When it got into its stride, the next major war – Vietnam – would be fought on the screens of the world's living rooms as well as in print and cinema newsreels.

above: Ed Murrow and his production crew pose for a picture during the filming of 'Christmas in Korea' for CBS News during December 1952.

The Vietnam War

Today, 'Vietnam' is once again just the name of a country. However, for two decades it was first and foremost the name of a particularly ghastly war. To the correspondents who were there it became both, and it exerted an almost unique influence on them, not least on Jacques Leslie:

Within a few days after my arrival in Saigon in January 1972, even before I'd traveled outside the capital, I could feel the war's seductive shimmer. I saw Saigon as the world's cockpit, at the heart of the most important story in the world, and believed I was carrying out a mission to convey its wretched truth to American readers. Adrenaline gushed through me day after day, and when it didn't, drugs – usually marijuana, rarely opium – did. Like many of my colleagues, I loved the war and hated it and hated myself for loving it. By the war correspondent's macho standard, my experience was mild: I was wounded once (an American colonel standing next to me was killed in the attack), shelled repeatedly, teargassed occasionally, and finally expelled from South Vietnam for having embarrassed the South Vietnamese government with my stories one too many times.[18]

Together with the complementary wars in Laos and, particularly, in Cambodia, the conflict in Vietnam killed more correspondents than any other, with the ongoing exception of Iraq. The War Rem-

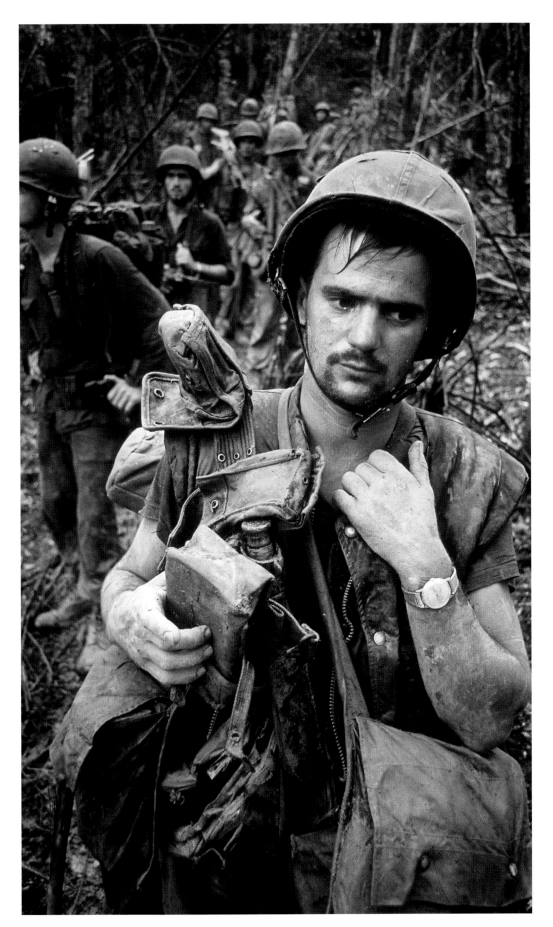

opposite: Nick Ut captures ARVN soldiers rushing to the US helicopter that will airlift them out of Cambodia following a sweep east of Prey-Veng in June 1970.

left: Unmistakably by Larry Burrows, a tired and dirty US Marine patrolling with his squad near the Demilitarized Zone.

nants Museum in Ho Chi Minh City, formerly Saigon, has a room devoted to the work of photographers killed in the war. Over the door is an inscription, the sentiment of which is equally applicable to the reporters, photographers and cinematographers: 'Each came for a reason and died taking a chance. All lived for the next picture; it could be the best one of all. It is for their photographs, not their dying that the world remembers them.'

Vietnam was the first war to be defined by images, still and moving, many of them memorable, shocking and calculated to disturb anyone turning on the television for the evening news or opening a morning newspaper. Photographers and cameramen who worked alongside journalists achieved equality, no longer being introduced as 'my cameraman' or 'my photographer' as though they were merely part of the baggage.

'From a war correspondent's perspective', wrote Jacques Leslie, 'Vietnam was in many ways ideal. We could travel wherever we liked. We faced no censorship and no restraints on coverage except for the minimal, reasonable ban on reporting troop movements in advance of battle (something I was never interested in reporting anyway). To a large degree we could choose when to be in danger, by moving into a battle zone, then retreating whenever we wished to a place such as Saigon where the risks were minimal or non-existent.'[19]

As a result of that freedom, relations deteriorated rapidly between much of the press and both President Diem's government of the Republic of Vietnam (South Vietnam) and the US Mission in Vietnam. When the New York Times' David Halberstam arrived in Saigon in August 1962, his first engagement was at a farewell party for the veteran French photographer François Sully, who had been served with an expulsion order by the South Vietnamese regime over a report that criticized the progress of the war. Nobody from the US Mission attended, and there was already a serious credibility gap between military and government communiqués and observable facts.

A major factor in this was 'Cable 1006' – a document issued in February 1962, which instructed the US commanders to stress to correspondents that the war in Vietnam was a South Vietnamese conflict and the US Mission was providing help only through its advisors. Because this was contradicted by the evidence on the ground, such as the involvement of American helicopter pilots at the Ap Bac debacle (see page 148), the journalists began to lose confidence in official briefings.

Correspondents thrown together in a war zone invariably gravitate into small social or professional communities, but in the early 1960s a group that included Halberstam, Neil Sheehan of UPI (later the New York Times) and the AP photographer Mal Browne went further by pooling their information. It was the only way to compensate for the deficiencies of official sources.

The official briefings were known as the 'five o'clock follies'. Late in the war, after the US withdrawal in 1973, Philip Caputo attended those held by the Army of the Republic of Vietnam (ARVN):

> Officers standing on a stage in crisp, starched uniforms and speaking nonsense while they pointed at a big lighted map covered in military symbols – the sessions were the Five O'Clock Follies all over again, minstrel shows in yellow face. The North Vietnamese had been stopped, said the briefers, who had been Through the Looking Glass so long they couldn't remember what it looked like on the other side. The Arvin were pulling themselves together … if need be, they would turn Saigon into another Stalingrad ….[20]

There were, of course, some correspondents who were content to remain in Saigon and regurgitate 'dope' in their dispatches. The best did not.

THE USA IS DRAWN IN

The French had been reinstalled as colonial masters in Vietnam in 1945, only to find themselves fighting against a communist independence movement led by Ho Chi Minh. Following France's withdrawal after the Battle of Dien Bien Phu in 1954, Vietnam was partitioned and a civil war between the north and the south broke out, one in which the anti-government guerrillas of the communist National Liberation Front (NLF) in the south also supported the north's aims for a country united under communist rule. The NLF fighters were better known in the West as the Viet Cong, or Vietcong (VC).

As the period of French colonial rule was coming to an end, Life magazine needed someone to provide relief photographic coverage in the region, and it turned to Robert Capa. In financial difficulty, fresh from a hedonistic period in Paris and trying to validate his American passport in the face of US investigations into his 'subversive' activities, Capa had accepted a lucrative, safe assignment in Japan. Although he had little enthusiasm for another war

zone, having once told Martha Gellhorn that he hoped to stay unemployed as a war photographer until the end of his life, he agreed to cover Vietnam.

On 25 May 1954 Capa crossed the Red River with a French column, taking significant risks to get the pictures he wanted and rescuing a wounded soldier while under fire. Then he went ahead, out of sight, and used his Contax to photograph men on a dyke. It was his last shot: a landmine blew off one leg and inflicted massive injuries. He was only 40 when he became the first American correspondent killed in Indo-China. The legacy he left was not just of great images but also an example that served as an inspiration to other aspiring photographers.

The USA, which had previously sent 'military observers' to assist the French, deployed increasing numbers of advisors during the early 1960s to help the ARVN, before it decided to commit combat troops in 1965. Ten years later, as the Americans pulled out their troops[21], Saigon fell to the forces of the Democratic Republic of Vietnam (North Vietnam). The conflict had also extended to neighbouring Laos and Cambodia; after 1975 the latter was taken over by the communist Khmer Rouge, which it is estimated had killed one-third of the country's inhabitants by the end of its reign of terror in 1991.

CHAPELLE IN CAMBODIA

Neighbouring Cambodia lured Dickey Chapelle. Vietnam's neighbour was the scene of a secret war in which American advisors and money were used to prop up the government against the Soviet-backed Pathet Lao insurgency movement. Reporting for the *Reader's Digest*, a magazine very close to the US government and, allegedly, the CIA, Chapelle's task was to cover the guerrilla war – and obtain military intelligence. At Vientiane she made the contacts to get herself airlifted in and out to cover the troops behind enemy lines, and she was allowed to stay on when other correspondents were ordered out for their own safety. An outstanding reporter on the subject of special operations, her understanding

of the wider situation became inversely proportional to her courage. She wrote stories about the bravery of American troops and was furious that *Reader's Digest* refused to use them – because to do so was to betray the nature of US involvement. Restlessly, she went from Laos to Saigon and Cambodia, blinded by patriotism and unable to understand the war in Vietnam. She parachuted with the South Vietnamese and, armed, went on patrol with them, sometimes at night, through the swamps and under fire. On 23 October 1965 she joined them for Operation Red Snapper, to clear Viet Cong from a position north of Da Nang, no longer a group of individuals but:

Now as a night patrol on suspect earth, we are something more. It is an entity committed to steady movement across space. We cannot go quickly, and yet we have become inexorable as an organism on one course with one will. ... As long as I can half see, half sense the sergeant in front of me, I walk in faith: if there are bogey men, they cannot frighten me in this company or in this place.[22]

Chapelle was killed in action on 4 November 1965, at the age of 46, during a patrol, when the US Marine walking ahead of her tripped a wire that set off an explosion. Henri Huet took a photograph of her as she received the last rites, an image that sums up her life, even to the glint of her pearl earring. Divorced from the husband she had met when he was her photographic teacher, but who became secondary to her career, and still determined to be judged for her toughness, though concerned that age was against her, she died in combat fatigues and wearing the delicate earrings with which she reminded people she was nevertheless a woman.

LARRY BURROWS BRINGS THE WAR TO LIFE

Larry Burrows arrived in Vietnam in 1962, and during the almost nine years he spent covering the war he created an unrivalled portfolio of images, many in colour. However, his most famous in-depth feature – 'One Ride With Yankee Papa 13' – was shot in black and white in 1965, by which time American combat forces were engaged.

The young photojournalist accompanied Helicopter Squadron 163 of the US Marines on a single operation. With reverse superstition, he deliberately chose the helicopter with the call-sign Yankee Papa 13 (YP-13), and photographed two of the young crew off duty in Da Nang, as if introducing them to a readership which, unlike himself, had not known them for weeks.

previous page: Photographers and cameramen recording the capture of Viet Cong prisoners taken by the ARVN at Xuan Loc in 1975.

above: Chaplain John McNamara administering the last rites to the mortally wounded Dickey Chapelle. The photograph was taken by AP's famous Henri Huet.

opposite: The crew chief of Yankee Papa 13, Lance Corporal James C. Farley, mans a M-60 machine gun during the mission.

To give himself a range of camera angles during the flight, he mounted a rig on the helicopter's gun, pointing back into the body of the aircraft at the crew chief, Lance Corporal James C. Farley. Tucked out of sight, Burrows operated the camera using a remote cable and spoke the captions into a tape recorder.

The operation was simple: to airlift ARVN infantry a distance of 20 miles (32 kilometres) to oppose Viet Cong troops. It could have been routine; it proved the opposite. The Viet Cong were along the treeline, and opened fire as the helicopters disgorged their troops. Two wounded men from YP-3 ran over to Burrows's helicopter and were taken onboard. When Farley made a dash to see what had happened to the pilot, Burrows ran with him through the gunfire. There was nothing they could do: the pilot appeared dead. Braving the fire again, they raced back and Yankee Papa 13 took off for base. During the flight, one of the wounded died; Farley stood cursing and crying with frustration at his inability to recover the pilot of YP-3. The operation ended back at base with the 21-year-old breaking down in the semi-privacy of a supply hut. Later they found out that another crew had reached YP-3 and managed to extricate the pilot.

The 24 images of 'One Ride With Yankee Papa 13,' a perfect storyboard for a feature film, brought home in an unprecedented way the reality of life for US combat troops.

The head of $Life's$ bureau in the Far East, John Saar, told the managing editor that Burrows's concentration and commitment was frightening and that he took enormous risks because he was a perfectionist. During an incident of 'friendly fire' in early 1971, when cluster bombs were dropped on ARVN forces, Burrows rushed to take dramatic images against the backdrop of burning fuel and exploding ammunition as well as to lend a hand with the wounded. It was his final assignment. On 10 February he was killed when the helicopter in which he was travelling was shot down over Laos. Killed with him were Henri Huet (AP), Kent Potter (UPI), Keisaburo Shimamoto (Newsweek) and Tu Vu (ARVN official photographer).

LARRY BURROWS, 1926–1971

above: Larry Burrows attaches a camera to helicopter YP-13 in preparation for shooting his famous sequence of photographs.

opposite: The complete collection of images that made up Larry Burrows' 'One Ride with Yankee Papa 13' appeared in the 16 April 1965 edition of *Life* magazine.

In 1942, two years before Robert Capa took his famous D-Day images, the young Larry Burrows joined *Life* magazine's London bureau as a messenger and worked his way up to become a darkroom technician. Inspired by Capa's work, some of which he had been permitted to print, he set out to become a photojournalist and served his apprenticeship as a war photographer in the Congo. At the time of his arrival in Vietnam, in 1962, he was accomplished; by 1965, he was great – some argue that he is the greatest war photographer of all time. Burrows was also exceptionally versatile, and *Life* would regularly pull him out of the conflict to photograph the wildlife and stunning scenery and culture of Southeast Asia.

Life gave him what many of his rivals lacked – time. He was not under pressure to feed a daily or weekly output to his employer. Although sociable in Saigon, where he painstakingly made his contacts, he did not work alongside his colleagues and instead he would disappear without telling them what he was doing or where he was going.

On 25 January 1963 *Life* featured Burrows' first major work of Vietnam reportage: headlined on the cover as 'The Vicious Fighting in Vietnam'. Before his departure for the war, *Life*'s editor, Hugh Moffatt, had suggested he set a precedent by photographing in colour, and that exposed readers to a far greater realism than previous images had offered. The project had taken him six months to complete, and he had flown almost 50 missions in fighter-bombers and helicopters. To capture a napalm attack from the air he persuaded the pilot to fly so low that the aircraft went through the upper edge of the fiery explosion. He kept rolls of film handily stuffed into his socks, and while on ground patrols he wore steel-soled shoes to protect himself against the sharp bamboo and steel spikes planted by the enemy.

His best-known work is 'One Ride With Yankee Papa 13', but his output covered all aspects of the war, from the civilian cost and the strain on the troops to the air campaign; and his images of war range from stark realism to highly artistic, even beautiful.

Burrows became a three-times winner of the Robert Capa Gold Medal, an award instituted in 1956 for 'superlative photography requiring exceptional courage and enterprise'.

LIFE

By LARRY BURROWS in VIETNAM

WITH A BRAVE CREW IN A DEADLY FIGHT

Vietcong zero in on
vulnerable U.S. copters

In a U.S. copter
in thick of fight—
a shouting
crew chief,
a dying pilot

APRIL 16 · 1965 · 35¢

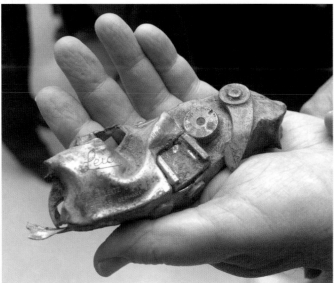

Halberstam's first important dispatch was filed on 2 January 1963 after US helicopters airlifted ARVN troops into Ap Bac in the Mekong Delta to engage enemy units. The operation turned into a fiasco in which five helicopters and three pilots were lost. Rumours of the debacle had reached the correspondents in Saigon in the afternoon. Neil Sheehan and a colleague hastily drove to the scene and spoke to Brigadier General York on the ground, only to be caught up in the last of the fighting. Halberstam and Peter Arnett drove to the helicopter base to interview the returning pilots, before flying in a helicopter over the scene of the engagement. They then went to the command post, where they found:

> … a brass-plated, white-helmeted honor guard paying tribute to General Cao, who had not bothered to visit the battlefield. General Harkins was also there, about to leave for Saigon, and we asked him what was happening. 'We've got them in a trap,' he said, 'and we're going to spring it in half an hour.' We looked at him, completely bewildered. The enemy was long gone, the Government troops were so completely disorganized that they would not even carry out their own dead, a province chief was shelling his own men – and a trap was about to be sprung? As on so many other occasions in Vietnam, we never knew whether Harkins believed what he was saying, or whether he felt that it should be said.[24]

Halberstam's focus on the helicopters caught the attention of an American public that had been fed on assertions that the war – in which, officially, the US had only observers and advisors – was going well. It made him very unpopular in official circles.

Neil Sheehan's dispatch for UPI, which was carried on 7 January by the *Washington Post*, also reflected personal experience of Ap Bac and it challenged 'Cable 1006':

> … United States military advisors charged today that Vietnamese infantrymen refused direct orders to advance during Wednesday's battle at Ap Bac and that an American Army captain was killed while out front pleading with them to attack. The Vietnamese commander of an armored unit also refused for more than an hour to go to the rescue of 11 American crewmen of downed helicopters and an infantry company pinned down by Communist small arms fire, they said. …

LET SLIP THE NEWSHOUNDS OF WAR

'How,' asked Halberstam rhetorically, 'do you add up thirty minor engagements each day, almost all of them in places you've never been to, and with no substantive information to cast light on the significance of the situation?'[23] The answer was not to sit in Saigon but, like the photographers, go to the front.

The Mekong Delta, in which the war would be won or lost and where ARVN's 7th Division was based, lay 40 miles (64 kilometres) from Saigon. Halberstam jumped with ARVN forces to spend time there, exploring the paddyfields, mud, canals and rivers. There were no bridges over the canals, just bamboo poles – off which this large man fell several times in one day, to the amusement of the South Vietnamese platoon. The sun burned his neck and the wet ground turned his feet white, because he had brought only a single pair of boots and had nothing dry to change into.

Lt. Col. John Paul Vann, senior U.S. advisor with the 7th Vietnamese Division, quickly rounded up 60 American advisors, cooks and communications men from his headquarters and sent them to the aid of the major. The Americans were under strict orders not to fire unless fired upon. They rescued the major and captured 17 guerrillas without suffering any casualties and then returned to their regular duties.[25]

Another major story that tested correspondents during 1963 came in June during a period of Buddhist-inspired anti-government demonstrations. Halberstam received an urgent tip-off and, taking a UPI man with him, ran to the scene. At first he saw just the orange-robed Buddhist monks; then he realized: 'Flames were coming from a human being; his body was slowly withering and shrivelling up, his head blackening and charring. ... I was too shocked to cry, too confused to take notes or ask questions, too bewildered even to think ... I had never felt such conflicting emotions. One part of me wanted to extinguish the fire, another warned me I had no right to interfere, and another told me that it was too late, another asked if I was a reporter or a human being.'[26]

Mal Browne of AP had captured the story on his Minolta and the image of 73-year-old Thich Quang Duc swept around the world, as the media-savvy Buddhists had anticipated.

The young American journalists in Saigon at this time, whose average age was around 27, had come to Vietnam with similar patriotic ideals, wanting and certainly expecting the USA to be on the winning side. They quickly decided that even with American help the Diem regime would not achieve a victory; it was both corrupt and lacking the support of its own people. The dislike and suspicion was mutual. Diem's sister-in-law, Madame Nhu, who had shocked many people by publicly alluding to the Buddhist burning as a 'barbeque', told Marguerite Higgins that, 'Halberstam should be barbequed I would personally be happy to supply the fluid and the match'.

Halberstam wrote a long article, printed in the *New York Times* on 15 August 1963, expressing his disquiet:

South Vietnam's military situation in the vital Mekong Delta has deteriorated in the past year, and informed sources are warning of ominous signs. Essentially, those military sources say, a communist Vietcong build-up is taking place in the Delta. They find it

opposite above: Waiting for the fatal helicopter lift in Laos: (left to right) Keisaburo Shimamoto, Henri Huet, Larry Burrows and Kent Potter.

opposite below: Identified by its serial number as that of Larry Burrows, the battered Leica was found in Laos in 1998 at the helicopter crash site.

above: In at the deep end: David Halberstam wading through a river.

above: Mal Browne's celebrated photograph of Buddhist monk Quang Duc burning himself to death in Saigon, 11 June 1963.

particularly disturbing because it has persisted since an American build up 20 months ago....

The political, administrative and military wrath of the USA fell on his head. The *New York Times* cabled that Secretary of State Dean Rusk had insisted that the war was going well. Halberstam replied that he stood by the story and was sorry Rusk did not believe him. Even some journalists attacked it, in particular Marguerite Higgins of the *New York Herald Tribune*, now married to a United States Air Force (USAF) general and a friend of the Kennedy family. During a short visit to Vietnam at the same time, she interviewed General Harkins and reported his robust rebuttal of Halberstam's assessment, before going further by accusing her Saigon colleagues of wanting to see the war lost just to prove their point.

Higgins had visited Vietnam on several occasions before that trip. She had been in the forward unit in 1954 when Capa was killed, and since then she had travelled widely, possibly to get over the death of her premature baby daughter. She returned for the last time in late 1965 and during her flight home she was taken ill with what proved to be leishmaniasis, caught from the bite of a sandfly. She died on 2 January 1966 and was buried at Arlington National Cemetery.

Halberstam, who had won a Pulitzer Prize for his 1963 reporting, turned to writing books after his return from Saigon. He was killed in a car crash in 2007.

THE DEDICATION OF DAVIS

After 8 March 1965, when President Johnson sent the first official combat troops, Vietnam grew into a massive international news story. Most correspondents, particularly the Americans, covered the conflict as an American war. There were comparatively few British journalists; not even a respected Sunday paper such as the *Observer* could afford to put its own man in the field. Photojournalist Don McCullin initially operated in Vietnam as a freelance for other print media, also using the opportunity to produce affordable material for the *Observer*. Australia's Neil Davis covered the war by following the ARVN.

At the age of 20, Davis had been shooting 35mm newsreels for the Tasmanian Film Unit – a valuable apprenticeship, because its small budget had taught him to use film economically. After three years with the Australian Broadcasting Corporation (ABC), Davis was hired by the forerunner of Visnews, and he spent the rest of his life covering conflict in Indonesia, Borneo, Laos, Cambodia and Vietnam. Visnews, with whom he stayed for 11 years, let him script his material after filming, which gave him greater autonomy than most of his rivals enjoyed. He rapidly became one of the best-loved and most respected cameramen of his day.

Davis worked alone in Vietnam, making his own sound recordings rather than taking a soundman with him. This left him free to concentrate on his work and his own safety, rather than having to be responsible for another human life. He ascribed his survival to 10 percent luck and 90 percent experience, and took the opposite view to those who believed that the odds on being killed increased with every risk taken. He cultivated the sixth sense that alerted him to real danger, and once saved the life of a fellow correspondent by warning him to travel in a Huey helicopter rather than in a slow and vulnerable Chinook.

Offered the choice of filming with the ARVN or the US Army, he chose the South Vietnamese, whose contribution was widely viewed as inferior to that of the US, even though Davis could recall only three weeks in ten years where the US forces took higher casualties. More significantly, he had empathy with the ordinary

people of Vietnam, disparagingly called 'gooks', 'dinks' or 'slopes' by most Americans and 'noggies' by the Australian troops. Unbeknown to his fellow reporters, he supported a London-based charity for Vietnamese orphans and helped to finance an operation in Germany on a small girl's withered leg. When the war was over, he and other correspondents publicized the plight of children fathered by American troops, and at the time of his death he was trying to arrange for his Cambodian driver to emigrate to Australia.

For a correspondent, life was harder with the ARVN than with the US troops. Davis could be in the field for perhaps three days, with no more food than he could carry and only tablets to purify the water. By contrast, US forces were resupplied by helicopter – even pizzas and ice-cream were flown in, despite the fact that aerial activity provided the enemy with information on US troop positions.

As well as rations, Davis carried his equipment: a hand-held, clockwork-powered Bell and Howell camera, sufficient 100-feet (30-metre) reels of 16mm film, each lasting for two minutes, and a small cassette recorder to capture the sound. Film and tape would be flown to London, where it was the task of the editor at the London office to synchronize the picture and the sound. Davis possessed a sound-on-film camera, but it was too big for combat patrols, during which mobility was vital.

The intensity of Davis's work is evident in this detailed description of one routine assignment, sent to Visnews after they queried his commitment:

ARVN Search VC cradle: Filmed 4–6 July 1969

The 'cradle' is the birthplace of the Viet Cong, an area in the Mekong Delta where few troops still venture. It is alive with booby traps. It is totally VC. It is difficult and dangerous to even reach there, and obviously dangerous when one is there. Our opposition have never covered this area. The filming was actually done 4–6 July, but I left Saigon city at a little after 0600 on 3 July. Could only get to Can Tho in the Delta that day, where I received an up-to-date briefing on the area I was interested in. Before dawn the next day I left again and finally arrived at My Tho, the ARVN 7th Division HQ. Finally there I was able to get a jeep to Ben Tre (by road and ferry) through VC-controlled territory. From Ben Tre I hitched a ride on a chopper to the field, where a reconnaissance company of the Vietnamese 7th

(bribe) the package aboard an aircraft before noon. I managed to get a shower by 1400. On 1–2 July I made at least six different calls (in person) to obtain full permission for this coverage. So besides 3–6 July out of Saigon (and two nights in the jungle), at least several hours were spent on this job on 1–2 July. We obtained exclusive footage….[27]

Like Chapelle, Davis learned to copy the soldiers. If they hit the ground, so did he, but facing death was natural for a man who, as a teenager, had caught polio and fought for his life in an iron lung. In July 1965, in Saigon, he had contracted the worst case of hepatitis the doctor had ever seen – so severe that Jack Langguth of the *New York Times* compared him to a giant corn-on-the-cob. The following year he slipped a disc and had to wear a steel-ribbed back brace for almost two years in order to carry his equipment. Then there were the numerous combat injuries, the worst of which occurred in 1974 in Cambodia when a mortar bomb exploded nearby. His tape-recorder saved him from being disembowelled, but one leg had multiple breaks and was ripped apart below the knee, with the main artery severed. A lieutenant gave him a pistol so the Khmer Rouge would not take him alive in the event of an evacuation proving impossible. A local dressing station carried out a transfusion using coconut milk, and after he was brought to the capital the Americans flew him to Bangkok. The leg was saved, but thereafter he had no feeling below the knee.

Division was operating. Reconnaissance companies in the Vietnam war mean those that precede a larger sweep in order to seek out and engage the enemy, then hold them off whilst the larger units can reinforce. I spent the night of 4 July in the field in Kien Hoa province – sometimes walking, sometimes catching a 'rest' in a swampy paddy field. From before dawn on 5 July till at least one hour after dark we operated non-stop through paddy fields and jungle, across streams, through VC villages – all studded with booby traps. I spent the night of 5 July the same as 4 July. On 6 July we started again (of course) before dawn, and I managed to get a chopper out at 0800. This was the first resupply since I landed – I carried food for the time spent in the jungle as always. By great good luck I managed to get three quick chopper rides and arrived back at Tan Son Nhut airport by 1000 – the fastest I can remember from the Delta. I did complete shot lists and scripting immediately and managed to 'buy'

Davis once tried to film a Viet Cong soldier trying to shoot him as he lay badly wounded; one of his friends, Joe Lee, had his leg blown off at the knee by a landmine but managed to film his dying soundman and then his own leg. Like Lee and many cameramen before and since, Davis felt there was little that should not be filmed. He kept the cameras rolling on his friend Nguyen Van Phuc, grenade-thrower for a South Vietnamese platoon, after he was hit and fell dying. On the other hand, when a group of soldiers offered to execute some prisoners so he could film it, he put his camera down. Don McCullin was another who refused to film executions for ethical reasons.

PUSHING THE BOUNDARIES

Indeed, a new and disturbing element was now creeping into warfare: a readiness on the part of some belligerents to carry out actions in front of the camera that they had previously preferred to commit out of sight. If the correspondent recorded the event in the defensible belief that everyone should understand what was happening, critics could claim he was encouraging the perpetrator

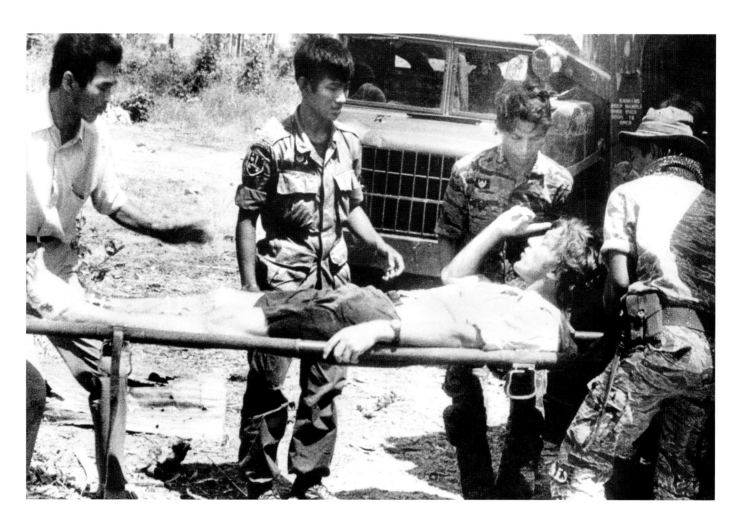

by giving publicity to a campaign of intimidation and terror. The message to the other side would be clear: stop fighting us, or this is what will happen to you. Photographs of the massacre of Vietnamese civilians by US soldiers at My Lai exist because a military photographer, Ronald Haeberle, accompanying Charlie Company took some officially and added more on his personal camera. The presence of the cameras was no deterrent.

Shared danger and horrors made for black humour among friends. Donald Wise of the *Daily Mirror*, an ex-commando, had left Vietnam to cover another story, and he returned to Saigon in June 1965 at the time when the new military government was publicly executing black marketeers and war profiteers, in front of the wives and children who screamed and wept as they tried to reach their menfolk over the barbed wire. He asked Davis to take him on a tour and brief him on the situation. Davis drove via the central market, where Wise spotted five posts surrounded by sandbags. Wise knew there had been executions of Viet Cong terrorists and war profiteers, but not that it was happening in groups: "'My God. Five executions!' Donald Wise is a sensitive man, who abhors vio-

opposite: A helmet makes a handy drinking vessel for Neil Davis during the Communists' Spring Offensive in the Mekong Delta in 1972.

above: Wounded by the mortar blast, Neil Davis is taken for emergency medical attention.

overleaf left: A US Soldier reading a copy of the *Pacific Stars and Stripes* on 21 March 1970. The headline refers to the infamous My Lai Massacre.

overleaf right: ITN reporter, Michael Nicholson's dog tags.

Palace, built in 1880 in French Colonial style. Larry Burrows put up at either, always requiring a twin-bedded room so he had a bed on which to lay out and clean his cameras and lenses. Don McCullin put up at the Hotel Royale, full of old furniture and one of the few hotels where the male journalists, who made up the overwhelming majority of the press corps, were forbidden to have women in their rooms. In the villa that they rented from a German diplomat, Halberstam and Horst Faas (AP) enjoyed a garden and servants, and they held dinner parties.

Saigon was full of cafés and good restaurants, as well as bars and shops full of tacky souvenirs appealing to the escalating number of American troops. Beggars and orphans were everywhere; pollution was increasing rapidly and the roads were becoming clogged by military traffic. Like the drugs trade, the sex industry flourished in the testosterone-rich miasma. Leslie wrote:

> *Sexuality was as palpable in Saigon as the late-evening artillery serenades audible from my window; it was the city's fuel, as much a propellant as the diesel oil whose fumes settled over the capital, mingling grittily with our sweat.... For Americans, Vietnam was a sexual testing ground, a place for acting out fantasies far less easily realized at home. … Dave Elliott theorized that if Vietnamese women hadn't been so attractive … the Americans would have quit the war years earlier. The only difference between me and everybody else was that I was ashamed of my obsession.*[29]

lence and discrimination, but covers his feelings with a rather black sense of humour. I said, "Not only that, Donald, five in one go the other morning." "Did you see it?" "See it? I filmed it, old fellow!" Wise was silent for a moment. "Christ," he said. "You have all the luck!"[28]

SAIGON – THE 'WARCO' CAPITAL OF EXCESS

The food was excellent, and opportunities for satiating appetites for sex and drugs were plentiful.

Jacques Leslie

The correspondents were based in Saigon, a vibrant city of tree-lined avenues, the look of which, in the early 1960s, still owed much to the French. Some 'warcos' rented apartments or villas, and those working for significant organizations might also have an office. Many stayed at hotels such as the Caravelle, opened in 1959 but bombed by the Viet Cong in 1964, or the Continental

Independent Television News's (ITN) reporter Michael Nicholson used to return to his hotel, throw his dirty clothes to the laundry boy and have 'a shower and a shave and then lobster and salade Niçoise at Ramuntchos, the French restaurant on Lam Son. Dolly girls, five dollars a body, another twenty later for the doctor, dance clubs providing the strangest partners whose jockstraps bulged from sequinned limb-clinging dresses, a night-time's whoring and drinking, business as usual. Saigon went dollar-crazy, competing for the GIs' time and money. When was there ever a war like it?'[30]

Smart streets quickly became red-light districts. Leslie reported on the city's first topless restaurant, earning himself a promise of death from the ex-GI who owned it if he dared to go there again. He interviewed one Madame Hieu, who ran a clinic offering eye, nose and breast enhancement, to give Vietnamese women a Western appearance, and hymen reconstruction, which allowed prostitutes to charge their clients more for sex with a virgin. The

Los Angeles Times practised its own cosmetic surgery on Leslie's relatively prosaic dispatch, turning it into something more titillating. Although he could write about Madame Hieu's seedy business, he found it impossible to write about another plastic surgery clinic, the Barsky Unit, which dealt with children suffering from burns and diseases that wasted their skin: '... it was so straightforwardly virtuous that it lacked an element of the drama I sought to portray. Suffering, not healing, was my obsession....'[31]

Among Saigon's other vices, the black market was well established. Davis allowed an Indian money changer to operate out of his office, but there were currency restrictions. On one occasion Davis was arrested at the airport while carrying undeclared US dollars, and beaten up by American guards. An influential American correspondent reported the matter to his ambassador, who promised that if attacks on correspondents continued he would reveal the names of all American officials who were dealing on the black market.

Official corruption, too, was widespread. Based on a tip-off and his own secret interviews, Jacques Leslie investigated the lucrative smuggling of scrap brass out of Vietnam, which implicated ARVN generals and the US Embassy's Property Disposal Branch. It was an unglamorous story, but one that involved large sums of money, and he was warned his life was in danger. The story appeared in three newspapers in 1972, but instead of sparking demands for an inquiry, it sank like a stone.

CONSCIENCE IN A BRUTAL WAR

I feel guilty about the people I photograph.... Why should I be celebrated at the cost of other people's suffering and lives?

Don McCullin in *Shaped By War*, 2010

Now 58 years old, Martha Gellhorn felt compelled to see the war for herself, and subsequently she concluded that Vietnam was the only war she had ever covered from the wrong side. Her three weeks gave her material for six primarily humanitarian articles, all written in September 1966.

... if any neutral harmless-looking observers went through the provincial hospitals and asked the people how they were wounded and who else in their family was killed, I believe they would learn that we, unintentionally, are killing and wounding three or four times more people than the Vietcong do, so we are told, on purpose.[32]

Gellhorn's message bursts through her rigid self-restraint. She desperately wanted the articles to be published in the USA, but only two were accepted. The series appeared in full in Britain, in the *Guardian* and cost her any hope of renewing her visa to return to Vietnam.

Despite the massive build-up of US troops from 1965, the NLF coordinated a series of attacks aimed at 100 towns, cities and military centres in South Vietnam on 31 January 1968. They hoped that this Tet Offensive, as it was called, would gain the support of the ordinary South Vietnamese and thus end the war quickly, but although it shook the US military, and dismayed the US public, which had been somewhat deceived as to the remaining capability of the communist forces, it did not achieve its aim. However, from a journalistic perspective, the upsurge of fighting in February brought the war onto the front pages, producing the first of two images from the war that both stunned the world and encapsulated the conflict's brutality.

Eddie Adams had served in the US Marines during the Korean War as an official photographer. Now a civilian photographer working for AP, he had first come to Vietnam in 1965 to cover the US Marines as they landed, and his sympathies lay with the ordinary soldier. Shortly before the Tet Offensive he returned for a third stint, and on 2 February was in Cholon, a Saigon suburb, when soldiers brought a man out of a building. General Nguyen Ngoc Loan approached the prisoner with his pistol raised, intending, or so Adams assumed, to interrogate him. Instead, he fired.

The roll of film was developed at AP's office and evaluated by the bureau's best-known photographer, Horst Faas, who was filling in as photo editor while recovering from injury. Adams's camera had caught a summary execution, with one image that was taken at the precise instant the general's bullet entered the prisoner's head. The images were transmitted the following day by the radiophone – essentially a fax machine – that AP shared with UPI, and the key photograph was shown around the world. Immediately, it became a powerful image for the increasing numbers of anti-war protestors. Film crews had also captured the execution, but the moving image lacked the stark, frozen quality of the still. Adams won that year's Pulitzer for on-the-spot photography, but the image always troubled him because it took no account of the context and it ruined Loan's post-war life.

The United States was losing the propaganda war, but the exposure of the most infamous event of the whole war – the massacre at My Lai of up to 504 civilians by US soldiers on 16 March 1968 – was not the work of any Saigon-based war correspondent but of journalist Seymour Hersh back in the USA.

THE DISTRESSING EXPERIENCES OF DON MCCULLIN

By the time Don McCullin returned for a second stint in Vietnam in 1968, the dyslexic boy from North London was a 32-year-old world-class photojournalist.

Forced to leave art school at 14 after his father's death, he began work in an animation studio before spending most of his National Service with the RAF in Kenya, developing photographs during the Mau Mau rising. He returned home as the proud possessor of a twin reflex Rolleicord camera, and took photographs of the neighbourhood gangsters. When a local murder focussed press attention on the subject of gangs, McCullin took some of his images to the *Observer*. Overnight he became a Fleet Street photographer. A trip to Berlin produced stunning images of the construction of the Berlin Wall. In Cyprus he learned to photograph death and grief with empathy and resilience – and won the World Press Photo Award for his work. He then went out to one of the most vicious war zones of the twentieth century, the Congo, to report on the mercenaries, before the brief visit to Vietnam in 1965. He always carried three cameras (one a reserve) and 30 rolls of film. The cameras were manual – motordrives ate up reels of film too quickly.

So many correspondents were covering the fighting in Khe Sanh in 1968 that McCullin, by now with the *Sunday Times*, opted for the old city of Hue, still held by the communists, and attached himself to D Company, 1st Battalion of the 5th US Marines Regiment. Prior to Vietnam he had thought that combat photography was something he would like to do every day, but:

Hue was to teach me a terrible lesson. The Americans had told me they were going in for a 24-hour operation. As the days turned into a week, and then a

second week, I suddenly became an old man. I had a beard. My eyes were sunken. I was sleeping under tables in tin shacks, on the floor, shivering with the cold at night. I never took off my clothes, and I kept my helmet close by me, and a flak jacket for a blanket.

A worse experience was about to happen. While on patrol with a US Marine a shell came over:

We both jumped into a foxhole by the wall … we were cowering under our helmets when the American said, 'Goddammit, there's an awful smell here.' I noticed that this hole was not firm underfoot. Even though we were in sand, it was too soft. I looked down and saw a row of fly buttons by my boots. We were both crouched on the stomach of a dead North Vietnamese soldier and our weight had caused the stomach to excrete….[33]

Two years later, McCullin was in Cambodia, at Prey Veng, and his life was saved by one of his Nikon cameras when it stopped a round from an AK-47. A few days later he was hit in the leg and groin. Uppermost in his mind was a determination not to be captured by the Khmer Rouge; unlike Neil Davis, he did not have a pistol with which to kill himself if necessary, so he 'crawled for about two hundred yards on my stomach, dragging my cameras. I thought that if the Khmers suddenly tried to move in, I was going to leave my cameras and make it into the river and swim. I passed a bridge … then some Cambodian soldiers dragged me into a house, stuck morphine into my leg and bandaged me. I was bleeding from the crotch, so I was concerned about that.' On the way to the hospital he steadied himself by taking photographs, including images of the man who had taken the brunt of the mortar shell:

He was dying. He sat up screaming. His abdomen was covered in blood and full of holes. He was making his last pleas and I took a picture. The truck was bumping its way back and by then it was dusk so I was having a job with the exposures. I vividly remember arriving at the hospital and the man's head was down the other side of the truck and all I could see were his bare feet next to my head, shaking with the bumps of the road, and I knew he was dead.[34]

In the interval before his return to Indo-China in 1972 he had been in Venezuela, Guatemala, East Pakistan, Northern Ireland (during

The Troubles) and Uganda in the time of Idi Amin's brutal dictatorship, when he was arrested and imprisoned along with other correspondents in a notorious prison.

DEALING WITH THE ENEMY

Jacques Leslie interviewed refugees from the Battle of Quang Tri who had spent three months living in bunkers, believing they would die, most probably as a result of American bombing raids. The *Los Angeles Times* published his dispatch on 23 July 1972, and in a letter to his family he wrote feelingly:

> I'm proudest of the story I did on refugees, wherein I
> managed to drop the fact that American bombing
> had killed 'at least 5000' civilians, and probably more
> than twice that number, in Quang Tri alone. I can't
> put this sort of thing in the lead, though, I don't think.
> Or my story on minibase operations in the delta,

THE TERROR OF WAR (1972)
NICK UT, 1951–

The second of the two defining images of the Vietnam War (alongside the one by Eddie Adams, see page 157) was taken by a young South Vietnamese who became known as Nick Ut.

Ut's story is remarkable. Born Huyn Cong Ut in Saigon in 1951, he had an elder brother who worked for AP but was killed in late 1965. A few weeks after that, the 14-year-old joined AP, and although he knew nothing about photography, in less than a year had demonstrated considerable talent.

On 8 June 1972, the day that made him a household name and a Pulitzer Prize winner, he had driven in an AP minibus out of Saigon along Route 1 towards the border with Cambodia. At the village of Trang Bang he joined other traffic as South Vietnamese units tried to dislodge North Vietnamese troops ahead. A South Vietnamese Skyraider aircraft made a bombing run, dropping napalm and white phosphorous bombs. Suddenly, the civilian casualties came screaming down the road, among them 9-year-old Phan Thi Kim Phuc, who had ripped off the napalm-soaked clothes that were burning her. Ut went into action with his Leica and Nikon cameras. Close by him, Le Phuc Dinh of NBC (National Broadcasting Company) and Chris Wain of ITN started filming. A photographic scoop then became a mercy mission as Ut got the girl and her family into the AP minibus and drove them to hospital in Saigon.

After the reels were developed, eight pictures were chosen for the radio photocast – but the image of Kim Phuc was initially rejected because full-frontal nudity was unacceptable. Horst Faas, head of AP's photo department in Saigon, arrived back at the office and argued vehemently over the telex with the New York head office. The importance of the story overrode all other considerations. The print was taken to Saigon's Post and Telegraph Exchange where AP had its transmitter and AM/FM converter. The telephone number was manually dialled, and 14 minutes later the image had been sent, line by line, to AP's Tokyo bureau. From there it went by land and

right: The Leica 35mm rangefinder was the most common piece of kit for war photographers in the 1950s and 60s, known for flexibility and reliability – essential qualities when the moment of capture was both fleeting and precious. In Vietnam, AP photographer Nick Ut had procured a Leica M2 with a 35mm Summicron lens, typically shooting on Kodak 400 ASA black-and-white film.

submarine wires to the New York and London offices who sent it on to media outlets around the world. Atmospherics sometimes hindered transmission, but Ut's picture was lucky. However, his integrity was questioned in high places, as he recalled: 'President Nixon once doubted the authenticity of my photograph when he saw it in the papers on June 12, 1972.... The picture for me and unquestionably for many others could not have been more real. The photo was as authentic as the Vietnam War itself. The horror of the Vietnam War recorded by me did not have to be fixed.'[63]

Chris Wain's colour film footage of the incident was widely shown, although colour television was not universally available and the majority of viewers were still watching television on monochrome sets. The still image is the better known, simply because it appeared in so many newspapers at the time and in almost every book about Vietnam.

Ut now lives in the USA and still works for AP. Kim Phuc underwent 17 operations at the Barsky Hospital on her third degree burns and still experiences pain. While training in pharmacology in Cuba she married a fellow Vietnamese student, and obtained asylum in Canada where the couple now live. She has remained in contact with Ut, and in 2010 she met Wain for the first time since he put down his camera and joined Ut in pouring drinking water over her skin to ease her pain.

above: The picture that shocked the world. Nine-year-old Phan Thi Kim Phuc, centre, running down a road near Trang Bang, Vietnam, after a napalm attack on her village. Also pictured is her older brother Phan Thanh Tam (aged 12; far left), younger brother Phan Thanh Phuoc (aged 5; background left, looking back), and younger cousins Ho Van Bo and Ho Thi Ting.

showing that things had deteriorated there as a result of the offensive. … For some reason I seem to care how this war is reported….[35]

Towards the end of his 14-month assignment Leslie was invited to interview a group of political detainees just released from prison on Con Son Island. All had atrophied limbs caused by years of incarceration in the notorious 'tiger cages', where conditions were too cramped to move, fed rotten food, beaten, forced to drink urine and sprayed with lime. He found it a strange but ultimately liberating experience:

What gave me pause was their serenity, their lack of distress at their deformation. They not only insisted on displaying their fleshless legs, but they were always smiling, as if pain had no purchase … somehow they'd faced death and come out the other side. Deprived of everything but their lives, they had learned how to take pleasure in simple existence: they were the first free men I'd ever met.[36]

On 27 January 1973 a ceasefire came into effect that allowed US troops to evacuate Vietnam during the spring. This gave Neil Davis the idea for the first of his two major scoops of the war, although contact with the 'enemy' was not condoned. With the help of a trustworthy double agent and a US major who promised to stop any bombing strikes on the area, he was able to film in a Viet Cong village. Hardly had he been escorted back to the safety of the main highway to Saigon than he was arrested by the South Vietnamese who had clearly been tipped off about his activities. A captain, whom he knew, ordered him to surrender his film, but considerately gave him a few minutes alone in which to secrete the *exposed* reels and cassette tapes inside his trousers. The officer then confiscated the unexposed film and Davis hastened to get his reels out by air. They were shown around the world.

Although Davis obtained the first footage, Jacques Leslie and Véronique Decoudu of Agence France Press claimed the honour of being the first correspondents to enter a Viet Cong village. After careful negotiations, they were escorted in, offered dinner and then invited to an entertainment:

… we heard the buzz that a crowd makes, and the buzz grew ever louder. We reached a clearing and saw a large crowd, in front of a stage with a Viet Cong flag for a backdrop, and flashbulbs went off in our faces, the old kind that newsmen in '30s and '40s

movies used, and the crowd applauded, the crowd cheered, several thousand people cheered. The reception both astonished and pleased me: most people, after all, pass their lives without receiving an ovation from a crowd of strangers, much less from people of a different civilization and language.[37]

Despite having had two hours sleep in 48 hours, Leslie wrote and filed his story as soon as he reached his apartment. It took up the front page of the *Los Angeles Times* on 1 February 1973 under the headline: '"We Are Friends." Viet Cong Tell Visiting U.S. Newsman.'

THE WAR ON THE SMALL SCREEN

The BBC's television news monopoly ended in 1955 with the founding of Independent Television News (ITN), of which former Spanish Civil War correspondent Geoffrey Cox became News Editor. Well funded and dynamic, the new service attracted first-rate talent.

One such was Michael Nicholson, who in August 1968 was reassuringly quoting the Geneva Convention to an Ibo POW captured by Nigerian government forces during another of Africa's vicious wars – moments before the young Ibo's captor cold-bloodedly executed him in front of the ITN camera. Leaving his cameraman and soundman in Port Harcourt to allay suspicion, Nicholson went to Lagos and smuggled the film onto a plane for London. Shortly after its transmission the three men were summoned to identify the killer, who was then executed in front of them. Initially, they had been ordered to film the firing squad at work so that they could finish what they had started. They refused, and the BBC crew shot the footage – at the last moment asking for a slight delay while a flat battery was changed. The whole business left Nicholson feeling guilty that a man had been killed because of a report he had made.

A year later, Nicholson was in Vietnam:

[and] despite the jetlag, full of enthusiasm, you know. This was my first major foreign war, and to be sent to Vietnam by your company was something of a privilege; it was something everybody wanted. And I stood on the roof of the Caravelle hotel, and that morning there had been some 122 mm rockets, and they had caused a bit of damage in the centre of Saigon, and as I was describing these rockets and what they did, suddenly we heard this SWOOSH

SWOOSH and they came over our heads. [We] didn't see them of course because they travel so fast, but we heard them and we felt them.... And that was my first introduction to Vietnam, but not my last meeting with 122 mm rockets.[38]

Television crews were highly active in Vietnam, not just providing news broadcasts but also making influential, often ground-breaking documentaries. John Laurence spent five years in Vietnam for CBS and in 1970 he produced an Emmy Award-winning television documentary entitled 'The World of Charlie Company', about a group of US Army 'grunts', the young men conscripted into the US Army to serve in Vietnam for 12 months. He and his crew went with them on their patrols, filming their lives, the harsh conditions and, most significantly, their dissent. Ordered to leave an area in readiness for a US air strike, the 'grunts' refused to climb into their

helicopters and the air attack had to be called off so that they did not fall victim to 'friendly fire'.

Two months later, in September, another award-winning documentary on the same subject was aired, this time on British television and made by a young Australian journalist at the start of his vocation. 'The Quiet Mutiny' was the first of many documentaries by the *Daily Mirror's* correspondent, John Pilger. Reporting from Camp Snuffy, near the border with Cambodia, he interviewed young grunts with long hair and love-beads who were willing to speak on camera about their ignorance of why they were in Vietnam, their resentment against the 'lifers' – regular soldiers – who were leaving them to bear the brunt of the fighting, and their reluctance to kill people they had nothing against. In Saigon, Pilger went to the US Army's discredited press briefing, noting that it was very sparsely attended by the correspondents, and asked the press officer a series of statistical questions relevant to his documentary, only one of which was answered: the number of US troops serving in the country at that time.

WAITING FOR THE END

After a year of top-secret bombing missions, the US had controversially invaded neutral Cambodia in 1970, which destabilized the country and led to its fall to the Khmer Rouge on 17 April 1975. Most of the correspondents left before then. Outside the capital of Phnom Penh, Cambodia had long been a dangerous place for journalists. Sean Flynn, son of the Hollywood actor Errol Flynn, and Dana Stone had been captured in 1970 and were believed to have been brutally murdered, possibly the following year. Françoise Demulder (AP), Ennio Iacobucci (freelance) and Sydney Schanberg were among a tiny handful who covered the entry of the Khmer Rouge and were afterwards deported.

Philip Caputo returned to Vietnam just before Saigon fell. His first tour had taken place in 1965–66 when he was a lieutenant in the US Marines and had sent men off to kill. Now he was back as the military correspondent of the *Chicago Tribune*:

[his driver Hoang] pulled up in front of the Continental Palace, oozing mildewed colonial splendor. The

ground floor, an expansive terrace with arches opened to the street, was known as the Continental Shelf. It had always been the social center for Saigon's community of journalists, diplomats, and double, triple, and quadruple agents, but the journalists claimed it exclusively on that day. There appeared to be hundreds of them, boisterously slaking their thirsts with tart citron pressés, keeping off the malaria with gin and tonics, and creating, as journalists always do en masse, an atmosphere of cheap excitement ... it was like a class reunion. Every newsman who had spent more than a week in Vietnam had returned. 'All come for end,' Hoang said to me with his cheerful smile.[39]

When Saigon fell to the North Vietnamese communists 12 days later (after Phnom Penh), Brian Barron of the BBC ignored orders to evacuate. He was at a radio station in Saigon and talking to London when the building trembled and plaster came down as defecting aircraft attacked the nearby presidential palace. Anxious for their man's safety, the BBC immediately ordered him to get on the first available helicopter out. He ignored the command: he had no intention of missing such a vital story – particularly given that his rivals were in place.

Michael Nicholson reported from the last front line. With his crew, he had covered the war for ITN alone; suddenly Sandy Gall was sent to share the work, so the pair alternated between reporting the fighting and covering the political stories. The two men had lunch together – lobster, strawberries and white wine – and Nicholson drove off on what should have been his 'political' assignment. Instead, he ran into trouble. 'Today,' he wrote in his diary, 'my French crew, Jacques Chaudensen, Lucien Botras and I filmed the last fighting of the war, the very last, and we had it to ourselves. There must be around thirty international television crews here in Saigon but for some reason no one else turned up. Perhaps they have already packed, ready to go, their fighting done. It was on New Port Bridge, spanning the Saigon river on Highway One, the last the communist army have to cross to enter Saigon. A lot of men on both sides of it died today, but I am glad not to have missed it, now it is over. That is an epitaph and it is Vietnam's.'[40]

The Central Intelligence Agency (CIA) advised correspondents of the evacuation arrangements. A coded message would be given over US forces' radio: 'The temperature in Saigon is rising to 112 degrees.' After that, a record of Bing Crosby singing 'White Christmas' would be played, and everyone must walk nonchalantly to their assembly point and avoid looking as though they were departing.

opposite: Although war correspondents were not supposed to carry arms, more than a handful did in both Korea and Vietnam, including Sean Flynn.

above: Caught in the fighting on Newport Bridge, a television crew races to safety.

The ITN crew drove to the US Embassy as the last helicopters were evacuating the Western diplomats and civilians. The area was packed with desperate Vietnamese looking for a way out:

> But the people clawing the gates were those who had believed in the Americans, who had worked with the Americans and fought for the Americans... They began to climb the walls to get in and we did the same. We fought and clawed our way toward the hands of the marines who were hauling only Westerners over the top. And we did fight and we did claw. I was not proud of what I did that day. No one who was there can feel anything but shame at what they did and what they allowed to happen to others around them. Marines lined the top of the wall by the back gate on Hong Thap Tu, pulling us all up and booting down the rest. They lunged with their bayonets at young girls, knocked children unconscious with their rifle-butts, stamped with their boots and broke the fingers of those who reached the top. But they pulled us up.[41]

Evacuated from Phnom Penh by helicopter, Neil Davis was not going to miss the fall of Saigon either, and he drove through a back gate into the grounds of the presidential palace and waited for the communist tanks to arrive. His camera caught the first tank break-ing down the front gates and a soldier jumping off with a Viet Cong flag. As he was filming, 'out of my left eye – the one not to the camera – I could see a very determined communist soldier racing straight towards me and calling out something. Because of the sound of the tank, I couldn't hear what he was saying, but I could imagine what he was telling me to do.' Davis decided to keep the camera going, and he filmed until the communist reached him. 'Then I did stop, and put my hands up, still holding my fifteen-pound [7-kilogram] sound camera in my hand, so I couldn't keep my hands up for very long. As quickly as I could, I got off my Viet-namese welcoming speech, which was, "Welcome to Saigon, comrade. I've been waiting for you!"'[42]

Davis continued to report from the Far East. In 1985 he was killed in a Bangkok street during a failed coup attempt, and was mourned by the entire press corps.

In recent years, the idea of going to a country such as Vietnam to 'find oneself' has become a something of a tired cliché, but during the course of the war many correspondents did take away far more than their memories and their scars. Leslie had arrived in Vietnam lacking in confidence, wondering if he even had the courage to be a war correspondent. Fourteen months later he left believing that he had become a professional journalist who had shown some insights and displayed a modicum of courage when it was needed. Perhaps more important, he came to understand the meaning of his encounter with the prisoners from the 'tiger cages', and it helped him to overcome his own demons.

However, for one correspondent the demons proved too strong. Ennio Iacobucci had been a shoeshine boy and male prostitute in Rome until he was taken up by Derek Wilson of the BBC, who, Pygmalion-like, turned the illiterate youth into a photographer – but at a heavy price. Wilson was homosexual and Iacobucci was not, but he consented to the relationship to escape his poverty and obscurity. From the Six-Day War in the Middle East, he went with Wilson to Vietnam and began to make a name for himself. After conquering his initial terror of coming under fire, he produced raw images that were widely used and he married a Vietnamese girl. Vietnam gave him everything he craved: respect, love and security – even a Pulitzer nomination in 1975. But the end of the war marked the end of his marriage and he returned to Rome where, all but unknown, and unable to establish himself, he hanged himself two years later.

There will never be another war like Vietnam, in as much as there will never be another war that allowed journalists so much freedom to report it. Every country, every government, every military in the world learnt from Vietnam that if you give journalists, especially cameramen, free access to what you're doing, they'll be a greater enemy than the enemy you are fighting. It is suicidal to allow journalists total freedom, not because they are going to give away secrets to the enemy, they don't know secrets to give away, but what they will do is report, not often fairly, and not often without prejudice, what they see, and that can be, as you know, wholly detrimental to the military operation.

… The casualty figures, like the body bags, were well hidden by the Americans. I think if the American public had been aware of American casualties earlier on in the war, the war would have been concluded much earlier. … But every government from then on realized that to allow the press access, uncontrolled access, to what is going on, is the quickest way to lose your war. Maggie Thatcher learnt that in the Falklands, the Israelis eventually learnt that in the Middle East, and every government since, including the Americans, who are now extremely strict about what they allow the press to see and say. So that was the last free war for the communicator.[43]

opposite: Evacuees boarding an Air America helicopter as Saigon falls to the Communists.

above: Braving the barbed wire and armed US soldiers, desperate people try to reach evacuation helicopters inside the US embassy in Saigon.

War in the South Atlantic 1982

You bastards are the lowest priority rating – at the bottom of the list, and as long as I'm here, that's where you'll remain!

An officer of HMS *Hermes* to Michael Nicholson,
quoted in *A Measure of Danger*, 1992

A CRUISE TO NOWHERE

As the Royal Navy task force assembled over the weekend of 3/4 April a group of irritated correspondents was breakfasting in the wardroom of HMS *Nelson*, the main shore base at Portsmouth. Some were complaining vociferously about the ships to which they had been allocated, feeling that, if Britain was going to war to retake the Falkland Islands, their rightful place was aboard the flagship, the aircraft carrier HMS *Hermes*. At a nearby table, the Fleet Air Arm (FAA) commander responsible for those allocations, as duty officer for the Third Flotilla, prudently kept his head down and concentrated on his own breakfast.

Everything had happened within a couple of days of Argentina's invasion of the islands (on 2 April 1982) to which they claimed sovereignty. ITN's Michael Nicholson's holiday was cut short by a message telling him to phone London. Half an hour later he was being driven to a private airfield to catch a flight to the south coast of England. Next day he was on *Hermes*, along with the BBC's correspondent Brian Hanrahan, cameraman Bernard Hesketh and soundman John Jockell, plus ITN's engineer Peter Heaps, and two from the Press Association (PA): Peter Archer and photographer Martin Cleaver. A quintet of print journalists, including A.J. McIlroy of the *Daily Telegraph* and Tony Snow of the *Sun* embarked on the second carrier, HMS *Invincible*. A further three joined other ships.

From Ulster's Troubles, via the well-trodden path of Indo-China, culminating in the fall of Saigon, and the Arab–Israeli wars, Max Hastings was working on another military history book, and thinking: firstly, that the idea of going to war over the Falklands was ridiculous; secondly, that at 36 he was too old to be reporting another conflict; thirdly, that he was desperate to go. Robert Fox of

BBC News was planning his trip to study local radio in Newfoundland and thinking that those who went on the ships would merely be bored. Few people seriously expected a war to be fought over a distant colony of a mere 1,800 people.

Prime Minister Margaret Thatcher had insisted, against the wishes of the military, that correspondents accompany the task force. The war in Vietnam had ended only seven years earlier, and there were still those who considered the media, particularly television, to be responsible for the US defeat. However, quarantining a small number of correspondents on the ships, from where they had no access to the outside world except via Royal Navy-controlled communications, seemed a reasonable compromise – and one that would satisfy the public and ensure the right story was told, even if the right story was not necessarily the true one. Admiral Woodward, already with more than enough responsibility on his shoulders and no experience of handling journalists, was ordered to cooperate with the press but not to give it any information.

Initially, only 17 press representatives were accredited, but when the P&O liner *Canberra* was requisitioned, a further 13 places became available, making room for Fox and Hastings, the latter with a contract from the *Evening Standard*. There were no representatives of the foreign press, not even those from close allies. When CBS intimated they would charter a ship they were informed that the vessel would be sunk.

If the correspondents on *Canberra* expected a luxury cruise they were disappointed. The ship had been stripped of excess comforts, including its catering team, and only a reassessment of the effect on public relations saw the press switched from depressing berths in the liner's bowels to passenger accommodation. This gave them an advantage in comfort over the group on *Hermes*, who were too close to the action: right beneath the flight deck from which the Sea Harriers took off and landed on, their engines screaming; where the helicopter rotors thrashed; and on which the Royal Marines trained. Communications on *Canberra* were an improvement, too, because while the carriers preserved radio silence, the merchant ship's telephone link was operational.

Quickly the aircraft carrier correspondents discovered that it was spasmodically possible to hitch a lift in a helicopter over to the nearest support ships equipped with MARISAT/IMARSAT, which was a godsend to the TV correspondents in particular, because it at least allowed their voices to be heard even if they had no way of transmitting the accompanying footage. Whereas radio messages could be intercepted, satellite transmissions could not, because

they were beamed up to a satellite and down to the recipient, allowing ships to maintain communications.

The helicopter trip was not for the faint-hearted: in rough conditions, journalists were winched down onto a deck that could be pitching and rolling, and the return schedule was so haphazard that Hanrahan invariably took his toothbrush. If the weather was too bad, or the ship out of helicopter range, they were marooned, sometimes for days, during which they fretted over what great story they were missing, and the crews got used to running a hostel. Later in the war, when Commander Tim Gedge went aboard LSL[44] *Sir Bedivere*: 'The RFA [Royal Fleet Auxiliary] Radio Officer onboard said to me that they had been inundated with press who had used every excuse to get aboard in order to use this scarce [telephone] facility.'[45]

ITN's engineer Peter Heaps left *Hermes* at Ascension Island when it became clear there was little for him to do. The original intention had been for him cover the entire operation and send back live or at least semi-live television pictures, but doubtless to the relief of the Ministry of Defence (MOD), this proved impractical. *Hermes* was equipped with the new SCOT (Satellite Communications Terminal) technology, but to send back even black-and-white footage, without any sound, would have required the entire bandwidth available for the fleet's communications.

The long voyage gave correspondents an unparalleled opportunity to get to know some of the units, and as honorary officers they had entrée to the wardroom. On *Invincible* A.J. McIlroy and John Witherow (*Daily Telegraph*) established a rapport with 'Sharkey' Ward, commanding officer (CO) of 801 Naval Air Squadron (NAS), but a suggestion from the *Sun*'s Tony Snow that the Sea Harriers' missiles be decorated with insulting messages for the Argentinians – amusing after a few beers – was rejected. Hanrahan quickly found the way to an officer's heart, and even before *Hermes* sailed he had clambered onto the counter of the wardroom bar, introduced himself and his team, hoped that they would learn to trust the press, and, crucially, offered to buy a round of beer. Hastings, a failed paratroop cadet, struck up good relations with the officers of the Commando Brigade and the Parachute Regiment. This would serve them all well, and by the end of the war there was more amity between the press and the units to which they attached themselves than within a press corps that had become fractious, frustrated and resentful.

Only one journalist asked to return home. Martin Lowe of the *Wolverhampton Express and Star*, the one representative of the

provincial press, told his astounded colleagues he had no wish to go to war, and he flew back from Ascension Island. He was replaced by Derek Hudson of the *Yorkshire Post*, who shared cabin A86 with David Norris of the *Daily Telegraph*. The rest worried that the imminence of war would now bring an avalanche of seasoned reporters, from John Pilger to Don McCullin.

THE REALITY OF WAR

From the military point of view, the lives of soldiers are more important than facts or the media's clamour for their right of free speech. The troops must endure shells, missiles and bullets, while reporters face only the wrath of their editors.

Hugh McManners in the Independent, 2003

After regrouping and further provisioning at Ascension Island, the main task force sailed on 17 April, and on 20 April Argentina rejected a peace proposal. The mood on the ships grew grimmer – something that could not be reported. All that the press had had

to record was continual training and life on board. The emergency drills, which always included the correspondents, became more serious. Anti-flash gear had to be worn at action stations and an order went out on *Hermes* that everyone had to be clean-shaven to ensure their gas masks fitted correctly. Correspondents were trained in first aid and survival ashore – from the vitamin contents of seals' eyes to the theory of turning a dead cow into an emergency shelter in the Antarctic winter. McIlroy tried to send a cable to New York to close his US bank account, but he was not allowed to do so in case this was a coded message to his paper to say the invasion was starting.

If relations with officers at the sharp end were good, those with the higher command were less so. Press conferences with Admiral Woodward had produced headlines and articles highly displeasing to the government and MOD. The first briefing was judged too optimistic; when Woodward duly provided a more downbeat assessment of the conflict, they accused him of negativity. Michael Nicholson caught the fallout and was nearly sent packing after broadcasting his report on an attack by frigates on Argentin-

ian emplacements. He had ended with a throwaway line, to the effect that such success might lead to a second attack. Without waiting to see the transcript that proved Nicholson had said no more than had been approved, Admiral Woodward accepted the judgement of the commander-in-chief back at Northwood, and he announced to the whole ship that Nicholson was to go. When the exonerating transcript duly arrived, no such action was taken, but no apology, public or private, was made.

The worst problems were the inconsistency of censorship and the lack of trust aboard *Hermes*. The press was told to hold back a story, only to discover that the MOD had released the details in London. Material passed as suitable for reporting on one ship was classed as secret on another. A frustrated Nicholson wrote later:

> *… we were treated by some as if we had found a secret way to transmit information home, or even, I suspect, to Buenos Aires. One evening in the wardroom, a senior air control officer, three gins the worse, loudly accused us of 'giving too much away',*

previous page: Prime Minister Margaret Thatcher is interviewed by the BBC's 'Panorama' programme in Downing Street about the Falklands War

opposite: British soldiers are filmed boarding a troop ship for the ITN production 'The Falklands War'.

above: TV crew wearing anti-flash protection while accompanying the Task Force.

of being 'as good as Argentinian intelligence agents'. Our cameraman, Bernard Hesketh, a genial man, exploded. White and quivering with rage, he pulled up a trouser leg to show a long and vivid scar. 'This,' he said, 'I got in the last war fighting for my king and country. Don't you ever dare call me a spy again!'[46]

What they did not know at the time was the amount of misinformation they were being fed. The classic example is the one that affected the reporting by both Hanrahan and Nicholson of the RAF bombing of the runway at Port Stanley. Unskilled in the interpretation of reconnaissance photographs, they had to accept in good faith what they were told, and duly reported that the runway was completely out of action. It was not.

Some censorship was reasonable, the more so when accompanied by explanations. The Argentinians would have given much to know that many of their bombs had failed to explode. In the event, the MOD gave out that information and the Argentinians began using a different type of bomb, one of which exploded by the hospital at Ajax Bay, East Falkland, killing ten men. Fox, the BBC man on the spot, was the target of the angry leader of the RAF's bomb disposal team, but he was exonerated by the executive surgeon of the hospital who pointed out that Fox had been '"at the Goose Green punch-up. It's probably one of those civil servants again, leaking it to the defence correspondents, just to show they're in on the act and have got balls as big as aircraft tyres." An explanation which the Flight Lieutenant seemed disposed to accept.'[47]

A particular mention of fog was forbidden, because the only fog in the area at that time was that under which the task force lay. It was also known aboard ship that soldiers from the SAS were operating on the islands a month before the main landings, but no mention was to be made of it. A fourth example of justified censorship gave rise to the most famous quote of the war.

On 1 May the Harrier squadrons made their first offensive sorties, attacking Goose Green and the airfield at Stanley. Watching 800

NAS landing on, Hanrahan asked Woodward if he could say how many aircraft had taken part in the sortie. Woodward suggested he say only that they had all returned safely. When it was his turn to broadcast that night (by agreement with Nicholson he always broadcast first because BBC news went out an hour ahead of ITN), Hanrahan reported first the Vulcan raid, then the take off and return of the Sea Harriers: '... the pilots said there had been smoke and dust everywhere, punctuated by the flash of explosions. They faced a barrage of return fire, heavy but apparently ineffective. I'm not allowed to say how many planes joined the raid, but I *counted them all out, and I counted them all back*. Their pilots were all unhurt, cheerful and jubilant, giving thumbs-up signs. One plane had a single bullet hole through the tail; it's already been repaired....'[48] The phrase slipped effortlessly into common usage.

Jubilation on the ships gave way to solemnity with the torpedoing of the Argentinian cruiser, *General Belgrano*, on 2 May, and the loss of HMS *Sheffield* to an Exocet missile the following day. Hesketh filmed the survivors coming aboard *Hermes*; some of the flag-

opposite: ITN's Michael Nicholson on the way to the Falklands Islands aboard HMS *Hermes*.

above: HMS *Sheffield* after being struck by an AM.39 Exocet missile on 4 May 1982.

being defused. He processed and printed the photographs and sent them back using a Muirhead drum transmitter, similar to that used for Nick Ut's famous Vietnam picture (see page 159). But instead of the dial-up connection available in Saigon, Cleaver could use Stromness's MARISAT to transmit the image to London. The image was shot in black and white because that 'was the only film stock which I stood a chance of processing in the field and at the time was first priority. Colour was very much a second choice and of a much lower priority, something to be shot when time allowed'.[49]

YOMPING AND HITCHING

Back on the islands, the shipboard fraternization between units and correspondents had led to their acceptance by the men they were accompanying. Attached to the 2nd Battalion of the Parachute Regiment (2 Para) for the landings, Robert Fox and David Norris got to know their commanding officer Lieutenant Colonel H. Jones during the two weeks preceding his death and were with him on the P&O ferry *Norland* as she crept into San Carlos Water: 'We were looking through night-vision telescopes to see if there were enemy lights on the foreland. "How do you think the boys will stand up to it?" we asked. "I don't know how they'll face being strafed and bombed from the air out in the open" – sharing his innermost worries without a hope of getting any expert advice from us.'

Just before the attack on Goose Green, where Jones won his posthumous VC:

ship's younger officers called it ghoulish. The news of *Sheffield's* loss, like that of two Sea Harriers and a Sea King was withheld, and when it was released, it was announced by the MOD.

INTO 'BOMB ALLEY'

As D-Day approached, the correspondents were assigned to their units. Brian Hanrahan nearly missed it because his ID showed a bearded man, not the forcibly clean-shaven reality.

On 21 May Nicholson went into San Carlos Water – known as 'bomb alley' – aboard the assault vessel HMS *Fearless*, beneath a hail of bombs, one of which hit HMS *Ardent*. On the 24th, Martin Cleaver was aboard the store ship RFA *Stromness*, where he had rigged up a darkroom and from where it was now possible to transmit images. Previously he had been sending his unprocessed reels home. From *Stromness* he took the most famous photograph of the war: HMS *Antelope* exploding when a bomb went off while

... he turned to me and said, 'Where do you want to go, Robert? You can come with us or stay behind with the guns, here.' I said I had never been in a thing like this before but wanted to go with the main battle. He replied: 'Neither have I been in a thing like this, and I don't know how I will get on either.' The battle of Goose Green was heroic by any standards, because it was the courage of the men and almost nothing else which won the day. The thing I remember most was their companionship, helping the wounded, sorting out the dead, trying to round up prisoners. I cannot pretend these men are angels. In Port Stanley, when the tension of battle was over, the amount of 'proffing'[50] by British troops was considerable, some understandable, some not.... My perspective as a reporter, I know, was constricted by the enforced, but welcome, companionship of the field, the cold and the miles of marching across peat

bog, the occasional shelling and bombing, and the difficulties of communicating with an audience 8000 miles away the colour and circumstances of the rat-pack[51] war.[52]

Nicholson found Fox after the Battle of Goose Green in a dreadful state of shell-shock and cold, and wanted to interview him for ITN. Hesketh refused to film it because he and Fox were BBC employees and needed Hanrahan to make it 'fair'.

In theory, the Falklands should have been a television war. That there is very little footage of the land campaign was less down to censorship than to simple logistics and opportunity. Much of the fighting took place at night and was therefore unfilmable, and the new generation of television equipment was far too heavy to be carried around at the pace at which the troops moved when going into action, or withdrawing from it. Hesketh was using a modern ENG (Electronic News Gathering) system that was more cumbersome and heavier than the cine equipment it was beginning to replace, because it required the operator to carry a heavy cassette tape recorder as well as a camera. Even the stills photographers were weighed down with equipment in addition to the heavy packs that everyone carried. Film had to be sent back by mailbag and took a minimum of three weeks, so most viewers' memories of the war as seen on TV were of Hanrahan and Nicholson's voices set against old stock footage or simple stills, with all the important news breaking via the monotone voice of the MOD spokesman. Very little footage was seen until after the war was over.

There had been an imperative for the television men to stay close to a satellite phone in order to provide the sometimes hourly news fixes. That worked well enough until the landings. From one of the destroyers, Hanrahan had provided a vivid account of the night-time destruction of the Argentinian base at Pebble Island in mid-May:

The bulk of the island, black against a luminous sky, was suddenly lit up by star shells and red tracer lines from the sea; the ships threw out orange flame and covering fire: first, more star shells to show the attacking force the ground, then salvo after salvo of high explosive, each whining away into the darkness to land on the defenders, twenty at a time, one shell every two seconds – a tempo designed to terrify as much as destroy. The barrage was controlled by a Royal Artillery spotter ashore on an overlooking hillside. With his calm voice coming across the radio

opposite above: Martin Cleaver catches the violence of the explosion that destroyed HMS *Antelope* in San Carlos Water.

opposite below: Burial of the dead of 2nd Battalion, the Parachute Regiment, after the Battle for Goose Green, 28 May 1982.

above: BBC cameraman Bernard Hesketh in action.

above: Sea King helicopters were sent to rescue survivors from HMS *Coventry*. The upturned hull of the Type 42 destroyer is just visible in the sunset.

opposite: Paul Haley, official photographer for the British Army *Soldier* magazine, follows the troops.

the ship steadily moved its aim closer to the Argentinian positions.[53]

However, the action had now shifted almost entirely to the land with the two-pronged march on Port Stanley from the north, but the need to be close to the satellite phone precluded tramping for days around the island. Given the length of time that the films were taking to get home, Nicholson turned to radio-style reporting, buying a tape recorder for £20 and a tin of toffee from a rating, and travelling light, hitching lifts between units by helicopter. It proved more rewarding than speaking 'captions' to film footage that would not be seen for weeks.

On 9 June Nicholson was in a shed above Fitzroy with a group of gunners when an explosion blew off the roof. Some 400 yards (360 metres) away the landing ship HMS *Sir Galahad*, packed with soldiers and ammunition, was on fire and exploding after an Argentinian air strike. Royal Navy helicopters went into the thick clouds of smoke to winch people up, and they used the down-draught of their rotors to blow men in life rafts clear of the oil burning on the sea and towards the beach. Soldiers ran into the sea from their trenches to pull the wounded to shore. 'It was a day of tragedy, but I vouch it was a day of extraordinary heroism and selflessness by every man who witnessed it.'[54]

Derek Hudson went ashore at San Carlos with the 3rd Battalion of the Parachute Regiment (3 Para) carrying his backpack, 200 rounds of ammunition, two mortar bombs and with his portable typewriter hanging from his neck. The priority for him and his press colleagues Robert McGowan and Jeremy Hands was to dig a slit trench as an air-raid shelter, and later, while 3 Para and 45 Commando, Royal Marines yomped[55] for hours to Teal Inlet, the correspondents thumbed a lift on a passing helicopter and watched the guns set up on Estancia Mountain.

Hitching lifts in this way was not without its own hazards. The *Glasgow Herald*'s Ian Bruce hurled himself at a helicopter that was on the point of taking off, cracked his head on a machine gun mount and had to be pulled in unconscious. This incident would be remembered some years later by the helicopter's loadmaster, to Bruce's advantage (see page 206).

In the years after 1945, many war correspondents could claim some form of military experience, either of wartime combat or peacetime National Service. By 1982 that had changed, and yet few of the Falklands journalists were unwilling to follow their units into battle. Some preferred to do more than *follow*. McIlroy and Snow were two of the *'Invincible Five'* who went ashore without having been issued with Arctic clothing and who were sent back to the ships. After a week on an ammunition ship in 'bomb alley' they returned to the land and joined the 2nd Battalion, Scots Guards with whom they went through the hard-fought Battle of Tumbledown, surprising Lieutenant Colonel Scott by materializing as he finally reached the top of the mountain. They reminded him he had given them permission to go with them; he agreed, but said he had not expected them to be at the front.

On land, every correspondent had to be self-sufficient in the bitter cold and the snow. There was no communal dining: each man had to set up his own camp and cook on the small stove he carried. Bolt-holes and trenches had to be dug, and this, plus travelling, left little time for sitting down to write a dispatch. The cold was such that going to the toilet was an experience to be dreaded.

The second problem was finding the time to work amidst all the business of surviving and trying to move around on terrain with no roads and the continuous threat, often realized, of air attack.

Danger did not come only from the enemy. In company with an officer and a non-commissioned officer (NCO), Hudson walked into a blast of fury from two paras brandishing machine guns; they had strayed off the path and almost been mistaken for Argentinians. The *Guardian*'s Gareth Parry had a similar experience after leaving his trench one night and being confronted by the click of a bolt and a demand for the password, of which he apologetically had to admit ignorance.

After a helicopter lift back to *Fearless* to file his story, a bath and half a bottle of wine, Hudson was back on land, at brigade HQ on Mount Kent when the paras took Mount Longdon at the cost of 60 casual-

above: The image of Max Hastings that became synonymous with his Falklands reporting.

ties, 23 of them killed. HQ was attacked by Argentinian aircraft, sending journalists and soldiers diving for cover into the muddy slit trenches or whatever refuge came first. Hands and McGowan recalled that, between the bombing runs, Hudson politely requested permission to come into the trench. He maintained it was a joke, and he had every intention of jumping in. It broke the tension of the moment around the trenches, but as the HQ was shifting further up the snow-covered slope, news came over the radio that the Argentinians in Port Stanley were surrendering.

Before *Canberra* had left Ascension Island, Max Hastings had obtained reassurance that his life insurance had been increased to £200,000, a sum for which he was prepared to take some risks, and, while sea conditions allowed, he spent the early mornings running round the deck to improve his fitness. On 19 May he cross-decked to *Fearless*; at dawn on the 21st he went ashore with 40 Commando, Royal Marines, size 14 boots and a typewriter.

At San Carlos he had his first experience of digging a trench, and watched as the previous night's ceremony of raising the Union Jack was repeated for the benefit of the official Royal Marine photographer:

> Then Pete [Holgate] did me one of the biggest favours of my life. He took a photograph of a British correspondent, tired and still blackened with camouflage cream, draped in web equipment, helmet, cameras and binoculars, standing stick in hand on the Falkland Islands. That image was transmitted to London along with the shot of the flag-raising. It helped to make me quite famous for five minutes, and was reproduced again and again in a host of newspapers over the weeks that followed. I have cherished it ever since, of course, because it represents the war correspondent as he would like to see himself. It was a melodramatic moment, a melodramatic pose, and I have a thousand reasons to be grateful that Pete recorded it.[56]

A story is only worth writing if it reaches the newspaper, and Hastings had no faith in any other delivery system than 3 Commando Brigade's press officer or his own efforts, which included punching the telex tapes aboard whichever MARISAT-equipped ship he could hitch a helicopter lift to. His ability to operate within the army made him few friends among the correspondents, but many among the soldiers. Commander Tim Gedge of the FAA said of him:

Max Hastings made himself known to all the officers, bought drinks freely and organized himself conspicuously well. He got to know the people that mattered and I gather inveigled his way into aircraft on missions when the remainder of the press were, for good reasons of course, not allowed to fly. A case in point was on 13 June (the day before the surrender) when I had arranged to be dropped off by Sea King on Mount Kent, and the aircraft launched in the early hours in the dark with an over-full load of people and stores: I suddenly found Max amongst the 'passengers'. I am pretty sure he had not been given priority for this flight: he was just there and sufficiently well known to the crew not to be turfed off! I suspect everyone assumed that he had been properly authorized for this flight.[57]

Hastings spent a wretched sub-zero night on Kent, followed by the triumph of being offered the use of an SAS Satcom, essentially a mobile phone, to phone a dispatch through via the regiment's HQ in Hereford.[58] This created something of a stir and, like the helicopter lift to Mount Kent, it infuriated his rivals.

On the day that the Argentinians surrendered in Port Stanley, Hastings was with Major Dair Farrar-Hockley and 2 Para as they marched on the town. The unit was halted and the men started to make tea.

Stripping off his military equipment, Hastings walked into Port Stanley, asked the Argentinian commander if he was surrendering and then strolled into the Upland Goose pub for a drink. Unbeknown to him at the time, he had beaten a blanket ban on anyone entering Stanley, but afterwards he was able to get a military helicopter out to RFA *Olna* to transmit the scoop of the war. Kim Sabido of Independent Radio News (IRN) was there already, but, unfortunately, the Prime Minister had stopped all transmissions until after her announcement to Parliament. Sabido interviewed Hastings; the latter punched his copy, the ban was eventually lifted, and on 15 June the *Evening Standard* carried a front page: 'Max Hastings leads the way … THE FIRST MAN INTO STANLEY.' He was afterwards taken to task by a furious senior officer who pointed out that his action had endangered the lives of the commandos. Had he been mistaken for a combatant, a firefight could have ensued.

Ultimately, the Argentinians posed a lesser threat to Hastings than his colleagues. He had taken a whole sheaf of other corre-

spondents' dispatches with him to *Olna*. When British newspapers were subsequently flown out to the islands, it transpired that those dispatches had not been sent. Tempers frayed in the Upland Goose. Hastings later wrote:

There was dismay about the amount of space my dispatches had received in almost every title, as a result of the pool system. It was now that the charge was first made by some reporters in the bar, that I had conspired with allies in the marines to suppress their copy. I don't remember whether in truth I replied with a four-letter shrug, as Mike Nicholson alleges, but I hope I said something equally contemptuous. A little Glaswegian who had dined well rushed forward wielding a bayonet.[59] *He was led away by his mates. The Yorkshire Post man, though sympathetic to my assailant's objectives, said regretfully: 'This is neither the time nor the place to kill Max Hastings.' I understood how that Glaswegian felt. He had been an eyewitness of the greatest story he would cover in his life, suffered endless frustrations and privations and, at the end of it all, gained less attention than some great tall streak of an Englishman whom he thought a stuck-up middle-class woofter.*[60]

Perhaps more than in any previous war, the Falklands correspondents as a group experienced the life of the soldiers, particularly after the landings. There were no hotels or chateaux, only the trenches they dug with others and the food they cooked for themselves. Although they were able to hitch lifts back to the ships for baths and the occasional dinner, they often shared bitter nights on exposed hillsides and ran the same risk of being killed as the troops around them.

When the correspondents had joined the task force they had been shown copies of the *Regulations for correspondents accompanying an operational task force*, which dated back to the Suez Crisis in 1956. For all of them it had been the first war in which they had, as Mike Nicholson put it:

fought alongside British troops, and to begin with we started to say 'our troops', 'our aircraft', 'our pilots', 'our ships' and I was reprimanded by my editor: one must be more objective, and it's the British troops, the British government. And even recently, in the year 2002, I went back to the Falklands to do a piece on

MICHAEL NICHOLSON, 1937–

above: ITN's Michael Nicholson with a Scorpion light tank of 'B' Squadron, the Blues and Royals.

Michael Nicholson's career as an overseas and war correspondent began in 1968 with a posting to Nigeria at the height of the Civil War and its attendant humanitarian disaster in Biafra. Born in 1937, he had joined ITN after leaving university and worked his way up, at first behind the scenes and then as a home reporter.

Nigeria was followed by the civil war in Jordan, then the India–Pakistan conflict of 1971 and the Yom Kippur War in 1973. In July 1974 Nicholson was posted to Cyprus after the coup, when a Turkish invasion appeared likely. The ITN car broke down, gloating press rivals streamed past, but a short time later Nicholson saw hundreds of parachutes floating down: he was right in the middle of the invasion. By cordially welcoming the paratroopers, he gained permission to film and interview them, achieving unique footage that he and his team edited in secret, lest their rivals should resort to sabotage. From their base at Akrotiri the RAF flew the film home.

Nicholson and his crew covered much of the Vietnam War, evacuating at the fall of Saigon, and then Angola. A household name by 1982, when he became one of the voices of the Falklands War, he returned to the UK for a four-year spell as a newsreader. It was not a happy period: he was bored, and after an unfortunate slip of the tongue provoked criticism from viewers, he returned to the front line. His reporting of the First Gulf War in 1991 earned him an OBE.

Today Nicholson remains best known for his coverage of Bosnia, from where he engineered the evacuation and adoption of a 9-year-old girl from an orphanage. The story was told in Nicholson's book *Natasha's Story*, filmed as 'Welcome to Sarajevo'.

the landings ... and I wanted to remind viewers of the events ... and I talked about our losses and our troops, and the editor even now went apoplectic about it…. One became very understandably less objective because you were fighting alongside your Yorkshireman, your Cockney, your Scot, your Welshman…. Our people … my people. I have never understood why we are supposed to be absent of humanity because we happen to be journalists.[61]

In the meantime, Fleet Street had been running a separate 'Falklands' story. Ian Mather of the *Observer*, Simon Winchester of the *Sunday Times* and Tony Prime, an *Observer* photographer, had gone to Argentina in April to report on what at the time appeared to more of a diplomatic crisis than a prelude to war. General Galtieri's press secretary had given them carte blanche to go where they pleased, so they headed for the far south of the country, to Ushuaia, a town right on the Beagle Channel. Unable to reach the Falklands by any means, they decided to return to Buenos Aires, only to be arrested at Rio Grande airport with that great cliché, 'For you the war is over'.

Taken back to Ushuaia the trio found themselves in the hands of the naval authorities; the military ran Tierra del Fuego, and this was all during the period of dictatorship in which thousands of Argentinian political prisoners simply disappeared – and whose actual fate remains unknown. However, they were given numbers, which put them officially into the system and guaranteed that, however the espionage case against them turned out, they could not simply 'disappear'.

Concerned about Winchester's silence, the *Sunday Times* took up the matter with Argentina, and when news emerged of the arrests an international campaign gradually built up, beginning with the wives and eventually involving the Pope, schoolchildren, the international press, King Juan Carlos I of Spain, the United Nations and that great American journalistic institution, Walter Cronkite. British journalists suddenly found that having even a single Irish grandparent entitled them to Irish passports, and they used this 'neutral' identity to pay visits to the prison. The three prisoners were allowed a television and watched the war unfold.

When the General Belgrano was sunk we decided to write a note to [the prison governor José] Barrosso. Although we had been stripped of reading material during the night it had been decided that we could keep anything written in Spanish. So we used a

Spanish edition of Reader's Digest to help us compose a letter to Barrosso stating that while we remained British patriots we were personally deeply saddened by the loss of life and the distress of the families of those killed. Barrosso later told us he had been moved by our letter. A few days later the Argentinians sank the British guided missile destroyer, HMS Coventry, a terrible blow to Britain. We decided to write another note using the same copy of Reader's Digest to find the right words. The aim was to try to neutralise the hostility towards us that had developed as a result of the sinking of General Belgrano. We said that just as we had felt sympathy for those who had lost their lives on the General Belgrano we hoped the Argentinian authorities would understand that we felt exactly the same over the deaths of our compatriots on the Coventry. It paid off. Barrosso invited us into his office, where he offered us Argentinian whisky, which he pronounced 'Wikky', called 'Old Smuggler', pronounced with a heavy 'u' just as Lancashire people pronounce 'bus'. From then on our relationship with him became not only thoroughly professional, but also at times cordial.[62]

Shortly after the end of the war they were released. Subsequently, Mather returned to Ushuaia to renew acquaintance with those who had been involved in his captivity, in particular with the prison governor.

The Falklands War was a perfect template for the future embedding – the term did not yet exist – of journalists but a disaster for open journalism. Logistics played their part, but above all it was the control of technology that ensured a military victory over the press – the irony being that none of the press had any desire to reveal any military detail that could result in an incoming bullet or missile on which their names were engraved.

This was arguably the last war primarily for the printed media, and as television muscled in, many newspapers began to divest themselves of their expensive foreign news departments. Communications technology was on the brink of a revolution, and digital recording that allowed the swift transmission of text and photographs would soon extend to film. Extended television news coverage, live or delayed only long enough to fit in with news bulletins, would become the norm, with a significant impact on the status of those standing in front of the camera.

The job of the war correspondent has expanded to embrace much of the 'Spectrum of Conflict', but the depth of coverage of any one of the 150-plus conflicts of the post-Vietnam era has, as always, depended primarily on the ability of journalists to enter the zone and on the judgement of editors as to whether the events are internationally significant or of interest to a sizeable proportion of the audience. Some wars remain in the public consciousness simply because of the coverage by just one or two journalists working in extraordinary conditions.

I went into journalism towards the end of the most violent century in human history, and the new one is already going bad. If I wanted to do the big stories, it was impossible not to go to wars, and compulsory to understand them. Some wars are necessary, vital, unavoidable. But they are all seducers. They must be, or humans would not make war, dread war, enjoy it, even love it in the way that they do. It can be sickening, exciting, affirming and terrifying. It brings out the best in people, and the worst.

Jeremy Bowen (1960–), British war correspondent, in *War Stories*, 2006

WARS OF THE WORLD

The civil war in Lebanon dragged on from 1975 to 1990, and for a decade after 1979 Soviet forces unsuccessfully fought the

New World Disorder:

wars in a digital age

mujahideen in Afghanistan in order to maintain a pro-Soviet government in Kabul. In 1990, in what became known as the Gulf War (or Persian Gulf War; later known as the First Gulf War), Iraq invaded Kuwait, and was expelled the following year by a UN coalition led by the USA and Britain, while in 1994 horrific genocide convulsed Rwanda.

A complex series of conflicts broke out in the Balkans from 1991 onwards after the dismantling of the Soviet Union allowed long-repressed tensions in Yugoslavia to fracture the country along ethnic and religious lines. Slovenia and Croatia both successfully fought for their independence from Yugoslavia – effectively Serbia and Montenegro – before civil war broke out in Bosnia between the three main groups. The capital of Bosnia, Sarajevo, was besieged from 1992 until 1995 by Serbian forces from within and outside the state, and Bosnia was finally split into a Bosniak–Croat Federation and a Serbian Republic. During the Balkan wars, the UN's efforts to keep the peace were supported by NATO

peace-enforcement operations, but these interventions were fatally undermined by UN rules of engagement. When Kosovo, the autonomous region of Serbia, declared its independence in 1991, there began a campaign by Serbian forces that was directed against the majority population of ethnic Albanians. NATO was called in to drive out those troops, and Kosovo is still administered by the UN, with peacekeepers protecting the Serbian minority.

In response to the destruction of the Twin Towers in New York on 11 September 2001, by aircraft flown by Islamic terrorists acting on behalf of Al-Qaeda, a US-led coalition invaded Afghanistan. The aim of what the USA termed 'the war on terror' was to destroy Al-Qaeda's training camps and, as a secondary result, establish democracy in Afghanistan. Ten years later the war was still being fought, by troops from the USA, Britain, Germany, Canada, France, Italy, Turkey and other countries, all assisting the Afghan Army.

A second strand of the so-called 'war on terror' saw another US-led international coalition topple the Iraqi regime of Saddam Hussein in

above: The crew of a coalition Bradley Infantry Fighting Vehicle watch the smoke from burning oil wells sabotaged by the Iraqis during the First Gulf War, 1990–91.

2003 and occupy the country. The destruction of Iraq's infrastructure and institutions, together with an absence of planning for what would happen after the military phase of the conflict that became known as the Second Gulf War, left a dangerous power vacuum in Iraq that was still being exploited in 2011 by groups inside and outside the country as coalition troops disengaged.

Elsewhere in the Middle East, the conflict between Israel and the Palestinians is rarely out of the headlines, particularly when it spills over the border into Lebanon.

These were the wars which, along with the Falklands, gained high-profile coverage, particularly in countries whose troops were engaged, or where international interests were seen to be involved, but there were many others that also caught the headlines, including those in Sierra Leone, Somalia, Guinea-Bissau and Chechnya.

A significant change took place during the post-Vietnam period. According to statistics from the Committee to Protect Journalists, 850 correspondents have been killed since 1992, most of them

locals, and correspondents are increasingly seen as legitimate targets for murder and kidnap, their rights under the Geneva Convention meaning little to extortionists, insurgents or other paramilitary units.

However, far from deterring correspondents, the danger can be an irrelevance or even a lure to someone like Anthony Loyd. During the First Gulf War, he saw action as a soldier in the British Army, but found peacetime service unfulfilling, much like his risk-hungry great-grandfather Lieutenant General Adrian Carton De Wiart, who won the VC during the First World War. Loyd left the army, took a course in journalism and became involved with hard drugs before taking himself off to war in the shape of the Balkan conflict: 'hoping for a metamorphosis or an exit. I wanted to reach a human extreme in order to cleanse myself of my sense of fear, and saw war as the ultimate frontier of human experience.'[1]

At the opposite end of the spectrum was the *Guardian's* Maggie O'Kane, who reported wars for 12 years; initially, she did so with what she described as a 'Pollyanna' attitude to risk – essentially, a

naïve optimism. 'I didn't really understand risk and the amount of danger I was in, until afterwards.... People I knew began to be killed. I nearly lost my life in East Timor, and it became more and more dangerous to be a foreign correspondent, and it was that experience that changed my assessment. And a very good friend said once, "It's like a game of Russian Roulette, you know: you keep at it long enough and the bullet will get you in the end."'[2]

In 2002 everything came to a head in an incident on the road linking Pakistan and Afghanistan, a road thought comparatively safe because it was well used and carried military traffic: 'And one day the Taliban stopped a convoy of journalists going in, and they took three out of the first car, and two of them I knew and had been in wars with before. They took them to the side of the road and maybe 30 seconds later they were dead. They'd all been shot in the head. And it was that moment when I said to myself that ... as long as you do this you can be dead in 30 seconds.'[3] Freely acknowledging that she had lost her nerve, O'Kane chose to withdraw from war reporting before a bullet got her.

opposite: Embedded with the US Marines in Helmand Province Afghanistan, AP's Julie Jacobson photographed US Marines moving through a compound in Dahanesh in August 2009.

above: Despite an emergency MEDEVAC, NBC's 39-year-old correspondent David Bloom died in 2003 from a pulmonary embolism after a deep-vein thrombosis. He was famous for his reports made on the move, using a gyroscopically stabilized camera on his adapted military vehicle.

She was far from the only one to pull out. Scott Hillier, the BBC soundman in Grozny, Chechnya, did so because he had just become a father and he, too, could no longer reconcile his responsibilities to his family with the demands of combat journalism that had taken him to other dangerous areas during his career. Jeremy Bowen, who was the reporter on the BBC team at the time, later made a similar decision.

More journalists than ever before, particularly those whose faces appear nightly on television, have become household names, with their assessments and experiences providing the main source of information for millions. During the 1990s in Britain, variations on a joke began to circulate, the crux of which was that a conflict situation could only be considered serious when Kate Adie was sent to cover it. Every country has its own authoritative correspondents, broadcasting from a troubled region against a background of explosions, desperate civilians, shattered streets and military hardware.

At different times these correspondents may fall into any one of three categories: embedded correspondents attached to military forces; staff or freelance reporters accredited by specific news organizations; or independent, self-financing journalists.

IN BED WITH THE TROOPS

The purpose of embedding correspondents with units and formation headquarters is to enable the media to gain a deeper understanding of the operation in which they are involved, particularly through access to personnel and commanders.

From the UK Ministry of Defence's 'Green Book', 2010

Since the Falklands War the embedding of journalists has become far more organized, and every army has its own regulations to clarify the rights and responsibilities of both the military and the embedded press corps. In Britain, the MOD's 'Green Book' outlines the selection process, the facilities to be expected, reporting restrictions, the training for risk, the equipment required or provided, and medical and physical fitness criteria. Although special allowances may be made for older, senior correspondents, journalists 'must possess a standard of medical, dental, physical and mental fitness that equates to MOD civilian personnel or contractors deployed to the operational theatre'. The most suitable candidates should be able to complete a 1.5-mile (2.5-kilometre) course inside 22 minutes, while wearing body armour and carrying a helmet and a 13-pound (6-kilogram) day sack. Many health conditions, even those stabilized by medication, are sufficient to rule out a correspondent;

top: Journalists with the 1st Armoured Division write their reports at the Forward Transmission Unit (FTU) during the First Gulf War.

above: A film crew is shown what appears to be the fuselage of a missile during the First Gulf War.

opposite: Haute cuisine in the desert: an offical British Army cameraman eats lunch from a can in the back of a Landrover.

anyone with dental implants needs to be carefully assessed, and those with a Body Mass Index above 30 should lose weight prior to deployment. Helpfully, correspondents are reassured that, while war zones are inherently dangerous 'UK forces on operations will not deliberately target individual correspondents'.

Being embedded means more than just following the army. In the weeks leading up to the liberation of Kuwait in the First Gulf War, correspondents were rigorously trained until they were so exhausted that at night they crawled into their tent and struggled into their sleeping bags desperate for sleep. They participated in all the preparations, even to the extent of a night exercise that gave them more than a taste of what lay ahead. Along with fellow correspondents Brian Barron and Martin Bell, and cameraman Ian Pritchard who was filming, Kate Adie went on that exercise:

... on top of a Warrior armoured vehicle, hanging on for dear life .... We hurtled out into the desert and we could hear noise all around us: the scream of

armoured vehicles; the roaring tanks ... orders being shouted, radios going. We were absolutely bewildered – it was quite frightening in the dark. We were aware that orders were being given; people were lining up; people were doing mock attacks. There was the sound of explosions – they were firing blanks: there were great bangs and booms, and this had been going on for some considerable time, 25 minutes, and we were all totally disorientated .... And suddenly they sent up ... these huge great phosphorescent flares and it went like daytime and we couldn't believe our eyes: the whole desert was crammed with armoured vehicles ... there were infantry running around [and] people setting up artillery positions – it was a battlefield.[4]

BORDER CONTROL

'One of the best definitions of being a television reporter', suggests ITN's Michael Nicholson, 'is that it's 10 percent talent and 90

above: From the remote Afghan village of Rocha a Western journalist sends a dispatch by satphone watched by curious locals.

percent logistics, and trying to get in to a country and trying to get to the story and once you've got your story, trying to get it out again back to base is the major part of our employment. Covering the story itself is the easiest thing in the world; things are happening all around you and all you've got to do is point a camera and report what you see; there's no great secret about that, there's no great talent involved.'[5]

For correspondents not travelling with the military, not even a passport, visa and a press card are guaranteed to secure entry. Some regimes will not admit journalists; others ban specific broadcasters and newspapers. In the days when their passports stated the bearer's occupation, some British reporters classed themselves as authors or writers.

Jeremy Bowen arrived openly at Kabul without a visa, during the time of the Soviet withdrawal from Afghanistan, and was locked up for three days before being permitted to join his guards and share his whisky with them prior to being put onto a flight deeper into the country.

For others, clandestine entry or illegal papers were the only options. Guided by cross-border smugglers, John Simpson and Peter Jouvenal crossed into Afghanistan from Pakistan in 2001 wearing the *burkas* they had bought openly in Peshawar from a trader who had immediately recognized Simpson from his BBC television appearances. While he was working illegally in Zimbabwe in 2008, Simpson toyed with the idea of using a fake beard but he found it too inconvenient. Although he was recognized several times, once by a senior official in the ruling Zanu-PF, he was never betrayed.

For the independent journalist in a war zone, or any country where the foreign media is unwelcome, the prerequisites are a local driver and a 'fixer' – who can also act as interpreter. When freelance journalist James Fergusson first went to Afghanistan in 1996:

> *I didn't have a fixer. I just turned up and I hired somebody in Mazar-e-Sharif, a young chap called Mir. I still use him, and 15 years on he's become a great friend. He got into trouble because he was working for Westerners, and I helped him to get asylum in Britain where he has made a career for himself as a fixer for the BBC and Channel 4.*
>
> *We still go back to Afghanistan together; I couldn't possibly operate there without him. He's built up very good contacts with the Taliban. People will often only speak to you if they trust your interpreter, and Mir is very good. He comes from a good Pashtun family and has the right kind of social profile to be able to set up meetings with people who matter. When I go out into the wilds I depend on his discretion and his tactical sense. His antennae are keen enough to keep me safe. I trust him absolutely.*[6]

Something of an expert on the ground in Middle Eastern affairs, freelance Richard Engel left it too late to get a journalist's visa to enter Iraq in 2003, so entered initially on a 'peace activist' visa, although, as he pointed out, peace activists rarely travelled with $20,000 in cash. With the majority of his money strapped round his ankle and the rest hidden in a huge sport utility vehicle he was driven from Amman, the capital of Jordan, to Baghdad, accompanied on the second leg of the journey by an Iraqi intelligence officer.

COMFORT AND DISCOMFORT UNDER FIRE

Before the First Gulf War began, the Iraqi government expelled every major news-gathering organization, except Cable News Network (CNN), only to relent on the eve of the action. Brent Sadler represented ITN and was shortly joined by Alan Little (BBC Radio) and Jeremy Bowen (BBC Television) plus cameraman Rory Peck. They went to the BBC office in the Al-Rashid Hotel and climbed, remembered Bowen: 'a dark staircase by torchlight to the fourth floor with our supplies and the gear. Bags of rubbish were decomposing in the corners of the office. A half-eaten meal was fossilised on a plate. I had no idea how long our predecessors had been given to get ready when they had the order to get out.'[7] However, ITN had a generator, long-life meals from Marks and Spencer, and soft music.

The Al-Rashid was again a favoured hotel in 2003, although at $150 a night it was too expensive for Richard Engel who was recommended to stay at the Flowers Land, where he found an apartment with two balconies suitable for operating the satellite phone. What the hotel lacked in the quality of its breakfasts it atoned for in its 'business centre', which was run by an enterprising hacker who could give guests access to uncensored web-based e-mail. Having unpacked his chemical/biological/radiological suit, nerve agent antidote, satellite phone and, as bribes, baby clothes and a quantity of expensive tea, he proceeded to introduce such emergency supplies as a generator, earplugs, fuel for the taxi he had hired, oil for the generator and cans in which to store water.

Kate Adie spent the First Gulf War embedded with the British Army's 7th Armoured Brigade, sharing a 12-man tent with her male colleagues – in fact, the only woman among 2,000 men. With a field kitchen providing good food, some of it 'proffed' from unsuspecting American units, no cooking needed to be done (unlike during the Falklands land campaign), but tents and camp beds had to be erected in the darkness. Despite the presence of British troops all around, they were almost wiped out one night when a US tank strayed into the area and was climbing the dune above their encampment when it suddenly stopped and reversed away.

During the war in Bosnia, many correspondents in Sarajevo were based at the Holiday Inn, which, despite the fact that the top five floors were uninhabitable due to sniper fire, charged $100 a night. Jeremy Bowen checked in on the day in 1992 that CNN camerawoman Margaret Moth had her jaw seriously damaged by a gunshot, and he was almost shot himself by Serb snipers who, from their position overlooking the hotel, targeted the lift doors. There was no hot water, but several journalists used elements from old immersion heaters to heat up their bathwater. Later,

KATE ADIE, 1945–

above: Kate Adie on her way to join an army unit in 1996.

Kate Adie went into local radio journalism after leaving university with a degree in Scandinavian Studies, moving to national news in 1979, aged 34. The following year, on 5 May, she was the duty officer outside the Iranian embassy in London where for the previous five days Iranian separatists had been holding diplomatic staff hostage. Suddenly five SAS teams swung into action, and Adie, as much surprised as everyone else, provided a lucid but dramatic commentary that was aired as a live newsflash.

Although her coverage of the US bombing of Libya in 1986 was unpopular among those who thought she had lost her objectivity and sided with the Libyans, she nevertheless became the BBC's chief news correspondent in 1989. That same year she was widely praised for the com-

mentary and footage she managed to get out of China after the bloodshed in Tiananmen Square. Her arm was grazed by a bullet that killed the man next to her, and in order to reach the comparative safety of the hotel she scaled an 8-foot (2.5-metre) wall 'like a lizard ... propelled by terror', carrying her cameraman's precious videotape, and fought off two soldiers by the hotel doors. Once inside she hammered on a door. Julian O'Halloran, from 'Newsnight', opened it to find her covered in blood. She delivered her report over the telephone and then helped to edit the video footage, which was smuggled out on the first flight leaving Beijing by a friend of the team.

Adie's credentials as a combat reporter took her to war zones, including the First Gulf War, Bosnia, where she was wounded in the foot, Rwanda and Sierra Leone before she left the front line in 2003 to become a writer, freelance correspondent and presenter. She was awarded an OBE in 1993 to add to her many journalism awards.

when water became scarce, it was not unknown for the press corps to inherit used bathwater.

While filming in Afghanistan in 2001, John Simpson established his team in a filthy municipal building in Charikar, 25 miles (40 kilometres) from Kabul, which he nicknamed 'Bin Laden Mansions' and it turned out to be the base of Hajji Bari, an influential commander. An amicable agreement was reached with the commander that allowed the correspondents to make themselves at home and to turn:

> ... this Third World toilet of ours into a liveable if spartan base, cold enough for us to have to wear our warmest clothes, but clean and tidy and almost homelike. As the weeks stretched out the artists among us – chiefly Joe Phua and Peter Emmerson – drew on the walls the creature-comforts we missed most: a drinks cabinet, which we stocked from our imaginations, a television set, a really expensive Bose sound system, and dozens of CDs with humorous names. Also three flying ducks.... Belts had to be tightened at Bin Laden Mansions. There wasn't much edible food, and no alcohol at all. We lived off eggs, hard boiled or sometimes fried, large quantities of Afghan bread, fruit and vegetables of various kinds from the market, disgustingly fat, greasy and tough meat (though most of us turned aside from this with revulsion), gallons of tea, and the vegetarian curries which we had brought with us from India.[8]

In Beirut in 1982, during the civil war, Simpson was fascinated by the speed with which he became accustomed to the constraints of life under fire:

> We crawled along the corridors in the Hotel Alexandra in East Beirut because its windows were commanded by snipers, and we knelt on the floor of our editing room on the top storey of the hotel (the only place left by the time we arrived), while the picture editor reached up over his head to press the buttons on the edit machines.
>
> 'What was that?' Russ Crombie, the editor I was working with, asked absently. He was trying to do a particularly difficult sound-edit, and wasn't paying much attention to anything else.
>
> I looked up at the window.

> 'It's OK,' I said, 'just a bullet hitting the blinds and the wall.'
>
> I carried on writing my script.[9]

On the Front Line

LEBANON

After Vietnam, Philip Caputo had agreed with Nick Profitt never to cover another war from the front line, so in Lebanon they reported from the safety of their respective Beirut offices. The result was a stream of complaints from Caputo's newspaper demanding more action-packed reports and refusing to accept his protest that travelling varied from the very dangerous to the suicidal. On 25 October 1975 he went out and was targeted by two snipers with automatic weapons:

> I could hear every round fired and tasted blood in my mouth – the blood trickling from my head. Blood oozed down my back, down my left arm, down my left calf. Running zigzag, the way they trained us in the marines, I looked back and saw both men, only forty, fifty feet away, kneeling to steady their aim, and then the guns bucking, muzzles and gunmen's faces blurred by the pale haze of the smokeless powder. I was knocked down. I rolled and was on my feet and running again, enough adrenaline in me to outrun a deer. Down again, up again, hobbling instead of running, still zigzagging. A fragment or ricochet had hit my right foot. Then I felt a terrific impact in my left ankle, like a blast from a compressed air hose. I was flying, lifted off my feet by the round that had hit me solid, fair and square. No fragment or ricochet that time. I landed on my belly and, not stopping to check how badly I'd been hit, scuttled on my elbows like a crab.[10]

Emergency treatment was administered by a local doctor in a nearby house. As the firing continued Caputo was taken to a hospital in the Christian quarter and operated on without anaesthetic, and friends helped his wife and children to leave the country. A US Marine colonel brought out Caputo in a bullet-proof limousine. His Vietnam service had not been forgotten, and the US Marines always boast they never leave one of their own behind.

THE FIRST GULF WAR

Because of the expulsion from Baghdad of all significant Western broadcasters except CNN, which was allowed to broadcast censored reports, most of the remaining reporting was, therefore, from correspondents with the UN coalition forces.

The actual assault began with an artillery barrage. Adie and her team found themselves positioned behind one of the many tracked artillery pieces that extended in a line. Invited to observe the firing from inside, she climbed in and the order to fire was given. The shell jammed. As frantic attempts were made to free it, one of the soldiers inside with her began to pray. From outside, a sergeant hit the mechanism with a sledgehammer, until at last it was released. Adie emerged to find that there was nothing in sight around them, apart from the colonel. Everyone but she knew that a similar incident in the US Army the previous day had caused a massive explosion.

On the night of the attack, the army was organized into columns to go through designated gaps made in the huge defensive *berm*, or sand wall:

> I think we were meant to go through gap L at something-or-other time, with ordinary vehicles (in other words, not tracked) on our right-hand side. I ended up going through K, with tanks on my left-hand side .... This is a war zone; this is what happens ... we tore through ... driving to keep up, much faster than anybody had ever said. And there was chaos: tanks came crossing through, transporters coming back; there were people running around – there was absolute chaos. We had all our wits about us. It was just terrifying; we were going onto the field of battle, because the tanks were up ahead of us and firing.[11]

After leaving the Grenadier Guards, Vaughan Smith became a freelance photojournalist and cameraman in search of excitement, and as such was frustrated that the MOD would only allow accredited representatives of the news media to accompany the troops. Not one to be discouraged, 'I disguised myself as a British Army officer – I had been only five years earlier – and managed to get to the front line on completely forged documents, with all sorts of strange clothing that looked quasi-military, until I managed to get the proper stuff. I filmed for the better part of two months, and this was the only uncontrolled footage.'

From Baghdad Bowen did his best to report what was happening, in the teeth of Iraqi obstruction: 'Iraqi officials would stop the BBC using a small light for a piece to camera, on the grounds that it violated the blackout and would attract bombs, while twenty-five feet away CNN's Peter Arnett stood in a blazing pool of light, on air non-stop via a satellite dish.... The Iraqis loved CNN, and hated us.'[12]

The bombings were easy enough to report; information about everything else was hard to obtain and the BBC relied on AP's correspondent, an Iraqi national, for explanations. Then, on the morning of 13 February 1991, two US smart bombs targeted the Amiriyah, or Amirya, shelter, which at the time was crowded with civilians. Bowen was one of the first to be taken to the site, and afterwards he and cameraman Rory Peck went to Yarmuk hospital:

> [where] fragments of people, burnt pieces of meat, had been laid out in the car park. The headless torsos looked even more like blackened tree stumps that had been burned and ripped out of the earth. I noticed that Rory Peck was shooting some tight [close up] shots. I told him not to do it, because we would never be able to use them. 'I know, but I just want those bastards back in London who don't like the truth to see it.'

> On air that afternoon I was interrogated endlessly about what I had seen. The Pentagon and the Ministry of Defence were claiming that the Amirya bunker was a military command centre. The aggressive tone of some of the BBC anchormen surprised me. I was being treated like an Iraqi spokesman. In London, they must have been feeling the pressure. ... It was such bad news for America and its friends that it was time to shoot the messenger. Again and again I made the point that I was just reporting what I had seen and heard with my own eyes and ears. No, I hadn't seen any soldiers. The bodies were of women, children and old men. And there were hundreds of them.[13]

After pressurizing Bowen for several days, the BBC backed his version, but he still came under savage personal attack from the tabloid press in Britain. On the advice of his barrister brother, he sued Express Newspapers for libel, and accepted an out of court settlement.

BOSNIA

While the war in the Gulf was over in a few weeks, the conflict that was just flaring up in the disintegrating Yugoslavia ran for several years, with the reporting centred on Bosnia, and particularly its capital, Sarajevo.

'I have very clear memories,' said Kate Adie, 'of the nightmare [of] driving round the city: careering round hysterically over pavements, though people's back gardens, smashing down road signs, uproar all around … you just took the straightest line from A to B and went for it. It was quite fun, because Sarajevo was full of one way systems … but you frequently nearly clipped large armoured vehicles, which took no notice of anything and barged down the road. … There were shells [that] fell in the middle of the road in front of you – I had that twice.'14

Early in her six-and-a-half-week stint she was hit in the foot during a hair-raising drive to the airport, when a bullet came into the cabin though a gap between the armour plating. A French doctor treated her, without anaesthetic, and some fragments could not

above: CNN film a broadcast at the International Hotel in Dhahran, Saudi Arabia, during the First Gulf War.

was too dangerous, and withdrew, the peacekeepers were forced to abandon the attempt. Anthony Loyd and his companions later convinced a Croat leader, Ivica Raji, of their 'empathy' with his need to attack Muslim positions at the nearby village of Stupni Do, thereby flattering him into letting them enter the village, just at the moment the Swedes had forced their way in. In the smoking ruins he saw Swedish soldiers swearing savagely in shock and horror at the butchered children: '... the rage comes in like a hurricane and then you want them dead, the people who did this, you want the scum erased for this. You could do it yourself there and then at that moment, blast every one of them forward in a pink spray. And walk away to find some more.'[16]

The complexities of the war were hard to accept: some correspondents, seeing the results of ethnic cleansing and massacres by Croats, Serbs and Muslims alike, took the view that all three sides were equally guilty and might as well be left to kill one another unhindered.

HEARTS OF EVIL

Fergal Keane was one of the correspondents who covered the Rwandan genocide in May 1994. He entered the country via Nairobi, Kenya, where he met correspondents who had just come out of Rwanda:

And they were shattered. And I said, 'What is this?' And one of them pulled me aside and he said, 'It's spiritual damage, it's spiritual damage.' I didn't quite get it. I thought he was either drunk or in some kind of wild existentialist phase. I didn't get what he meant. But I sure do now. I really do.

And we came relatively late. It was the very end of May, the beginning of June. Most of the killing had been done. There were still pockets of Tutsis being hunted down in different areas. But to drive through those road blocks, and see the looks on people's faces. I will never forget driving from Butare to the Burundi border with the Tutsi orphans whose parents had been wiped out. They tried to get these kids out a couple of weeks before, and some had been dragged off and killed. These were kids! You know, five, six, seven years of age. And you are driving through these road blocks and, if only for the presence of international aid workers and the fact that they had been able to do a deal with the local prefect, those

be removed. She did not report it to the BBC, fearing that, so soon after Martin Bell's injury (see page 200), it would induce the BBC to cease coverage.

Correspondents were often glad of a military friend. Anthony Loyd found the Royal Anglian Regiment in Vitez helpful. 'As by now I was often the only journalist in central Bosnia they indulged my company long after the daily briefings were over, and expanded the often empty details of the UN's situation reports with insight and background. If I saw less of the real war that spring then at least I understood more of the UN's situation, not that it gave me any cause for optimism. The great post-war Charter body could not decide if the troops it sent to Bosnia were part of a trucking company or a fighting force, and was prepared to go to almost any length to preserving inaction at the expense of lives.'[15]

Swedish peacekeepers in Vareš tried to release Muslim prisoners, relying on the presence of BBC cameras to deter any Croatian moves to stop them. When the BBC crew decided the situation

kids would have been taken off and hacked to death in front of us. I never ever forget the looks on their faces. They were petrified because they didn't know, they had no guarantees. Rwanda was a country without guarantees.[17]

Two years later, in Sierra Leone, the Canadian journalist Ian Stewart was distressed by the bestial violence he encountered. The Revolutionary United Front (RUF) had sought to subvert the 1996 elections by chopping off the hands of voters, and their atrocities had continued even after the elections. Stewart was introduced to a 9-year-old former child soldier who had been abducted and taught how to murder and mutilate, asking his victims if they wanted long or short sleeves before cutting off their arms at the wrist or the elbow with his machete. Within sight of the boy-soldier he saw a small girl, her arms ending at the wrists in bandages, asking her mother if her hands would grow back. 'I shut my eyes tight and held them closed to hold back the tears that reporters are not supposed to show.'[18] He met a boy whose older brother

above: Refugees from the 1994 Rwandan genocide photographed in neighbouring Zaire by Italian-born photojournalist Dario Mitidieri.

opposite: A Sarajevo mother cradles her child as she runs across an intersection targeted by snipers in June 1995.

was forced to have sex with his mother – before both were murdered. In Guinea-Bissau, where Stewart was one of only three foreign correspondents, he wept at the cruel juxtaposition of a dying child and one born alive and healthy in a poorly equipped hospital. 'Despite my own increasingly dark mood, I was determined to tell the world about Adao and Gbadne and the many other nameless victims I met in that country.'[19]

In 1999 Stewart became a bigger story than any he had filed. After rebels overran Freetown, Stewart and his colleagues came under fire on the road on 10 January: 'With every round, I ducked lower behind our station wagon. My heart raced with that same exhilaration I always felt whenever I came under fire.'[20] Not long afterwards, an AK-47 opened up and Myles Tierney was killed immediately; Stewart took a bullet in the forehead. Nigerian peacekeepers flew him out of Sierra Leone and a Swiss air ambulance took him to London. Against the odds, Stewart not only survived but managed to overcome the challenges of his brain injury.

BACK TO THE GULF

The Second Gulf War provided a major boost to the careers of the BBC's Rageh Omaar and the freelance, Richard Engel. The latter was taken on by ABC who, like all US broadcasters, pulled out their staff following orders from the Pentagon. Omaar watched the evacuation.

It seemed that as each journalist left the city, the level of neurosis rose correspondingly. There was a widely held belief that those who stayed would be used by the Iraqi authorities as human shields. ... But even if these visions did seem paranoid and far-fetched, as the days passed there was plenty of ammunition to fuel them. The supplies of nerve agent antidotes and the unwieldy chemical and biological warfare suits began to arrive in boxes at our hotel, and with them the fears about weapons of mass destruction seemed to gain credibility.[21]

Reuters gave their Baghdad staff the choice of staying or evacuating. Bureau Chief Samia Nakhoul was one who wished to stay: 'Reuters had made emergency preparations. We had rented a house and we had put all kinds of provisions in it: food cans, a room full of bottled water, and also gasoline for the car, because we knew we needed that to escape, and we had all the equipment that we needed, like Thuraya [mobile satellite phone]. Saddam's government did not allow Thuraya – they thought it was a spying

tool. We were worried that warplanes might jam satellite reception so we wanted to have extra, like Thuraya, so if the telephones were jammed we could file by Thuraya.'[22]

The press centre ordered all remaining journalists to stay at one of the three major state-run hotels, and when Richard Engel returned to Baghdad, after a hasty trip to Jordan to gain accreditation, he moved, with all his supplies, from the Flowers Land into a 14th-floor room at the Palestine, the hotel furthest from any government building likely to be the target of a coalition air strike. 'By the end of the day, the Palestine Hotel was explosive with all the gasoline inside it.'[23]

Afraid of air strikes on the official press centre, correspondents shifted broadcasting equipment into the hotels, ignoring the prohibition on satellite phones. Omaar had to curtail one broadcast in order to hide the BBC phones. For many correspondents the most frightening part of the campaign was the build up to the main air attacks. Early bombing had produced casualties on the outskirts, to which the Iraqi press centre laid on escorted tours. To avoid surveillance, Engel took the advice of the Corriere Della Sera's triathlete Lorenzo Cremonesi: choose an overweight minder who smoked, and then walk him to exhaustion.

Omaar became famous for his reports from the hotel when the operation commenced with the infamous 'Shock and Awe' assaults:

Building after building ablaze, disappearing in cauldrons of fire and ash. Such was the ferocity of it all that within one five-minute period I counted at least thirty strikes. I kept talking to the BBC news presenters in London, who were watching live, trying as hard as I could to convey the sheer violence, the thunderous noise which rumbled through every street and avenue of the city, and the terrifying sight of plumes of debris being hurled at least 300 feet into the air. The fury was so spellbinding that it defied instant description.[24]

The drama in Baghdad brought fame to Engel, too, for being in the right place at the right time:

Like the other networks, ABC switched to continuous live coverage, and I was on air every moment I could be. ABC, however, initially had trouble figuring out how to describe me. At first the anchors made sure to

Although born in Mogadishu, Somalia, Rageh Omaar has spent most of his life in Britain, to which his wealthy parents emigrated when he was very young. Educated at a public school, he read Modern History at Oxford before joining *The Voice*, a newspaper aimed primarily at an Afro-Caribbean audience. After that apprenticeship, he persuaded the BBC's Africa Service to let him report as a stringer – on a freelance basis – and, armed with a tape recorder and microphone supplied by the BBC, he went to Ethiopia for a year in 1991. A short period in London was followed by an appointment as the BBC TV News Africa correspondent, during which he reported on the Ethiopia–Eritrea war, and in 2002 he provided live reports from inside Kabul as the city was recaptured from the Taliban.

Omaar's fluency in Arabic made him an ideal candidate to cover the Second Gulf War from Baghdad in 2003, and his syndicated reports brought him fame in the USA as well as Britain, his good looks earning him the nickname 'the Scud Stud' in the *Washington Post*. One of his most famous reports was of the toppling of Saddam Hussein's statue in Fardus Square, his calm tones in contrast to the visible excitement around him.

After leaving the BBC to work as a freelancer and for Al-Jazeera, Omaar controversially criticized Western reporting of the Iraq conflict, claiming that correspondents frequently provide commentaries to footage shot not by their own teams but by local Iraqi cameramen, because much of Baghdad is too dangerous for the Western media.

RAGEH OMAAR, 1967–

As the most high-profile Somalian in Britain, Omaar has come to be seen as representative of the community and he has also explored the position of his friends and family as Somalian Muslims in the wake of the bombings on the London Underground in 2005.

above: The Second Gulf War turned Rageh Omaar into a household name. Here he speaks to an audience at 'The Guardian Hay on Wye Festival' in May 2004.

identify me as a 'freelance reporter.' My assumption at the time was that the network wanted to maintain distance from me in case I was killed. After a few days, however, the network embraced me, calling me 'ABC's Richard Engel' and 'our' correspondent. It felt good to finally be loved. ...

Again on the second night, I watched the sound and light show from my balcony. I sat on a tank of gasoline (not the safest perch), talking on the sat phone as the Americans airmailed explosives to Baghdad and Iraqi anti-aircraft guns sprayed flak at them, as effective as spitballs. When the exchanges got especially heavy – pound, pound, crackle, crackle – I put on my flak jacket and helmet... During the day, I'd been broadcasting from IHA's[25] camera fixed to the second-story roof of the press center. It was transmitting live pictures as I spoke via sat phone from the hotel. Although I was only separated from the camera by a couple of miles, I suspect it may have been somewhat confusing to viewers, because I was describing one perspective of the city under attack while the camera was showing another. I wouldn't go near the press center at night, believing it would soon be transformed into a heap of rubble.[26]

Reuters were working round the clock in shifts. Samia Nakhoul remembers that the night of 7/8 April was unnaturally quiet.

Not a shot was fired, especially after midnight. There was an eerie silence. It was a strange time. You felt like there was something coming, like a storm ... then at dawn actually I was looking out of the 4th floor. Our offices in the Palestine hotel looked at Saddam's Presidential Guards compound, and one of his special forces used to be positioned there. In the first Shock and Awe of the war they hit that compound across the river, so I started seeing tanks pushing there and our TV director called me and he said, 'Samia, I can see tanks advancing from that intersection to the compound', so I immediately went to the 15th floor and I started seeing tanks rolling in and advancing ... I started working, trying to find out what was happening. Suddenly we couldn't see the minders in the hotel. Even our minders had disappeared. At 8 o'clock or 8.30, I got a colleague coming and he said he'd heard that they had fired at Al Jazeera offices near where we were – they did not have their bureau in the same hotel as us; and I called Dubai. And it was true, that they had killed Tariq Ayoub. He was filing his reports from Al Jazeera rooftop, and the American plane bombarded the Al Jazeera offices and he died while giving his commentary.[27]

Nakhoul postponed her morning phone call to her husband because she did not want him to be alarmed by the sound of the bombardment. As midday came, all the correspondents were getting ready to file their stories. Nakhoul was

... on the balcony of our offices on the 15th floor and looking at all of Baghdad and the Joumhouriyah Bridge where US tanks were advancing. I could see the American tanks pushing in ... and a colleague said, 'Samia, Samia, come and look!', and then I just ran to look and I saw a glow, an orange glow. I was looking to see who had fired – and suddenly that was the tank shell that hit our office. It threw us down. It felt like fire coming out of my face, it was so painful. I was screaming and my colleagues were screaming. We were all on the floor and we knew we were hit but we didn't know what had happened, and our colleagues started shouting for help. Our office inside was full of journalists because they were feeding live from our offices because we had live satellite transmission, and they were trying to pull us out because they were worried that there would be another one coming. I couldn't open my eyes, and I felt like I lost my sight. My face was burning.

Just below, Omaar had been on his balcony, on the point of broadcasting to London, and was knocked down by the blast. When his wits returned he went upstairs to offer help to Reuters:

There was nothing but a gaping and blackened hole where the doors to the balcony had been. Shrapnel and blast marks had shredded the wallpaper and ceiling. Taras Protyusk [sic, Protsyuk], the Reuters cameraman who had been filming the American tanks on the Joumhouriya Bridge, lay flat on his back, in a pool of blood. The flesh of his stomach had been ripped apart. There was hysteria and anger and everyone was shouting. 'Tear the fucking bedsheets off, he's going to bleed to death!' 'No! No! We have to get him to hospital now, for God's sake ... Jesus Christ, somebody get a car....' A small number of photographers and cameramen were in the corner of the room, recording the scene. With hindsight one can understand what they were trying to do – it was, after all, no different from what we had been doing in the city throughout the war. But at that

above: One of the most famous moments from the 2003 US-led invasion of Iraq: the toppling of the huge statue of Saddam Hussein in Baghdad on 9 April 2003, photographed by Robert Nickelsberg.

opposite: 'Shock and Awe' in Baghdad: footage of the US strikes on 27 March 2003 from Al Arabia television was broadcast on CNN.

RICHARD ENGEL, 1973–

above: Richard Engel speaks live via satellite to NBC host David Gregory from Sderot in Israel regarding the Gaza conflict on 4 January 2009.

By the time Richard Engel had graduated from Stanford University in 1996 with a degree in International Relations, the Cold War was clearly over. Convinced that the Middle East would provide the new headlines, the young dyslexic from New York established himself in a Cairo slum, learned to read and write fluent Arabic and made himself a popular curiosity in the crowded neighbourhood, absorbing the local life and the values and preoccupations of the region. He supported himself by editing a small newspaper and writing freelance articles.

He made his name in Baghdad during the Second Gulf War when he secured a retainer from ABC, whose staff correspondents were evacuating. Throughout the conflict he broadcast live to ABC's audience, from the press centre as it came under attack, and from the Palestine hotel, securing an exclusive interview with Tariq Aziz on his last day as deputy prime minister. NBC News then offered him a job as a foreign correspondent, promoting him to Chief Foreign Correspondent five years later in 2008. Most of his time has been spent in the Middle East, particularly Iraq, and on a trip to New York in 2007 he discussed the region at some length with President George W. Bush. His 2011 reports and analysis of the uprisings in Egypt were widely praised.

Engel has received industry recognition for his work, including the 2009 RTNDA Edward R. Murrow Award and the 2007 Medill Medal for Courage in Journalism.

In 2008 Engel returned to the badly damaged Palestine hotel from where he had watched the bombings in 2003, and recorded his thoughts in a video diary. Like many correspondents he had believed that reporting wars would make him a tougher, harder person, but while exposure to death and violence had thickened his skin, he had come to find the experience painful.

moment it was too much for many of us and someone shouted at them to get out. ...[28]

Nakhoul 'could hear the shouting: someone should ask the hotel to put the generator on because they couldn't carry us fifteen floors, so finally we went down ... they were calling for cars. There was still fighting and firing coming: I could still hear it; and they put us in a car and they sped to the hospital. I could hear bombardment and I wasn't sure we wouldn't be hit again on the way to the hospital. And first of all I kept on telling a colleague, "I can't see, I lost my eyesight", and my total panic was not [caused by] the pain I was suffering from, but because I couldn't see. It was all black.'

The first hospital to which she and Protsyuk were taken lacked the equipment to treat her, but it was there that she overheard that he had died. 'To lose somebody who was so very close to us.... We were hoping that we'd all cover this war and come out of it safe. The night before he was saying to me that he couldn't wait to go home because he wanted to see his son again. He had one son and ... there was his son waiting to see his father after the war, and a wife waiting, and to hear now that he died.... This was the last day; we heard that it was coming to an end, but it was not the end that we wanted for us.'

The second hospital discovered that Nakhoul had shrapnel in her brain, and sent her to a third where, finally, she was given life-saving surgery. Sixteen hours after her operation, she was back at the Palestine hotel: 'The doctor came and said, "you have to leave the hospital", because the looting started and they were trying to break into the hospital. So I had to be taken from the hospital to the hotel with all my drips and antibiotics and the doctor promised that if Reuters sent a car he would come and look at my wound every day and give me the shot I needed to have.'

Two days later, the Americans evacuated her to a field hospital, and from there to Kuwait. A second journalist, Jose Cousos was also killed in the shelling.

Baghdad continues to be a dangerous place for journalists. Iraqi correspondent Huda Ahmed has learned to take nothing for granted. Her advice is to avoid the dangerous roads and anywhere that the US Army, contractors or Iraqi forces operate; keep the doors locked and the windows open: it is vital to hear what is going on outside; do not wear a seatbelt, because in an emergency it increases the time taken to get out of the car; have a second car following behind and maintain unobtrusive radio contact; always have a security plan for every assignment. 'The female reporters should were [sic] conser-

vative clothes like loose, long sleeve shirts and skirts or loose pants, and wear a headscarf. The interviews should be quick and to the point. At the same time, your eyes and ears should look for any suspicious moves. Be ready to leave right away.'[29]

Moving around the city has become so dangerous for correspondents that hiring security guards is normal. Peter Beaumont of the *Observer* grew intensely conscious of the risks posed by Improvised Explosive Devices (IEDs):

At first, travelling in military convoys, the fear of these things is utterly exhausting. The anticipation is felt physically. It is not being hit that becomes the issue, but where in the body the fragments might strike. I worry about the Kevlar sides to my body armour, where I would take the blast, lacking the ceramic side plates of the US soldiers' armour. I worry about the flak jacket sitting too high on my waist, exposing my liver, about my unprotected legs and groin, the location of large arteries. You cannot live like that. And while I wonder at the sangfroid of the soldiers, after a time my body imposes the same stillness. It is a fraught calmness I recognise from bad moments in mountaineering, a fatalistic feeling of acceptance. Not bravery, or resilience, but the process of being conditioned like a lab rat.[30]

PROTECTIVE CLOTHING AND SECURITY MEASURES

From the First Gulf War onwards, correspondents were issued with protective equipment. Until that time, Martin Bell had relied on a collection of charms sent to him by various well-wishers – 'They all kept me alive, so they worked.'[31] – and on the trademark lucky white suits that he had first started wearing during the war in Croatia: '... there was so much lead flying through the air. I am so lucky to have survived, and in some ways it was more dangerous than the Bosnian war. And I ascribed my survival to the wearing of the white suit. It also sort of became a recognition symbol ... "there goes that daft Englishman in the white suit".'

The need for additional protection was brought home to him 1992 during the siege of Sarajevo, after he had been driving across the runway at the free-fire zone that was Sarajevo airport:

... I thought it was quiet, I was wrong. We got shot up in our Vauxhall Carlton, I've got a bullet that came right through the window, just right next to my head

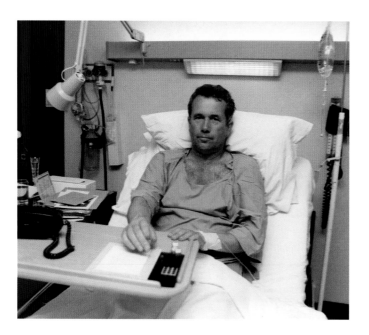

and another lodged in the door jam. And I wrote to [Vauxhall] afterwards, thanking them for making an armoured vehicle without knowing it. And as soon as I got to the safety of the other side I got onto the phone to London and I said 'Look we've got to have an armoured vehicle' and then they brought in body armour and everything.[32]

However, armoured vehicles only offer protection while the passengers are inside, and Bell was injured in 1992 when he went to investigate fighting around the city's Marshal Tito Barracks. 'I stayed out of the armoured vehicle too long and I got hit by some pieces of shrapnel. It was not a very serious wound, I was only in hospital for six days, but it was a bit difficult to gear yourself up for getting back after that. I took three months off. That was in August and I didn't get back until December, rather nervously I have to say, because clearly I was not immortal, contrary to what I might have thought before.'

When it comes to kidnapping there are, maintains James Fergusson:

… things you can do to avoid it. Most obviously: just keep a low profile. The worst thing you can do is to start hiring armed guards and putting on flak jackets and going about in a big 4x4. I've always taken the view that you're much safer if you try to blend in with the population. I've dressed locally; I've put on Afghan robes: the shalwar kameez, waistcoat, even a hat – and, these days, tried to grow a decent beard

before I go. It doesn't fool anybody at close quarters, but if you're sitting at the back of the car it's going to help. I would think hard before putting on a burka. The consequences, if you were caught, would be very serious.[33]

Engel, who joined NBC in May 2003, also favoured the low-key approach, travelling around Baghdad in 'Odd Job', a rusty pick-up fitted out as a mobile TV uplink and with a canvas rear cab. It blended in with the local traffic rather than advertising its presence with pristine white paint and TV company logos. However, by the end of 2004 he and the rest of the NBC team were travelling with professional security guards.

THE CONSTANT DANGER – KIDNAP

Arguably the first kidnap of a journalist to gain massive international attention was that of the *Wall Street Journal*'s American correspondent Daniel Pearl, who was beheaded by his Al-Qaeda captors in Pakistan in 2002 after the US government refused their demands.

In 2005 Italian journalist Giuliana Sgrena was abducted outside Baghdad University and held for a month by a group demanding the withdrawal of Italian troops from the coalition. Sgrena, a veteran pacifist reporter of *Il Manifesto*, was vehemently opposed to her country's involvement in Iraq, as her captors came to realize; they justified her kidnap on the grounds of having to use whatever means came to hand.

A month later she was informed she was to be freed. Left in a car, blindfolded, she was duly collected by Italian intelligence officer Major General Nicola Calipari and driven towards the airport. An American soldier at a makeshift checkpoint opened fire; Calipari threw himself over Sgrena. She was wounded in the shoulder; he became a posthumous hero. The US authorities claimed the car was travelling at 100 miles (160 kilometres) per hour and failed to stop when signalled to do so; Sgrena has continued to maintain that no such warning was given and that the speed was closer to 40 miles (64 kilometres) per hour.

Sgrena's freedom was achieved by negotiation, whereas that of the *New York Times*'s Stephen Farrell, in September 2009, was by force of arms. He had travelled to investigate the results of a NATO air strike on two fuel tankers, which had been hijacked near Kunduz by the Taliban. Afghan sources had claimed around 90 people had been killed and more injured, many of them civilians helping themselves to fuel. On 9 September he and his interpreter/assistant, Sultan Munadi, were captured by the Taliban, at the site of the air strike, held in a farmhouse compound and well treated, while their kidnappers opened ransom negotiations for Farrell. Four days later the compound was stormed by a joint force of men from Britain's SAS and the Afghan Army.

Munadi and Farrell ran out, the former shouting that they were journalists before he died in a burst of machine gun fire. Farrell hit the ground, yelling that he was a British hostage and flashing a torch. A few minutes later he was airborne, but celebrations died away. A 29-year-old SAS corporal, John Harrison, had been mortally wounded and Farrell had to look at his blood-soaked helmet during the flight. He thanked his rescuers, acknowledging afterwards that gratitude would always be inadequate, and when asked if he thought there was any obligation on the armed forces to attempt to rescue journalists, he offered an emphatic 'No'.[34]

During Farrell's four-day ordeal, his Taliban guards had alluded to the capture, in March 2007, of *La Repubblica*'s Italian-Swiss correspondent Daniele Mastrogiacomo. The 53-year-old was a veteran of Iraq, Palestine and Somalia as well as Afghanistan, and he had an experienced Afghan friend and 'fixer' with whom he had worked before – Ajmal Naqshbandi – as well as a Pashtun driver, Sayed Agha, who was reputed to be the best in Helmand province. The trio were seized while on the way to an arranged interview with a Taliban commander, and suffered brutal treatment including flogging. But infinitely worse was to come, when they were sentenced to death:

Sayed has been dragged in front of us. He is on his knees. Three, maybe four large men are standing right behind him. They push him down into the sandy desert floor. Sayed can't breathe. Now, they're on top of him, they turn him over and as they do so I see that the knife has already been drawn. One of our jailors holds it in his hand. I can't see the blade but I see something that cuts into Sayed's neck. A quick, neat cut. There are no spasms, no moans or cries; nothing: The scene plays out in an icy silence. Then, a hand. One of the Taliban works on Sayed's neck, front and back. Sayed's body is inert by now. His head is removed and they lay it on his torso. They clean the knife on his white tunic.[35]

In a deal negotiated by Italian surgeon Gino Strada, Mastrogiacomo was freed after two weeks in exchange for the release of five Taliban prisoners. Ajmal's release was likewise promised but

opposite: BBC journalist Martin Bell in hospital after being wounded in Sarajevo.

above: The *Wall Street Journal*'s Daniel Pearl in a photograph taken by his kidnappers prior to his murder.

above: Driver Sayed Agha, Daniele Mastrogiacomo and Ajmal Naqshbandi filmed by their Afghan captors. The footage was shown on Radiotelevisone Italiana (RAI) on 10 April 2007.

opposite: British freelance James Fergusson, wearing typical Pashtun clothing, with two lieutenants of Commander Abdullah, during one of his visits to interview the Taliban in Afghanistan.

overleaf left: A mud wall provides cover for US Marines and Afghan National Army soldiers in Helmand Province as Taliban insurgents open fire. A photograph taken by Julie Jacobson the day before her controversial image of the injured marine.

overleaf right: Resting on his pack, US correspondent Dexter Filkins files a story by satphone in November 2004 during the battle for Fallujah, just as a rocket is fired behind him.

the Taliban reneged on the agreement and beheaded him in April. In response to his murder, war correspondents ensured that the families of both Ajmal and Sayed were supported, and the Frontline Club has now organized a special fund to help fixers.[36]

In November 2008 David Rhode of the New York Times and Afghan journalist Tahir Luddin were captured outside Kabul and taken over the border into Waziristan, a Taliban-controlled area of Pakistan. Their captors were primarily mercenary and treated them comparatively well while ineffectual negotiations were conducted. Uniquely, the press preserved such a strict blackout that the first that the world knew of the kidnapping came seven months later when the two men used an old towrope to scale the wall of their compound in Miram Shah and walked openly down the street to a Pakistan military base where they asked for assistance.

Others have not been so lucky. French journalists Hervé Ghesquière and Stéphane Taponier have been held since December 2009. Harry Burton and Azizullah Haidari (Reuters), Maria

Grazia Cutulli (*Corriere della Sera*) and Julio Fuentes (*El Mundo*) were all murdered in 2001.

Aware of Afghanistan's dangers, not least from gun-wielding children stopping cars, James Fergusson has met the Taliban on several occasions:

> *The Taliban proper won't kidnap you because they would be shooting the messenger. They have a media agenda just as we do and they know that if they kidnap journalists they are just not going to get that message out.*

> *You have to make sure you know whom you're going to interview. If you go and interview some fake Taliban ... anything could happen. But if your contacts are good, and Mir's are directly plugged into the headquarters chain, I think it's absolutely fine. They do kidnap people sometimes if it is to their advantage, and I've discussed that with them – I did in October [2010]. I was talking to this commander, Abdullah, whom I'd met before, three years ago. One of his men piped up and said: 'I hope you don't take offence at this, but aren't you a bit worried that we might kill you?' I said: 'Well, not at all. I know you're good Pashtuns, and as good Pashtuns you're obliged to look after me because I'm your guest.' And they all nodded sagely and said 'Yes, you're quite right, but without Pashtunwali[37] we'd certainly kill you.'*

> *I've always been much more frightened of a stray bomb coming through the roof from our side.[38]*

Getting the Story Out

THE TRUTH AND NOTHING BUT THE TRUTH

Credibility still comes in two forms: accurate reporting from the front and the willingness of editors to give space to the story.

The faking of footage and images still goes on. John Simpson relates the story of picture editor Dennis Clarke who in 1980 showed him some footage which a foreign broadcaster had offered to the BBC. It purported to show a mujahideen attack on Soviet troops in Afghanistan but the editor's practised eye had

immediately identified it as a cobbled-together fake in which the 'Soviet' aircraft was easily identifiable as an American F-14.

A different type of fake cost Brian Walski, of the *Los Angeles Times*, his career as a combat photographer. He had covered numerous wars and been with troops in Basra, southern Iraq. A British soldier warned a group of Iraqi civilians to take cover from possible incoming fire. One man was on his feet with a child in his arms, and the soldier gestured and shouted to him to get down. The photograph, shot from a low viewpoint, was widely used. Then someone in the USA studied the picture closely, looking for known faces, and made the discovery that some of the civilians appeared more than once. The photograph that had been so much admired was created from two images. They told the story, but in one image the man with the baby was looking away from the camera; in the second, he is perfectly composed, but unfortunately the soldier's gun appears to be pointing at the baby's head.

Although the published image told no lies, it broke the *Los Angeles Times's* strict rules that no photograph may be doctored. Contacted by phone in Iraq in the hope that the photograph might be explained by gremlins on the satellite link, Walski admitted putting the two pictures together, and was promptly fired. Those who considered him to have been harshly treated pointed to the fact that reporters can make notes on a story and then write it up and tweak it before filing; others maintained that to allow manipulated images would be to destroy the credibility of combat photographers, which, in the words of Vincent LaForet of the *New York Times*, 'is all that we have'.

Even when a reporter tells the truth, and the censor (if there is one) lets it through, it is still far from certain that the story will reach an

audience. Considerations of taste, decency and public interest may intervene. The most shocking story filed by Ian Stewart was based on his interview with the widower of a pregnant woman in Sierra Leone whose house was invaded by rebels. They put a gun to the husband's head, stabbed his wife in the abdomen and pulled out the seven-month foetus, dead of stab wounds, and told them it was a girl – before slitting the woman's throat.

Stewart filed at 15:00 New York time and rang an hour later to check on his story, asking whether it was 'on the budget' – jargon for one of the main stories that AP was putting on the wire. "'Nope", I was told. "The General Desk feels it's just another story about a little war in Africa". "Well, if that's how they feel, then what the fuck am I doing here risking my life?" I barked back.'[39]

AP, which had released the emotive Vietnam image of Kim Phuc, released an even more controversial photograph, taken by embedded photographer Julie Jacobson in Helmand province, Afghanistan. It showed a US Marine after he had been hit by a rocket-propelled grenade, which took off one leg and destroyed another. With bullets flying over the scene, Jacobson lay flat on the ground, trying to get her pictures in the failing light that only allowed a shutter speed of half a second, and wondering if she should have been helping the dying casualty's comrades. Afterwards she argued that it was important to confront people at home with the reality of war, and that it is too

easy to read the story over coffee and then move on. It is harder to ignore a photograph.

The strongest criticism of the published image centred on the violation of the family's wishes for the picture not to be made public, though some have argued that it should not have been taken, much less considered for release.

News organizations generally associate credibility with objectivity and even-handedness. If 'side A' claims success in an engagement, 'side B' should be given the opportunity to comment; a massacre by 'side A' should be counterbalanced by an atrocity by 'side B'. It is a requirement that war correspondents have often found hard to equate with truthful reporting. As Vaughan Smith puts it: 'You can be subjective; you just have to be honest and open.'[40]

'In words that Martha Gellhorn would surely have approved, Maggie O'Kane described her job as:

… to try and paint a true picture, of what was happening in whatever war we were doing… [If you are] painting the picture of life in Sarajevo under siege then you are describing what life is like for people there; well, then you can be accused, as I was many times, of being lacking in objectivity and being anti … Bosnian Serb but I was painting that

objectivity and that life and those fears … the desperation that was there. So that wasn't objective but it was true. We need to be careful of objectivity because sometimes we can hide behind it, because we think oh I'd better not be seen to be too much this side or the other, when … you know that these tools are being often abused by the political leadership to paint an inaccurate picture.[41]

ON THE WIRE

The old maxim of 'the best story in the world is utterly useless if it's still in your notebook at edition time' was by then echoing dully and painfully through my brain

Ian Bruce

Since the early 1980s reporting technology has changed dramatically, to the point where the sounds and images of war can be relayed almost instantly to the consumer at home or on the move. Audiences are no longer dependent on their national television channels but instead have access to as many international broadcasters as their satellite dish can offer. New players including CNN and Al-Jazeera have joined the established television news media, and 24-hour channels bring breaking news from around the world.

Although the changing technology has brought advantages, it has also made the job of reporting with insight 'much, much harder', according to Michael Nicholson. ' … I have often had the luxury of sitting down in a hotel room for half a day, thinking about a story and writing it, and then people say "what a wonderful commentary that was". Well, I had time to do it. Nowadays kids have got to rush in front of a live camera having just stepped off an aeroplane.'[42]

Vietnam had given the BBC's Martin Bell his first taste of war reporting as early as 1967 and during the 11 conflicts he covered he, too, witnessed the communications revolution:

By the end of the mid-80s we were in the age of satellites as well, then you get satellite trucks, satellite dishes, the whole paraphernalia, which actually I welcomed because it gave me as a professional in the field a vast amount of freedom. In the old days … film would be sent home in packages in aircraft with a soundtrack. And when it reached London it would be processed and edited, the pictures set against the soundtrack. A fiddly process. But it also meant that if the editors wanted to fiddle around with or take bits out, substitute the middle for the end or something, they had the freedom to do it, which I found immensely depressing. Whereas, when the satellites came along, we edited in the field close to where the action had been. You negotiate lengths with London but it would only arrive there 10 minutes before the programme, they had no choice but to run it or drop it, they couldn't change it.[43]

During the First Gulf War, the British Army, unlike the Americans, allowed its embedded television correspondents to set up their own Forward Transmission Unit (FTU) and make live broadcasts. Although the BBC had taken a satellite dish into Afghanistan after the Soviet invasion, this was the first time that British television had carried one right into a war zone. General Sir Peter de la Billière, Commander-in-Chief British Forces, asked what would happen if the broadcasters were to be captured, and expressed himself satisfied by their assurances that by turning the dish upside down they could convince any captors that it was the wok they used for self-catering.

Military satellite phones were made available to embedded Iraq correspondents, and Ian Bruce, attached to the British 4th Armoured Brigade, used one to dictate copy to the *Glasgow Herald*. The weak link was not the technology but the competence of the copytaker at the other end, a problem that beset James Fergusson in Algiers in 1992. He managed to find a working phone in order to file his story, but had to watch his bill adding up at the rate of £1 a minute while the slow copytaker plodded away and even stopped work to get a cup of tea.

Bruce was an eyewitness to the carnage caused by the Serbian mortar that exploded in the main market in Sarajevo in 1994 and caused heavy casualties, and he was determined to transmit his story:

But there was no working phone in the entire city to which I could gain access. I hitched a ride back out to the coast on a UN helicopter and then thumbed

another ride out to HMS Coventry, a Royal Navy warship patrolling the Adriatic.

Once on board, I immediately sought permission to use the vessel's facilities to send out the story. Unfortunately, Malcolm Rifkind, the then Defence Secretary, arrived at about the same time and commandeered the ship's entire electronic communications' suite. Three other reporters from Fleet Street had also managed to worm their way aboard, intent on being first out with accounts of the atrocity. We sat together in the ship's wardroom for more than two hours, fuming at the delay, united briefly in our inability to call our offices and fretting furiously as deadlines approached. Just then, a helicopter crewman wandered up and asked me if I had a scar running just under my hairline and back towards my scalp. I said I did, amazed at how he knew … the crewman simply smiled mysteriously and whispered that I should follow him out a minute after he left the wardroom.[44]

The crewman turned out to have been the loadmaster who had hauled the unconscious Bruce into his helicopter during the Falklands War (see page 175):

[and] since we were fellow-Falklands veterans, he was prepared to let me use a ship-to-shore radio connection overlooked by the politicians.

It was a fragile link plagued with atmospheric interference, but it was the only link in town, as they say. At that point, I would gladly have accepted a carrier-pigeon if one had been made available. I should have known my luck was too good to last. When the connection with the office was made, Big Maggie answered the call at the copytakers, desk.

The result? My world exclusive datelined story read not 'From HMS Coventry off the Yugoslav coast', but simply 'From Coventry'.[45]

During the 1990s the wire services provided by Reuters, AP, UPI and so on had moved from the old, expensive cables to high-speed phone lines and satellite links. Their offices no longer rattled with the staccato chatter of the teletype machines, and their distant correspondents filed images and stories in a few seconds, a far cry from the five hours it once took to send a cable message from the Crimea to London.

Videophones that could send back images from remote locations were still new in 2001. Their quality, never of the highest order, was impaired by a poor satellite link, as John Simpson found out when he tried to send a video report out of Afghanistan, close to a Taliban outpost. The culprit was assumed to be the rough journey by truck and horse, and Simpson could only offer an audio report.

By the start of the Second Gulf War in 2003, correspondents went out with their laptops and satellite phones, but Ian Bruce, embedded with the troops, found that system far from perfect. Sandstorms and temperatures in excess of 100 degrees do not agree with laptops, and his machine died after two days, followed a day later by that of his colleague from the *Scotsman*. So it was back to the previous regime of hand-writing the dispatch for censorship before dictation by satellite phone to a copytaker in Harrogate:

> … [and] there were many catches to that method. The first was that passing jets tended to break the satphone signal. And it's a feature of front lines that fast jets tend to hurtle overhead annoyingly often. The second was that filing an 800-word piece could take up to an hour so it needed repeated redialling and the likely prospect of being connected to a different copytaker each time. This also meant the hassle of trying to ensure they joined up the disparate sections of story in the right order. The heat of the desert day and the freezing cold of the desert night also played havoc with phone batteries. Every call was a race against time. The temperature gradient meant that batteries which might be expected to work for up to three hours in the UK lasted barely 50 minutes in Iraq. Despite the newsdesk's sublime belief that we could just plug them into a magical recharger out in the sandy wastes, the real-life process was a trifle more complex.
>
> We stole a Land Rover battery and rigged up a Heath Robinson contraption involving an inverter and two elastic bands to restore power. But it took four to five hours to achieve a full charge for each satphone. That process dictated our lives.[46]

The Humanist Dimension

GETTING INVOLVED

> *I cannot understand the few journalists I have met who insist that, if confronted by casualties, their job is merely to film, photograph, or report without giving aid….*
>
> Anthony Loyd (1966–), British war correspondent, in *My War Gone By, I Miss It So*, 2000

For journalists face to face with the human cost of war, there is often an imperative to do something, however small, even if it helps just one person. Fergal Keane went back to Rwanda on several occasions to report on Valentina, a young women whom he had first seen as a traumatized orphan with terrible machete injuries and whom he thought certain to die.

The day before the attack on the Palestine hotel in 2003, Samia Nakhoul and the Reuters team had filmed 12-year-old Ali Ismaeel Abbas in a Baghdad hospital after a US missile destroyed his home, killed most of his family, and left him badly burned and with no arms. Her report went round the world, and led to his receiving treatment and prosthetic arms in Britain, paid for by Kuwait.

Of the day he drove a child, who had a gunshot wound to her head, to the nearest hospital, Anthony Loyd wrote angrily: 'Who were we to stand back and do nothing, justifying inaction by claiming with misplaced arrogance that our job was only to report? What good did reporting ever do in Bosnia anyway? … It was not sentimentalism that made us ditch our cameras and run back up the track to the UNHCR[47] house carrying the bleeding bodies. It was humanist logic. To do anything else would have been indefensible.'[48]

The most remarkable example of a journalist crossing the line between reporting and intervention, while still on assignment, arguably belongs to Michael Nicholson. At the main Sarajevo hospital a young doctor showed him the children who had survived a shell and told him tearfully: 'These are the innocent ones: these are the ones that must be protected … save the innocent ones.'

For Nicholson, this was a turning point. The story of the war in Bosnia was no longer about the politics – 'it was about the human casualties, and most especially the children. And we did that story, and it had enormous impact….' It also led to Michael Montgomery, an American reporter working for the *Daily Telegraph*, to suggest that Nicholson visit a Roman Catholic orphanage near the hospital,

SAMIA NAKHOUL, 1960–

above: Samia Nakhoul (left), Reuters photographer Faleh Kheiber (centre) and TV cameraman Paul Pasquale, prepare for their medical evacuation from Baghdad in a military ambulance on 12 April 2003. They had been badly wounded when a US Army tank shell hit the Reuters office in the Palestine hotel.

Samia Nakhoul was born in Lebanon and decided on a career in journalism while growing up during the long-running Lebanese Civil War. She worked for Beirut's *Daily Star* and the Arabic-language *An-Nahar* newspaper at the same time as she was studying for her degree in international affairs and journalism, and her first years as a war correspondent were spent reporting the hostage-taking, suicide attacks and car bombs that characterized the violent struggle in her country.

In 1986, she joined Reuters from UPI, and covered the First Gulf War from the Iraq-Jordanian border, before being posted to Cairo. There she spent almost five years reporting on the insurgency by Islamic Jihad and Al-Gama'a Islamiya and the subsequent government crackdown.

Following short periods in London and India she returned to the Middle East as Bureau Chief for Lebanon and Syria before being appointed Gulf Bureau chief in 2003. Fluent in Arabic as well as French and English, and familiar with Baghdad, she was keen to cover the Second Gulf War, having previously reported on the effect of UN sanctions. It was a choice that almost killed her when she was badly injured by shrapnel from a shell fired at the Reuters offices by a US tank.

After spending a few months recovering from her injuries she decided not to return to conflict reporting, but on a trip to Saudi Arabia to recruit correspondents and write some features she heard that al-Qaeda had taken a number of hostages. With no other Reuters journalist present, she went to cover the story, only to be caught in the firefight between al-Qaeda militants and Saudi special forces.

Samia Nakhoul is currently Reuters Middle East News Editor. In 2010 she received a prestigious Peace Through Media award. The prize is given to journalists whose work is of 'such quality that it has helped to foster a climate of peace and understanding' in the Middle East.

in which 200 orphans from another institution were now housed for their own safety in the cellar. 'So I did a story on it, and I remember saying that it's extraordinary, is it not, that you have 200 children living in a cellar in the front line of a war, children who could, in fact, be airlifted out to safety for the duration of the war to save their lives. It was easy enough.' An evacuee himself during the Second World War, 'I appealed on camera: "why can't these children be taken out?"'[49]

Among the children was a 'feisty little thing', 9-year-old Natasha whom he could not get out of his head. Nor, when he asked the authorities, could he get her out of Sarajevo, until a young Frenchwoman agreed to sneak Natasha onto one of the coaches that her charity had brought from Paris to evacuate children. Nicholson and his crew travelled with them, ostensibly to cover the mission.

At Zagreb, Nicholson added Natasha's name to his passport as his accompanied 'daughter', bought her suitable clothes, booked her on a business class flight with him to London and declared her at Immigration, where staff proved unexpectedly helpful. Natasha remained with the Nicholson family and was legally adopted by them.

Jeremey Bowen questions the motives of politicians who jump on the bandwagon when it comes to helping individual victims of war, but he also acknowledges journalists' motives may not stand the deepest scrutiny, either. Referring to the case of the Bosnian child whom he helped to evacuate, he wrote, 'We also intervene in people's lives, telling ourselves that the upshot of it all will be positive. What right had I to play God...? The answer is that I thought I was doing good, that I was righting a wrong.'[50]

THE SCARS OF WAR
A century and a half of war reporting can never prepare correspondents for what they themselves may experience when they venture into the field. A tough ex-soldier like Loyd saw the effect of Bosnia in the eyes: 'Whether it is your own or someone else's, the taste of evil leaves an indelible mark on the iris. You can see it flickering in moments of introspection as the muscles relax. I do not know if I would have recognized the pre-war picture on my own ID card – the open baby face, tousled hair and curious innocence – had I seen it lying on the forest floor that day. I find that man almost a stranger now.'[51]

Famous for some of the most moving reporting to have come out of conflict zones, Fergal Keane described his experience of Rwanda as:

... the defining experience of my adult life. There is no question about that. I had covered wars before I went to Rwanda. I had been in Angola. I'd lived in Northern Ireland. And I covered the township violence in ... Africa where thousands of people died. But nothing prepared me for what I saw in Rwanda.

... Just after the genocide, when I'd wake up in the night, this was a dream of being hidden under corpses, and a man with red eyes and a machete pulling the corpses away to get at me. And that was just born. I know where that came from. That came from the road blocks, and the looks on people's faces.

But now it's kind of waking up with a sense of failure as a human being.[52]

That sense of failure haunted CNN's Michael Ware, pushing him into post-traumatic stress disorder. For him, the trigger was an incident in 2007 in which US soldiers in Diyala province shot a young Iraqi carrying a gun. It was not the killing itself that caused him anguish – he regarded that as legitimate – but the fact that it took the youth 20 minutes to die from the head wound, during which neither the soldiers nor Ware himself took any action to ease the suffering. At the time, he was preoccupied with getting his pictures; afterwards he recognized the dehumanizing effect of war on himself and the soldiers, made worse when CNN not only refused to show the videotape but did not use the story. In 2010, he went on medical leave.

Samia Nakhoul believes she has been changed. 'I saw so much suffering and misery throughout my reporting ... I became so much more active. I feel that through my pen, through my writing, I can make a difference.... The panic of war gets to me, the fear. When I watch the television and I see what's happening in Libya, it gets to me.'

Looking back on 12 wars, Jeremy Bowen realized: ... that you cannot spend your time not just close to destruction but looking for it every day, and come out unscathed. And that makes you crazy too. The really mad thing is that I miss the thought of driving down a road towards the sound of gunfire and a horizon full of smoke, even though wars killed my friends and could easily have killed me. War reporting gave me some of my best moments, helped me build a career, made me a better journalist and most of all felt worthwhile. I was trying to shine a torch at the darkest places in the world; I thought it was a job that had to be done, and that I could do it better than anyone.'[53]

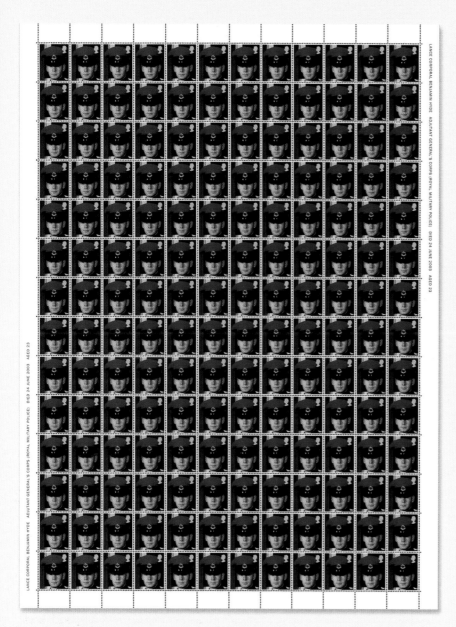

left: 'Queen and Country', 2007

Steve McQueen, 1969–
Steve McQueen set out to commemorate British soldiers killed in Iraq. He contacted their families, asking them to choose a photograph of their loved one in uniform, and from each image he created a sheet of stamps. The 160 sheets are housed in a wooden cabinet, in double-sided frames each of which can be pulled out by the viewer.

MODERN WAR ART

The official commissioning of artists to record British engagement in conflict continued after 1918, and during the Second World War it was administered by the newly established War Artists Advisory Committee under the chairmanship of Sir Kenneth Clark. Anthony Gross, Edward Bawden and Edward Ardizzone produced watercolour images from the foreign theatres of war, while Stephen Bone was appointed as the Royal Navy's official artist. Albert Richards, a serving paratrooper for four years, painted 'The Landing Hour minus six' (1944) after going in with the 9th Battalion, 6th Airborne Division on D-Day, and was later killed by a landmine *after* being released from military duties to concentrate on his art.

On the home front, artists as diverse as Kenneth Rowntree, John Piper and Henry Moore recorded everything from the Blitz to jam-making by the Women's Institute and the destruction of Coventry Cathedral.

In 1972 the Imperial War Museum established the Artistic Records Committee, which commissioned artists to commemorate a wide range of activity, from military tailoring to exercises. Early conflicts covered included the Northern Ireland 'Troubles' and the Falklands War – for which Linda Kitson sketched the troops in conté crayon, often in sub-zero temperatures.

In 1990, when 'war artists' were renamed 'official recorders', John Keane was commissioned to cover the First Gulf War. As well as sketch his ideas in situ, he used a camera and video recorder, and the 35 paintings that he created on his return were exhibited in the UK. Two were selected by the Museum: 'Micky Mouse At the Front' and 'Death Squad': a group of soldiers, masked against the sand, carrying a body bag.

The UN peacekeeping in Bosnia during the 1990s was depicted by Peter Howson, and his grotesque work provoked some disquiet

left: 'Mickey Mouse at the Front', 1991

John Keane, 1954–

'Micky Mouse at the Front' incorporates elements from the photographs Keane took in Kuwait City after its liberation: a broken palm tree; RPGs in a supermarket trolley; excrement on the ground. A Mickey Mouse model from a fairground ride sits incongruously among the devastation. The image can be interpreted as an attack on the cultural insensitivity of the USA, the weapons trade and the media circus that surrounds modern war.

below: The Imperial War Museum's official recorder of the First Gulf War, John Keane, works on a sketch.

because it depicted imaginary events. Controversy crystallized around the hard-hitting rape scene 'Croatian and Muslim', based on stories Howson had been told rather than an event he had witnessed.

Arabella Dorman became the first female war artist to go to the front line when in December 2006 she covered the Iraq war in Basra at the invitation of the Army, frequently coming under insurgent fire. Her aim was to evoke the emotional impact of war rather than its obvious horrors, and she came to have a great admiration for the soldiers among whom she spent her time. This respect was shared by the Turner Prize winner Steve McQueen, who also went to Iraq in 2006.

Why, in an age of photography, do we need war artists? The answer may be that a photograph is valid as a frozen moment; a painting or drawing, by contrast, is an impression, an interpretation, mediated by the human imagination and offering a complementary account of one of mankind's oldest impulses.

The internet is full of the images of conflict and protest uploaded by those who are caught up in it – constantly updated, and supplemented by blogs. It begs the question: is the day of the professional war correspondent coming to an end a mere century and a half after it 'officially' began? Has the very technology that made it possible for the war correspondent to bring a conflict into every home proved a treacherous friend by allowing anybody with a mobile phone and an internet-enabled computer to do the job even more quickly and far more cheaply? Is the public well served by its war correspondents?

The big players can afford to maintain a global network of often locally recruited correspondents ready to break a story and with sufficient knowledge to evaluate and interpret the raw information obtained on the streets. 'We are there before anyone else,' claimed Samia Nakhoul of Reuters, citing the 2011 revolution in Egypt as an example. 'People fly into places because they see a story is coming but we were there from the beginning in Tahrir Square. Our reporting highlighted that a big change was coming to this country.'[1]

The End of the Line?
the future of war reporting

JUST KEEP TALKING

When journalists are metaphorically parachuted into a developing situation, the importance of the story sometimes seems to be determined more by the quantity of the images and live commentary than the quality of the information. Michael Nicholson has sympathy for young correspondents. 'We blame them for their slightly downmarket, lightweight reports, but they don't have much time to think about them'.[2]

Maggie O'Kane shares these concerns, believing that it is a 'travesty that journalism has become so centred on delivering on the hour every hour ... that actually we aren't finding out things any more'. Her target is the Green Zone in Kabul and Iraq in which the military hold two daily briefings for the media, 'so everyone is hanging around like starving birds ... waiting for the press conference.... The demands of digital media are turning us into almost camera legs'.[3]

Live mobile phone conversations with civilians in war zones are dramatic, but not validated. Neither the studio anchorman nor the audience has any idea of the veracity of the interviewee, yet the mere fact that they are allowed to tell their story on a major news channel gives credence to their message. And the initiative lies with the willing interviewees who may have an undeclared agenda.

'If you don't have access, if you cannot see people, it's better to get in touch on the phone,' concedes Nakhoul, 'but there is nothing better than somebody *being* there, talking to the person in front of you. I remember the time I covered Iraq: there was a woman who lost three sons – I learned this story just by being next to her and hearing how she was mourning, and I don't think the telephone link would capture the enormity of what she had been through. She was consumed with grief; she was hysterical. Just sitting there with her and her family, listening to how she was mourning, was enough for me to write for the world what she was going through'.[4]

That opportunity does not exist for the embedded journalist. After working with the British Army, Vaughan Smith has concluded: 'they don't enable you to show the suffering of war. If you are there when a British soldier gets hurt, lots of soldiers, who appeared not to notice you before, suddenly get in the way of your camera. You are supposed to get the permission of the soldier who's been injured. Well, nobody seriously injured or anybody in any pain is going to want to give you permission'. The result is that wars have 'somehow become wallpaper wars: they carry on, and we don't really notice them. The quality of the pictures has been amazing, but we haven't seen the suffering of war'.[5]

above: RASC drivers, engaged in the difficult and dangerous job of bringing ammunition and petrol to the Allied troops in Libya, crowd round a portable radio set in 1942 in order to get the latest news on the fighting from the BBC.

LOSING THE WAR?

'We have not,' according to Smith, 'built a model for internet journalism that is working, and consequently the industry is starved of money, and that means that it is shrinking, cost-cutting, and it's losing its morale. In my view, we're failing to deliver the promise to inform the public at a time when we seem to be constantly at war; at a time when public relations has stuffed coffers and a lot of journalists who lose their calling ... move to PR. We cannot have healthy democracies without good quality journalism'.[6]

Perhaps the real future for war reporting lies with the freelances who can research their stories away from both PR manipulation and the voracity of the 24-hour news service. But they must sell their material in order to survive. Most news organizations are par-

tially or entirely funded by advertising; all are under pressure to give 'value for money'. Insightful, honest, often uncomfortable war journalism is not cheap, and will thrive only if the 'consumer', in a sound-bite society that prefers information to knowledge, thinks it is worth the cost.

'We are important to you,' maintains Nicholson. 'You should know what goes on in the Falklands; you should know what's going on in Egypt and Tunisia and Syria. You should know the facts as we see them because – forgive me for being sarcastic and perhaps too cynical – you won't hear it from our governments, and you won't hear it necessarily from our military. I'd like you to trust us'.[7]

notes

Full details of all books listed in the Notes can be found in the Selected Bibliography on pages 218–219.

THE TRAILBLAZERS

1 Dispatch dated 9 September 1854, published in *The Times*, 10 October.

2 Dispatch dated 2 January 1855, published in *The Times*, 24 January.

3 From a dispatch of 25 October 1854 containing the heading 'THE CAVALRY ACTION AT BALAKLAVA', published in *The Times*, 14 November.

4 From the *Commercial* newspaper, 20 June 1861.

5 Dispatch dated 22 July 1861, published in *The Times*, 6 August.

6 Monaghan, James, *The Man Who Elected Lincoln*, p.247.

7 A type of muzzle-loading rifle bullet named after its co-developer, Claude Etienne Minié.

8 Written at Cairo, Illinois, 1862, quoted in Griffis, William Elliot, *Charles Carleton Coffin: War Correspondent, Traveller, Author, and Statesman*.

9 Page, Charles A., *Letters of a War Correspondent*.

10 This reference is a quotation from Milton's *Paradise Lost*.

11 Page, *Letters of a War Correspondent*, p.145.

12 *Ibid.*, p.99.

13 'Fighting it out on this line' is a quotation from Ulysses S. Grant.

14 Page, *Letters of a War Correspondent*.

15 Raymer, Jacob Nathaniel, (Edited by E.B. Munson) *Confederate Correspondent: The Civil War Reports of Jacob Nathaniel Raymer, Fourth North Carolina*, p.39.

16 *Ibid.*, p.112.

17 Dispatch dated 4 July, published in *The New York Times*, 6 July 1863.

18 Blackett, R.J.M. (Editor), *Thomas Morris Chester, Black War Correspondent: His Dispatches from the Virginia Front*.

19 *Ibid.*

20 *Ibid.*

21 *Ibid.*

22 Steevens, G.W. (Edited by Blackburn, Vernon), *From Capetown to Ladysmith: An Unfinished Record of the South African War*.

23 According to Vernon Blackburn, who edited and wrote the introduction to *From Capetown to Ladysmith*.

24 Davis, Richard Harding, *With Both Armies In South Africa*.

25 *Ibid.*

26 Hales, Alfred Greenwood, *Campaign Pictures of the War in South Africa (1899-1900): Letters from the Front*.

27 *Ibid.*

28 Wallace, Edgar, *Edgar Wallace by Himself*.

29 A Joseph Rosenthal also filmed during the Boer War, but he should not be confused with the stills photographer Joe Rosenthal of Iwo Jima fame.

OUTLAWS AND CAPTIVES

1 Fyfe, Henry Hamilton, *My Seven Selves*.

2 Powell, E. Alexander, *The Fighting In Flanders* (2004 ed), p.4. (first published in 1914.)

3 Gibbs, Philip, *The Soul of the War* (1915 ed), p.40.

4 Villiers, Frederic, *Villiers: His Five Decades Of Adventure*.

5 Davis, Richard Harding, *With the Allies*, p.8.

6 Thomas, Sir William Beach, *The Way of a Countryman*, p. 106.

7 Davis, *With the Allies*, p.9.

8 Gibbs, *The Soul of the War*, p.124. Gibbs had gone to Germany in 1913 to discover what the attitude to England was. While he found the people personally friendly, he also realized that there were those who believed the two countries would go to war.

9 Fyfe, *My Seven Selves*.

10 The period 25–30 August saw occupying German forces in Louvain wantonly destroying buildings and carrying out mass shootings of unarmed civilians, regardless of age and gender.

11 Arthur Gleason was an American volunteer ambulance driver whose observations were published in *Golden Lads* and *Our Part of the War*, both in 1916.

12 Gibbs, *The Soul of the War*, p.183.

13 *Ibid.*, p. 194.

14 Powell, *The Fighting In Flanders*.

15 Mack, Louise, *A Woman's Experiences in the Great War*, p. 7.

16 Gibbs, Philip, *Now It Can Be Told* (1920 US ed).

17 Gibbs, *The Soul of the War*, p.350.

18 Palmer, Frederick, *My Second Year of The War*.

19 *The Times*, 10 July 1916, p. 9.

20 Thomas, Sir William Beach, *A Traveller in News*, p.109.

21 Gibbs, *The Soul of the War*, p.124.

22 Gibbs, *Now It Can Be Told*.

23 A private conversation, as quoted by C.P. Scott in his diary, 27 December 1917.

24 Gibbs, *Now It Can Be Told*.

25 *Ibid.*

26 Ruhl, Arthur, *Antwerp to Gallipoli: A year of war on many fronts – and behind them*.

27 Washburn, Stanley, *On the Russian Front in World War I: Memoirs of an American War Correspondent*.

28 Fyfe, *My Seven Selves*.

29 Fyfe, Henry Hamilton in the *Thames Star* newspaper, 21 September 1917, p.4.

30 Fyfe, *My Seven Selves*.

31 *Ibid.*

32 Ellis Ashmead-Bartlett in the *Sydney Morning Herald*, 8 May 1915, pp.13-14.

33 Fewster, Kevin (Editor), *Gallipoli Correspondent: The Frontline Diary of C.E.W. Bean*.

34 *Ibid.*

35 Ashmead-Bartlett, Ellis, *The Uncensored Dardanelles*, p.101.

36 Newspaper Publishers Association.

37 Ashmead-Bartlett, *The Uncensored Dardanelles*, p.247.

38 Fewster, *Gallipoli Correspondent*.

39 A trench dug to enable men to move up unnoticed by the enemy.

40 Malins, Geoffrey H. (Edited by Low, Warren), *How I Filmed The War*, p.85.

41 Gibbs, Philip, *Adventures in Journalism*, p.2.

42 Orpen, William, *An Onlooker in France, 1917-1919*.

THE PARTISANS

1 Davis, Frances, *A Fearful Innocence*, p.142. (The stories of Cardozo and Davis do not match in detail, but Cardozo mentions both de Jouvenal and Frances Davis as passengers. See Cardozo, Harold G. *The March of a Nation: My Year of Spain's Civil War*.)

2 Kaltenborn, H.V., *Kaltenborn Edits the News: Europe – Asia – America*, p.14.

3 The *Chicago Tribune*, 30 August 1936.

4 *News Chronicle*, 31 October 1936.

5 Cox, Geoffrey, *Eyewitness: A Memoir of Europe in the 1930s*, p.223.

6 *Ibid.*, p.228.

7 Killed in 1945 serving as a Lieutenant Colonel with the British Army in Southeast Asia.

8 *The Times*, 28 April 1937, p.17.

9 Martha Gellhorn in 'The Third Winter', November 1938, reprinted in Gellhorn, Martha, *The Face of War* (1998 ed), p.114. (first published in 1959.)

10 © BBC.

11 Ed Beattie's summation of the attitude of the Hitler Youth towards the press corps, in *Passport to War*.

'WARCOS' WARRIORS

1 Clare Hollingworth, IWM, Sound Archive, ref. 21130.

2 Associated Press dispatch, 1 September 1939.

3 Stanley Baron, IWM transcript, ref. 8877/4/1.

4 As quoted by Austin, A.B., *We Landed at Dawn*, p.78.

5 © BBC.

6 Acknowledgements to Chris Owen and Roger Beckwith.

7 Johnston, Dennis, *Nine Rivers from Jordan. The chronicle of a journey and a search*.

8 Noble, Ronnie, *Shoot First: Assignments of a newsreel cameraman*, p.24.

9 *Daily Express*, 18 May 1940.

10 Noble, *Shoot First*, p.25.

11 Divine, David, *The Nine Days Of Dunkirk*, p.222.

12 Beattie, *Passport to War*, p.252.

13 Robertson, Ben, *I Saw England: A journalist's account of experiences in England in 1940*.

14 *Ibid.*

15 Quoted in Finkelstein, Norman H. *With Heroic Truth: The Life of Edward R. Murrow*, p.78.

16 Tobin, James, *Ernie Pyle's War: America's Eyewitness to World War II*, p.57.

17 Robertson, *I Saw England*.

18 Technically, a legation.

19 Hollingworth, IWM, Sound Archive, ref. 21130.

20 St. John, Robert, *From the Land of Silent People*, p.227.

21 *Ibid.*, p.335.

22 Larry Allen, Associated Press, published in *The New York Times*, 16 January 1941.

23 Nixon, John, *Front-Line of Freedom*, p.16.

24 Larry Allen, Associated Press, published in *The News Of The World*, no date.

25 George Nixon, Reuters, published in the *Hampshire Telegraph and Post*, 25 September 1942.

26 Waldo Barnes of the *New York Herald Tribune*, no date.

27 Johnson, Stanley, *Queen of the Flat-Tops*, p.133.

28 Tregaskis, Richard William, *Guadalcanal Diary* (2000 ed), p.140. (published originally in 1943.)

29 Johnston, *Nine Rivers from Jordan*.

30 Moorehead, Alan, *The Desert War: The Classic Trilogy on the North African Campaign 1940-1943*, p.9.

31 *Ibid.*, page 96.

32 *Ibid.*

33 Hill, Russell, *Desert War*.

34 Hollingworth, IWM, Sound Archive, ref. 21130.

35 The Gazala line was divided into sectors – boxes – one of which was known as Knightsbridge, each with its own force to hold it, as a garrison holds a town or castle. At a press conference in Cairo the assembled correspondents had laughed when told that, 'The garrison of Knightsbridge has assumed a mobile role'.

36 Johnston, *Nine Rivers from Jordan*.

37 *Ibid.*

38 Frank Gillard, IWM, Sound Archive, ref. 10589/6/1.

39 Reynolds, Quentin James, *By Quentin Reynolds*, p.258.

40 Tobin, *Ernie Pyle's War*, p.258.

41 Gillard, IWM, Sound Archive, ref. 10589/6/1.

42 Probably loaned to him by the Americans.

43 Vehicle with conventional wheels at the front for simple steering, and tracks, like a tank's, at the rear for supporting weight and crossing difficult terrain.

44 ohnston, *Nine Rivers from Jordan*.

45 Capa, Robert, *Slightly Out of Focus* (2001 ed), p.103. (published originally in 1947.)

46 Campbell, Doon, *Magic Mistress: A 30-year affair with Reuters*, p.40.

47 Gellhorn, Martha, *The Face of War* (1998 ed), p.114. (published originally in 1959.)

48 Tobin, *Ernie Pyle's War*, p.153.

49 Johnston, *Nine Rivers from Jordan*.

50 Cronkite, Walter, *A Reporter's Life*, p.103.

51 LST represents Landing Ship, Tank.

52 Campbell, Doon, IWM transcript, ref. 9577.

53 *Ibid.*

54 Doon Campbell in the *London Evening News*, 9 June 1944.

55 Capa, *Slightly Out of Focus*, p.148.

56 Robin Duff, © BBC.

57 5 Parachute Brigade, Operations in Normandy June–September.

58 Guy Byam, © BBC.

59 'A Pure Miracle' dispatch of 12 June 1944 quoted in Tobin. *Ernie Pyle's War*, p.265.

60 Gellhorn. *The Face of War*, p.122.

61 © BBC.

62 Quoted in Finkelstein, *With Heroic Truth*, p.107.

63 *Manchester Guardian*, 19 June 1944.

64 From 'Invasion of France' by Ollie Stewart in *This is Our War*. The Afro-American Company: Baltimore, 1945. (Extracts available online at www.demovisions.com/afro2/OurWar/stewart1.html)

65 *Ibid.*

66 © BBC.

67 © BBC.

68 IWM, Sound Archive transcript, ref. 10589/6/1.

69 Ed Murrow, CBS Broadcast. Cited in Finkelstein, *With Heroic Truth*, p.112.

70 © BBC.

71 Noble, *Shoot First*, p.79.

72 *Daily Express*, 5 September 1945.

THE GREAT GAME

1 Cutforth, René, *Korean Reporter*, p.148.

2 Deane, Philip, *Captive In Korea*, p.36.

3 *Ibid.*, p.222.

4 Published in *The Times*, 12 August 1950.

5 'The Quiet Exit of Homer Bigart', © *American Journalism Review*, November 1999, by kind permission.

6 May, Antoinette, *Witness to War: A Biography of Marguerite Higgins*, p.155.

7 Published in the *New York Herald Tribune*, 18 September 1950.

8 Thompson, Reginald, *Cry Korea: An account of the author's experiences as a war correspondent, 1950*, p.85.

9 Cutforth, *Korean Reporter*, p.51.

10 Thompson, *Cry Korea*, p.195.

11 *Ibid.*, p.198.

12 Cutforth, *Korean Reporter*, p.174.

13 Noble, *Shoot First*, p.149.

14 *Ibid.*, p.160.

15 Alan Lambert's unpublished paper 'Korea: A War Remembered' quoted in Torney-Parlicki, Prue, *Somewhere in Asia: War, Journalism and Australia's Neighbours 1941–75*, p.125.

16 Wilfred Burchett to George. H. Burchett (his father), 16 April 1951. Wilfred's letters folder, Box 3, Burchett Papers. Cited in Casey, Stephen, 'Wilfred Burchett and the UN Command's Media Relations During the Korean War 1951–52', *Journal of Military History*, Volume 74.

17 Thompson, *Cry Korea*, p.339.

18 Leslie, Jacques, 'Continuing Reverberations of the Glorious War', an unpublished essay.

19 Jacques Leslie to the author, 2011.

20 Caputo, Philip, *Means Of Escape: A War Correspondent's Memoir of Life and Death in Afghanistan, the Middle East and Vietnam*, p.272.

21 Australian troops were also deployed but were pulled out during 1972–1973.

22 A Dickey Chapelle dispatch filed for the *National Observer*, quoted in Ostroff, Roberta, *Fire in the Wind: The Life of Dickey Chapelle*.

23 Halberstam, David and Singal, Joseph, *The Making Of A Quagmire: America and Vietnam during the Kennedy Era*, p.48.

24 *Ibid.*, p.89.

25 *The Washington Post*, 7 January 1963, cited at www.americanwriters.org – see 'Battle of Ap Bac' in *A Bright Shining Lie* in 'works'.

26 Halberstam and Singal, *The Making Of A Quagmire*, p.127.

27 Bowden, Tim, *One Crowded Hour: Neil Davis, Combat Cameraman*, p.191.

28 *Ibid.*, p.138.

29 Leslie, Jacques, *The Mark: A War Correspondent's Memoir of Vietnam and Cambodia*, p.96.

30 Nicholson, Michael, *A Measure of Danger: Memoirs of a British War Correspondent*.

31 Leslie, *The Mark*, p.54.

32 Martha Gellhorn in 'A New Kind of War', September 1966, reprinted in Gellhorn, *The Face of War*, p.255.

33 McCullin, Don (with Lewis Chester), *Unreasonable Behaviour: An Autobiography*, p.99.

34 McCullin, Don, *Shaped by War*, p.125 (both the indented quote and the embedded quote earlier, above).

35 Leslie, *The Mark*, p.92.

36 *Ibid.*, p.6.

37 *Ibid.*, p.150.

38 Michael Nicholson, Independent Television News, IWM, Sound Archive, ref. 21537.

39 Caputo, *Means Of Escape*, p.267.

40 Michael Nicholson's diary, quoted in Nicholson, *A Measure of Danger*, p.140.

41 Nicholson, *A Measure of Danger*, p.169.

42 Bowden, *One Crowded Hour*, p.337.

43 Nicholson, Independent Television News, IWM, Sound Archive, ref. 21537.

44 LSL denotes Landing Ships Logistics. *Sir Bedivere* was one of six such vessels.

45 Commander Gedge to the author, February 2011.

46 Quoted in Nicholson, *A Measure of Danger*, p.227.

47 Robert Fox in *The Listener*, 9 July 1982.

48 This author's italics highlight the famous phrase from the BBC News broadcast, printed in Hanrahan, Brian and Fox, Robert. *I Counted Them All Out and I Counted Them All Back: The Battle For the Falklands*, p.20.

49 Cleaver to the author, January 2011.

50 Looting.

51 'Rat-pack', referring to the ration packs everyone carried.

52 Robert Fox in *The Listener*, 9 July 1982.

53 Brian Hanrahan, Sunday 16 May, transcript printed in Hanrahan and Fox, *I Counted Them All Out and I Counted Them All Back*, p.34.

54 Nicholson, *A Measure of Danger*, p.259.

55 Royal Marines' term for a long march with full kit, possibly an acronym of '[at] your own pace'.

56 Hastings, Max, *Going to the Wars*, p.307.

57 Commander Gedge to the author, January 2011.

58 This was at a time when the general public had hardly heard about mobile phones.

59 Ian Bruce. Nicholson also claimed that everyone scattered when someone shouted that Robert McGowan had gone to

fetch a gun. Many such souvenirs were acquired by correspondents and troops alike during the war – and afterwards subjected by the Royal Navy to the 'floating test' before being allowed home.

60 Hastings, *Going to the Wars*, p.381.

61 Nicholson, Independent Television News, IWM, Sound Archive, ref. 21537.

62 Mather, Ian. *For You the War is Over*.

63 Nick Ut – source unknown.

NEW WORLD DISORDER

1 Loyd, Anthony, *My War Gone By, I Miss It So*, p.136.

2 Maggie O'Kane, Interview for the IWM exhibition 'War Correspondent', February 2011.

3 *Ibid*.

4 Kate Adie, IWM, Sound Archive, ref. 20901.

5 Michael Nicholson, Interview for the IWM exhibition 'War Correspondent', February 2011.

6 James Ferguson to the author, February 2011.

7 Bowen, Jeremy, *War Stories*, p.75.

8 Simpson, John, *News From No Man's Land*, p.364.

9 Simpson, John, *Strange Places, Questionable People*, p.271.

10 Caputo, *Means Of Escape*, p.334.

11 Adie, IWM, Sound Archive, ref. 20901.

12 Bowen, *War Stories*, p.76.

13 *Ibid.*, p.84.

14 Adie, Kate, *The Kindness of Strangers*, p.317.

15 Loyd, *My War Gone By, I Miss It So*, p.205.

16 *Ibid.*, page 151.

17 An interview with Fergal Keane at www.pbs.org/wgbh/pages/frontline/shows/ghosts/. Extracts by kind permission of Frontline.

18 Stewart, Ian, *Ambushed: A War Reporter's Life on the Line*, p.62.

19 *bid.*, p.107.

20 *Ibid.*, p.16.

21 Omaar, Rageh, *Revolution Day*, p.97.

22 Samia Nakhoul to the author, March 2011.

23 Engel, Richard, *A Fist in the Hornet's Nest: On the Ground in Baghdad Before, During*

and After the War, p.86.

24 Omaar, *Revolution Day*, p.185.

25 A Turkish company providing a satellite up-link service.

26 Engel, *A Fist in the Hornet's Nest*, p.94.

27 Nakhoul to the author, March 2011.

28 Omaar, *Revolution Day*, p.185.

29 From 'A Day in the Life of a Female Iraqi Journalist in Baghdad: Part One' by Huda Ahmed in *The Huffington Post*, 24 July 2007.

30 Beaumont, Peter, *The Secret Life Of War: Journeys Through Modern Conflict*, p.148.

31 Martin Bell, IWM, Sound Archive, ref. 22149.

32 *Ibid*.

33 Ferguson to the author, February 2011.

34 Stephen Farrell to the author, January 2011.

35 Mastrogiacomo, Daniele, *Days of Fear: A Firsthand Account of Captivity Under the New Taliban*, p.185.

36 The Frontline Club is a London-based club for war correspondents. A video on the role of the fixer and featuring Najibullah Razzaq, Alan Little, Jeremy Bowen and Martin Bell has been made by The Frontline Club (© Frontline) and is available at: http://frontlineclub.com/activities/2008/10/a-special-event.html

37 The Pashtun code of honour.

38 Ferguson to the author, February 2011.

39 Stewart, *Ambushed*, p.228.

40 Vaughan Smith, Interview for the IWM exhibition 'War Correspondent', 2011.

41 O'Kane, Interview for the IWM exhibition 'War Correspondent', February 2011.

42 Nicholson, Interview for the IWM exhibition 'War Correspondent', Februay 2011.

43 Bell, IWM, Sound Archive, ref. 22155.

44 Reproduced by kind permission of copyright-holder Ian Bruce.

45 A city in central England. Passage reproduced by kind permission of copyright-holder Ian Bruce.

46 Reproduced by kind permission of copyright-holder Ian Bruce.

47 United Nations High Commission for Refugees.

48 Loyd, *My War Gone By, I Miss It So*, p.228.

49 Nicholson, Independent Television News, IWM, Sound Archive, ref. 21537.

50 Bowen, *War Stories*, p.169.

51 Loyd, *My War Gone By, I Miss It So*, p.7.

52 An interview with Fergal Keane at www.pbs.org/wgbh/pages/frontline/shows/ghosts/. Extracts by kind permission of Frontline.

53 Bowen, *War Stories*, p.3.

THE END OF THE LINE?

1 Nakhoul to the author, March 2011.

2 Nicholson, Interview for the IWM exhibition 'War Correspondent', 2011.

3 O'Kane, Interview for the IWM exhibition 'War Correspondent', 2011.

4 Nakhoul to the author, March 2011.

5 Vaughan Smith, Interview for the IWM exhibition 'War Correspondent', 2011.

6 *Ibid*.

7 Nicholson, Interview for the IWM exhibition 'War Correspondent', 2011.

selected bibliography

Adie, Kate, *The Kindness of Strangers*, Headline Book Publishing, London, 2005

Ashmead-Bartlett, Ellis, *The Uncensored Dardanelles*, Hutchinson & Co. (Publishers) Ltd, no date

Austin, A.B., in *We Landed at Dawn*, Harcourt, Brace and Company, New York, 1943

Beattie, Ed., *Passport to War*, Peter Davies, London, 1943

Beaumont, Peter, *The Secret Life Of War: Journeys Through Modern Conflict*, Vintage Books, London, 2010

Blackett, R.J.M. (Editor), *Thomas Morris Chester, Black War Correspondent: His Dispatches from the Virginia Front*, Louisiana State University Press, Baton Rouge, 1989

Bowden, Tim, *One Crowded Hour: Neil Davis, Combat Cameraman*, HarperCollins, Sydney, Australia, 1987

Bowen, Jeremy, *War Stories*, Simon and Schuster, London, 2006

Campbell, Doon, *Magic Mistress: A 30-year affair with Reuters*, Tagman, London, 2000

Capa, Robert, *Slightly Out of Focus*, Modern Library, New York, 2001

Caputo, Philip, *Means Of Escape: A War Correspondent's Memoir of Life and Death in Afghanistan, the Middle East and Vietnam*, The Lyons Press, New Guildford, Connecticut, 2002

Cardozo, Harold G., *The March of a Nation: My Year of Spain's Civil War*, Eyre and Spottiswoode Limited, London, 1937

Cox, Geoffrey, *Eyewitness: A Memoir of Europe in the 1930s*, University of Otago Press: Dunedin, 1999

Cronkite, Walter, *A Reporter's Life*, Alfred A. Knopf, New York, 1996

Cutforth, René, *Korean Reporter*, Wingate, London, 1952

Davis, Frances, *A Fearful Innocence*, Kent State University Press, Kent, Ohio, 1981

Davis, Richard Harding, *With Both Armies In South Africa*, Charles Scribner's Sons, New York, 1900

Davis, Richard Harding, *With the Allies*, 1915

Deane, Philip, *Captive In Korea*, Hamish Hamilton, London, 1953

Dickson, William Kennedy Laurie, *The Biograph In Battle. Its story in the South African War*, T. Fisher Unwin, London, 1901

Divine, David, *The Nine Days Of Dunkirk*, Faber & Faber, London, 1959

Engel, Richard, *A Fist in the Hornet's Nest: On the Ground in Baghdad Before, During and After the War*, Hyperion Books, New York, 2004

Fewster, Kevin (Editor), *Gallipoli Correspondent: The Frontline Diary of C.E.W. Bean*, Allen & Unwin, London, 1983

Finkelstein, Norman H., *With Heroic Truth: The Life of Edward R. Murrow*, Clarion Books, New York, 1997

Fyfe, Henry Hamilton, *My Seven Selves*, G. Allen & Unwin, London, 1935

Gallagher, O'Dowd, *Retreat In The East*, Viking, 1942

Gellhorn, Martha, *The Face of War*, Granta, London, 1998

Gervasi, Frank, *The Violent Decade*, Norton, New York, 1989

Gibbs, Philip, *Adventures in Journalism*, William Heinemann, London, 1923

Gibbs, Philip, *Now It Can Be Told*, Harper: New York, 1920

Gibbs, Philip, *The Pageant Of The Years*, Heinemann, London, 1946

Gibbs, Philip, *The Soul of the War*, William Heinemann, London, 1915

Griffis, William Elliot, *Charles Carleton Coffin: War Correspondent, Traveller, Author, and Statesman*, Estes & Lauriat, Boston, 1898

Halberstam, David, and Singal, Joseph, *The Making Of A Quagmire: America and Vietnam during the Kennedy Era*, McGraw-Hill, New York, 2007

Hales, Alfred Greenwood, *Campaign Pictures of the War in South Africa (1899–1900): Letters from the Front*, Cassell & Co., London, 1900

Hanrahan, Brian, and Fox, Robert, *I Counted Them All Out and I Counted Them All Back: The Battle For the Falklands*, BBC, London, 1982

Hastings, Max, *Going to the Wars*, Pan Books, London, 2000

Hawkins, Desmond, *War Report – D-Day to VE-Day*, BBC, 1985

Hill, Russell, *Desert War*, Alfred A. Knopf, New York, 1952

Institution of Engineering and Technology, *A History of Telegraphy: Its Technology and Applications*, Stevenage, 2000

Jeffries, J.M.N., *Front Everywhere*, Hutchinson, London, undated

Jenkins, Roy, *Churchill*, Macmillan, London, 2001

Johnson, Stanley, *Queen of the Flat-Tops*, Jarrolds, London, 1943

Johnston, Dennis, *Nine Rivers from Jordan. The chronicle of a journey and a search*, Derek Verschoyle, London, 1953

Kaltenborn, H.V., *Kaltenborn Edits the News: Europe – Asia – America*, Modern Age Books, Inc., New York, 1937

Leslie, Jacques, *The Mark: A War Correspondent's Memoir of Vietnam and Cambodia*, Four Walls Eight Windows, New York, 1995

Loyd, Anthony, *My War Gone By, I Miss It So*, Anchor Books, London, 2001

Mack, Louise, *A Woman's Experiences in the Great War*, T.F. Unwin, London, 1915

Malins, Geoffrey H. (Edited by Warren Low), *How I Filmed The War*, Herbert Jenkins, London, 1920

Mastrogiacomo, Daniele, *Days of Fear: A Firsthand Account of Captivity Under the New Taliban*, Europa Editions, New York, 2010

Mather, Ian, *For You the War is Over* (Self-published), 7 Grand Avenue, London N10 3AY, 2010

May, Antoinette, *Witness to War: A Biography of Marguerite Higgins*, Beaufort Books, New York, 1983

McCullin, Don (with Lewis Chester), *Unreasonable Behaviour: An Autobiography*, Jonathan Cape, London, 1990

McCullin, Don, *Shaped by War*, Jonathan Cape, London, 2010

Ministry of Defence, *Working Arrangements With the Media* (commonly called The Green Book), 2010

Monaghan, James, *The Man Who Elected Lincoln*, Greenwood Press, Santa Barbara, California, 1956

Moorehead, Alan, *A Late Education*, Granta, 2000

Moorehead, Alan, *The Desert War: The Classic Trilogy on the North African Campaign 1940-1943*, Aurum Press, London, 2009

Nevison, Henry, *Ladysmith: The Diary Of A Siege*, The Echo Library, Teddington, 2006

Nicholson, Michael, *A Measure of Danger: Memoirs of a British War Correspondent*, Fontana, London, 1992

Nixon, John, *Front-Line of Freedom*, Hutchinson & Co., London, 1942

Noble, Ronnie, *Shoot First*, Pan Books, London, 1957

Omaar, Rageh, *Revolution Day*, Penguin Books, London, 2005

Ostroff, Roberta, *Fire in the Wind: The Life of Dickey Chapelle*, Ballantine Books, New York, 1992

Page, Charles A., *Letters of a War Correspondent*, L.C. Page and Company, Boston, 1899

Palmer, Frederick, *My Second Year of The War*, Dodd, Mead & Company, New York, 1917

Powell, E. Alexander, *The Fighting In Flanders*, William Heinemann, London, 1914

Raymer, Jacob Nathaniel (Edited by E.B. Munson), *Confederate Correspondent: The Civil War Reports of Jacob Nathaniel Raymer, Fourth North Carolina*, McFarland & Co., London, 2009

Reynolds, Quentin James, *By Quentin Reynolds*, Heinemann, London, 1964

Robertson, Ben, *I Saw England: A journalist's account of experiences in England in 1940*, Alfred A. Knopf, New York, 1941

Ruhl, Arthur, *Antwerp to Gallipoli: A year of war on many fronts – and behind them*, G. Allen & Unwin, London and New York, 1916

Simpson, John, *News From No Man's Land*, Macmillan, London, 2002

Simpson, John, *Strange Places, Questionable People*, Macmillan, London, 1998

St. John, Robert, *From the Land of Silent People*, Doubleday Doran & Co. Inc., New York, 1942

Steevens, G.W. (Edited by Vernon Blackburn), *From Capetown to Ladysmith: An Unfinished Record of the South African War*, William Blackwood and Sons, Edinburgh and London, 1900

Stewart, Ian, *Ambushed: A War Reporter's Life on the Line*, ABC Books, Sydney, 2003

Stowe, Leland, *No Other Road To Freedom*, Alfred A. Knopf, New York, 1941

Thomas, Sir William Beach, *The Way of a Countryman*, Michael Joseph, London, 1944

Thompson, Reginald, *Cry Korea*, Reportage Press, London, 2009

Tobin, James, *Ernie Pyle's War: America's Eyewitness to World War II*, University Press of Kansas, Lawrence, 1998

Torney-Parlicki, Prue, *Somewhere in Asia: War, Journalism and Australia's Neighbours 1941-1975*, University of New South Wales Press, Sydney, 2000

Tregaskis, Richard William, *Guadalcanal Diary*, Modern Library, New York, 2000

Tregaskis, Richard William, *Invasion Diary*, University of Nebraska Press, New York, 2004

Villiers, Frederic, *Villiers: His Five Decades Of Adventure*, Hutchinson & Co., London, 1921

Wallace, Edgar, *Edgar Wallace by Himself*, Hodder and Stoughton, London, 1932

Washburn, Stanley, *On the Russian Front in World War I: Memoirs of an American War Correspondent*, R.Speller and Sons, New York, 1982

http://www.ladysmithhistory.com/

http://randallbutisingh.wordpress.com/2008/10/25/conductor-rudolph-dunbar-of-guyana/

http://opinionator.blogs.nytimes.com/2007/09/25/which-came-first-the-chicken-or-the-egg-part-one/ [research into Fenton's 'Valley of the Shadow of Death' images]

http://www.mathewbrady.com/photos.htm

http://www.btinternet.com/~roger.beckwith/bh/menu.htm

acknowledgements

This book is very much a team effort. I am particularly grateful to Terry Charman, Senior Historian at the Imperial War Museum London for casting his authoritative eye and red pen over the manuscript, and to my ruthless editor, Chris Westhorp for his good-humoured zeal. Jennifer Veall's picture research and Georgina Hewitt's design are no less important to the overall creation than the words on the page.

I also want to thank Felix Rowe for providing additional research and Jo Garnier, Amanda Mason and Peter Taylor at the Imperial War Museum for their liaison. As always, my thanks go to the staff of the British Library, particularly those at the Newspaper Reading Library at Colindale. May I acknowledge everyone – publishers, organizations and individuals – who gave permission for extracts to be used, answered queries, or contributed material: Martin Gibbs, Jacques Leslie, Roger Beckwith, Chris Owen, James Ferguson, Ian Bruce, Commander Tim Gedge AFC RN Rtd, Brian Kaighin,

Robert Quirk, Ian Carver, Les Crawley, Rodney Pinder of International News Safety Institute, Jo Crosby and Samia Nakhoul of Reuters, Peter Heaps and the BBC.

Friends and family have also played an important role: Judy, Peter and Sarah with their spare room near London, David in Australia, and, above all, my husband George who has seen his passing acquaintance with the ironing press and vacuum ripen into inseparable friendship over the past months.

Ten years ago I sent the manuscript of my first factual book to John Lee at Conway, little dreaming, even after it was accepted, that it would be the first of six titles that he would usher into the world. To him and to Senior Editor, Alison Moss, I owe a very special debt for their confidence in me and the continuing opportunity to do what I love doing.

picture credits

index of names